We Cry Out

We Cry Out

✦

Living with Developmental Disabilities

*Susan Dahl, M.S., John DeFrain, Ph.D.,
and John S. Campbell, M.D.*

iUniverse, Inc.
New York Lincoln Shanghai

We Cry Out
Living with Developmental Disabilities

iUniverse books may be ordered through booksellers or by contacting:

iUniverse
2021 Pine Lake Road, Suite 100
Lincoln, NE 68512
www.iuniverse.com
1-800-Authors (1-800-288-4677)

ISBN-13: 978-0-595-38733-5 (pbk)
ISBN-13: 978-0-595-83115-9 (ebk)
ISBN-10: 0-595-38733-0 (pbk)
ISBN-10: 0-595-83115-X (ebk)

Printed in the United States of America

A book for medical practitioners, individuals with developmental and acquired disabilities, their loved ones, and friends

Susan Dahl, M.S., was a counselor and educator who devoted many years to serving children with developmental disabilities and their families at the Child Guidance Center and other agencies in Lincoln, Nebraska. Susan endured spinal muscular atrophy, which caused severe scoliosis, from the age of 7.

John DeFrain, Ph.D., is an Extension professor of family and community development at the University of Nebraska-Lincoln. He has written and edited 20 books and more than 90 professional articles on family strengths and families in crisis.

John S. Campbell, M.D., a board-certified family physician and board-certified pediatrician, was a practicing physician for 29 years, 26 of those years as a family physician and three years as a pediatric resident in training. He has had a career-long research interest, and has done extensive reading and thinking about issues related to: the experience of living with chronic illness and disability; the psycho-social and psycho-neurological aspects of illness and health; the essential nature of the physician/provider-patient/client relationship; the role of grieving in the healing process in illness and disabilities; and the history and politics of medical care and health care. Dr. Campbell lives in Lincoln, Nebraska.

Contents

Stories told by individuals and family members who have been challenged by a developmental disability for just a few weeks up to five years. It seems like "only yesterday" when their journey began....

What have we learned about developmental disabilities? And, what can we do together as a nation-wide community to help individuals and family members live a better life in the future?

Dedicated to our families and our friends.

I'm determined to be alive when I die.

FOREWORD

✦

WHY THESE STORIES MUST BE TOLD

By John S. Campbell, M.D.

When I met Susan Dahl as a patient in the mid 1980s, I initially felt anxious about my ability to care for her. She clearly had complex medical problems. That was obvious just looking at her sitting in her motorized wheelchair—her body permanently twisted, her arms and legs with severely limited motion and function. I reminded myself that I was Board Certified in Family Practice and Pediatrics, and that my Pediatric residency experiences included significant exposure to Developmental Pediatrics, which consists of managing neurologically and developmentally handicapped children. I took a deep breath and decided to do the best I could as an empathetic primary care physician, using consultation with specialists as needed.

At first I saw Susan as a disabled patient, but soon I was able to know her as an interesting, intelligent, and personable woman with disabilities. I remained her family physician until her death in 1995. Susan faced her life and death with bravery and humor. She lived as fully as she was able within the limits of her disability—and she tested those limits regularly. She did not let anyone else define these limits for her, no matter what their expertise, because she knew herself better than anyone else could.

Susan touched others' lives as a professional counselor as well as friend. I believe she experienced a good deal of happiness in her life, and maintained a generally optimistic outlook, along with the realistic fears and anxieties inherent in her complex medical problems and disabilities. Even after being struck by a bus carrying people with disabilities while crossing a street in her motorized wheelchair in downtown Lincoln, Nebraska, resulting in a severe concussion and post-concussion syndrome, she never gave up trying to live as best she could. Susan never gave up living until she died.

Susan was a person to be respected because of who she was, not because she was a person with a disability. Many people, including professionals who should know better, cannot see past the disability to know the person. I have learned more about how to be a competent, caring physician from Susan Dahl and my thousands of other patients over the 29 years in medical practice than I learned in my traditional medical education. And, Susan Dahl taught me more than any *individual* patient I can think of.

We Cry Out is an important book for you to read. It is a compilation of narratives about the real lives of real people with serious developmental disabilities from birth, childhood, or early adulthood, and thoughts from members of their families. Some of these people could have been better helped to happier, more productive lives by better information, better medical, psychological, social, and spiritual support.

The research done by Susan Dahl and John DeFrain speaks for itself—I should say the affected people and their families speak for themselves in their responses to the research questions Susan and John posed. John DeFrain and I hope in this foreword to provide a *frame* of information for the *picture* presented by this emotionally moving, compelling collection of stories of personal and family tragedy, grieving, and attempts to recover enough to continue with life. We will propose some questions to consider in reading these narratives. We will specifically ask how these individuals and families could have been better helped by professionals, as well as by family and friends, to survive these complicated and sometimes overwhelming problems. They specifically needed help to *heal* as much as their disability allowed and to learn to better live with their burdens. There is no way to improve upon the collection of narratives because individuals tell their own stories as they want them told.

The advantage to the use of written testimony is that it allows the individuals and families to answer the questions they want to answer. In this way it is better, in my opinion, than a face-to-face interview because many people are more likely to be honest anonymously on a questionnaire than when exposed to the social pressure inevitably involved in an interview setting. I believe that this is true no matter how " objective" and dispassionate the interviewers may assume they are. There is no pressure to answer questions they do not feel comfortable answering, and no hesitation in answering questions in a critical and emotionally honest manner. This approach provides a valuable, much needed, critique of our health care and social systems in the United States. Their written responses get at how these affected individuals and families *feel they have been cared for by the medical system—or not. The emotional reactions to their management are very important if we are to improve our health care for and social support of these multiply-handicapped people.* Potentially happier and more productive citizens and families could be the result.

The organization of the narratives provides additional insight by being categorized by how long the individual and family have been living with the aftermath of the traumatic event. The repercussions for all involved are clearly life-long. Severe traumas in fact have continuing and, in many ways, unpredictable effects on people's lives. This has not been adequately discussed in medical literature and professional conferences—especially specifics of how to try to help in the process of grieving and *healing*.

Physicians are taught early in medical school the importance of taking a good history. Over the three decades since I graduated from medical school the "siren song" of technology has given the impression to many of my colleagues that sophisticated tests are the so-called modern scientific way to arrive at proper diagnoses and treatment plans. But taking a history is not a simple act, because it involves establishing a therapeutic relationship between patient and physician. This relationship, which ideally also includes the patient's family, affects treatment and therapeutic choices and outcomes.

These points are well illustrated and documented in the lists of additional references at the end of *We Cry Out*. Physicians who have written about their own experiences of suffering significant health problems are especially insightful. The importance of the therapeutic relationship between physician and patient is emphasized, as well as the patient's emotional reaction to their illness, and its effect on their family and social relationships. The consequences to the patient's self-concept and self-image are discussed in the books by Oliver Sacks, very specifically in *A Leg to Stand On*. [1] The *healing effect*, which has been called the "placebo effect", is in fact a very powerful result of the interaction between clinician and patient with genuine beneficial consequences to the lives of patients, their intimates, and their families.

One significant weakness of the way modern medicine is practiced is that it is episodic and office-based. In the past, the doctor often made house calls and knew people in more depth—in the context of the lives they actually lived. To make matters worse, the instability of health insurance coverage over the past 25 years has led, in many cases, to frequent changes of primary care physician and specialist. This has further resulted in physicians being even less likely to understand the impact of illness on the lives of their patients. This impact can only be understood by knowing the patient over some significant period of time. In fact, the client's history really cannot be accurately understood in one or a few visits because people are unlikely to tell important personal and emotional information until they trust their doctor. Trust takes time in just the same way making friends with someone takes time. People are naturally cautious about revealing personal, emotionally-charged information until they have gotten to know each other.

Unfortunately, physicians often do not know what they do not know about their patients. Instead, physicians tend to focus on people's lack of compliance with medications and treatments. I am painfully aware that I have not always done as well as I should have in trying to understand the complexities of my patients' problems over my years in medical practice. The need to know sensitive information needs to be balanced against respect for the patient's privacy. The patient must be ready to tell the physician about painful aspects of their life history. In some cases, it has taken years for patients to trust me enough to raise some of these important issues. Time pressure felt by almost all physicians, exacerbated by relatively low insurance compensation for spending time discussing important life issues with patients, as opposed to performing procedures on them, is another significant barrier to understanding individual and family needs.

Medical care is handicapped by linear, episodic thinking rather than looking at the true fabric, the woven threads of experiences which make up real lives. Understanding the complexity of illness as it interacts with families, intimates, self-perceptions, and views of the past, present, and future are all factors especially critical in helping the severely affected people and their families who are the basis for this book. Real empathetic listening is an essential step in beginning to truly help these people.

WHY THE AUTHORS CREATED THIS BOOK

Books are written with a variety of motivations based on the educational and life experiences of the authors. Susan Dahl had an obvious interest in researching the lives of people with developmental disabilities similar to hers, as well as her professional interest as a student with the goal of being a counselor. John DeFrain met her and started his collaboration and friendship with her in that context. He was her professor.

My interest started as part of being a practicing family physician. Over the years, I read books about living with chronic illness and disabilities and the importance of the patient-physician relationship. I realized that these issues were not comprehensively discussed in my medical training, continuing medical education conferences, or in the standard medical literature—specifically the psychosocial, family, societal, and spiritual issues related to the illness experience. My interest was professional and intellectual. My goal was to better help my patients live with their illnesses. In 1997, I suddenly developed a much more personal interest after I found myself with a serious and unusual autoimmune disease, characterized by a combination of abnormal blood counts and immune system malfunctions. It is so unusual that the Immunology specialist who cares for me has so far heard of no one else who has quite this combination of problems. I am well aware of the irony of being a physician suffering an unnamed illness which makes me very susceptible to viral illnesses. I now try to avoid exposure to people who might be contagious as much as possible, whereas in the past I didn't think at all about walking into an examination room containing a coughing, miserable person. I have now experienced the fear, suffering, self-esteem and self-image problems I previously had only read about. I was forced to learn to live with frequent blood tests, visits to specialists, routine intravenous therapy, and other indignities patients with chronic illness suffer. I sensed that some of my physicians felt uncomfortable treating another physician with a serious illness. Over these years, I have made progress in changing my self-image to accommodate the loss of the ideas and dreams of how my life would have been if I had not developed this illness. I have grieved these losses. I now realize how little I really knew previously about the emotional aspects of learning to live with chronic illness. My personal experiences broadened and deepened my understanding and acceptance of these essential dimensions of any chronic illness.

Over the 37 years since I started medical school these matters were only discussed in bits and pieces. In recent years there has been more discussion of grief in relation to terminal illness, but not so much in relation to chronic illness. The discussions generally are related to specific disease entities without, in most cases, comprehensively dealing with the common features of learning to live with these illnesses.

The metaphor that most readily comes to mind in suddenly facing a serious life-threatening illness is that of a *personal natural disaster*—a personal earthquake, tornado or hurricane. Such a catastrophe is also comparable to dealing with the aftermath of an accident, a fire, or the death of a close relative or friend. It turns your life upside down and inside out. The experience has severe, long-lasting, often life-long, effects on the person, the family, and social and professional life and relationships. The crisis itself is only the beginning of a long, time- and energy-consuming process of grieving. This ideally is followed ultimately by *reinventing* a life which incorporates the changes which cannot be reversed. The healing process takes years and is a dynamic process, taking much longer than traditionally assumed. There are no prescribed easy steps to happiness and a new life.

The people and families portrayed in the narratives in this book have suffered devastating, catastrophic traumas with permanent or very long-lasting consequences. The amount of healing and adjustment to these life-changing events varies among the individuals and their families, and within families. Could interventions by professionals, friends, and family members have better assisted the grieving and healing? Could the lack of interventions have caused further harm to the affected person and their family? I believe the answer to both questions is yes.

WHAT HAS BEEN WRITTEN TO THIS POINT ABOUT THESE SUBJECTS?

Even before I developed my own chronic illness, for years I read books relating to people coping with chronic illness. I was also interested in the history of medicine and health care, and the intricacies of the physician/healer-patient relationship. In the past two years, I have researched these subjects more seriously with all the time I have had when I was too ill to work as a practicing physician, especially since my retirement with medical disability in March, 2002. It is rare to find medical literature which delineates the many common issues in the management of all chronic illnesses and disabilities. Indeed, many of my colleagues fail to acknowledge, write about, or discuss the difficult life adaptations involved in all chronic illnesses, disabilities, and health problems. We physicians, in fact, are educated primarily to differentiate between medical conditions, to diagnose, to try to define the medically-relevant aspects of clients' health problems. We are less educated in synthesizing the factors which very diverse medical conditions share in impacting the way our patients must accommodate their lives to their disabilities.

It is especially difficult to find discussions of the psychological, social, and spiritual aspects of helping people learn to live with their illnesses. It became obvious as I read non-standard medical books and nursing textbooks, which did deal with these issues, that a major reweaving of the threads of a person's life is what is really necessary to *heal*. The tapestry of life is thoroughly disrupted by serious illness and major repair and redefinition of one's life is what is essential.

In particular, nursing textbooks I studied dealt with more of the basic, common problems in the human aspect of living with chronic illness than the medical literature and textbooks. As a family physician, I know that much of the basic care of chronically ill people is done by generalists such as family physicians and general internists. This is even true of the very complex chronically ill and injured people such as those documented in the research of Susan Dahl and John

DeFrain in the main body of this book. Specialty consultation is variably avail-able and tends not to be long-term is many instances.

A recent review of the articles in the indices of the *Yearbook of Family Practice* for example, contained no articles related to the general topic of "chronic illness management" or "learning to live with chronic illness" or similar topics. Since the *Yearbook of Family Practice* is based on the world literature pertinent to family practice, I think this is a significant omission. That is not to say that important questions related to the psychosocial management of people with chronic illness are not contained in the articles abstracted. But, the topics focussed on were spe-cific health topics, specific illnesses, specific organ systems, specific disease pro-cesses, more than the generalities of the life impact of all these medical crises. In recent years, there have been more articles about health care delivery systems, end of life care, and pain control. Conferences I have attended over the years such as Family Practice Reviews, Family Practice Board Reviews, and annual meetings of the Academy of Family Physicians also had a similar orientation. These confer-ences featured excellent comprehensive coverage of specific illnesses and topics, with little emphasis on how to help individuals and families survive the major changes in their lives associated with the complex health challenges of chronic ill-nesses and serious injuries.

The traditional medical literature and conferences generally follow the linear thinking pattern of *diagnosis—>treatment—>prognosis—>management,* rather than dealing with the multifaceted, multifactorial, longitudinal-over-time, psy-chological, social, and spiritual aspects of serious medical problems. There is more focus on categorizing and defining the illness than on the actual impact on the person of the illness or injury in the context of all the facets of their existence. We need to address not just the medical-physical dimension, but the fabric of real people's lives.

Nursing textbooks generally feature a more comprehensive, multifaceted approach, in addition to dealing with specific illnesses and disease processes. Their approach is more patient-centered in the context of family and social con-nections. One example is a recent nursing textbook published in 2002, *Chronic Illness: Impact and Interventions* by Irene Morof Lubkin, and Pamela D. Larsen. The authors emphasize that "chronic disease is the nation's greatest health care problem". The financial and emotional toll that chronic illnesses take on individ-uals and families is comprehensively delineated. [2]

As in many nursing textbooks, the important point is made that our current health care system is not designed for chronic health care. It is primarily designed for acute and episodic health care. This textbook was especially clear in detailing the many personal, family, cultural, and social threads which make up the fabric of illness in any person. The authors emphasize that "biologically, the human body wears out unevenly." Therefore, we are witnessing the increasing burden of more and more chronic illnesses as all of us age. In addition, the authors elaborate an intuitively obvious point: "chronic illness affects all aspects of an individual's life" and is in turn affected by the kind of person the sufferer is, and social setting in which the person lives. "Each individual has a different and unique illness experience." This statement emphasizes and explains the complexity of caring for any person with chronic illness. [3]

A book entitled *Chronic Illness in Children and Adults: A Psychosocial Approach* by Debra P. Hymovich and Gloria A. Hagopian contains comprehensive charts illustrating personal and environmental factors interacting over time. The authors suggest that nursing assessments and interventions as well as social and family interventions are essential in the care of patients. This book specifically encourages integrating concepts from different professions, including psychology, sociology, nursing, and management. [4] It introduces the essential concept that "people behave according to the facts as they perceive them not as the facts are perceived by others" and the equally important insight that "health professionals need to assess their clients' perceptions and, at the same time, be aware of their own perceptions." Detailed discussions of the emotional and spiritual, as well as the biological, cognitive, and social influences in chronic illness are included in this textbook. [5]

All the nursing textbooks I studied included similar comprehensive evaluations based on the principles of management of these complicated chronic illnesses and injuries. Medical textbooks and medical literature generally do not cover in detail the kinds of common issues of disease management that the nursing books do.

Physicians, psychologists, other professionals, and people of diverse backgrounds who have themselves suffered chronic illnesses, or who have experienced family members suffering chronic illnesses have also written very insightful books. These authors obviously have a more comprehensive, emotionally sophisticated, and human view of the multiple, cascading problems resulting from illnesses and injuries impacting lives. These authors, as well as the professional nurses, tend to see the need for multispecialty, cross-professional teams in caring for complicated multiply-diseased patients.

The stories of people and their families documented in *We Cry Out* are very important because they illustrate many instances of failure to provide adequate medical, psychological, and social support for these individuals and families. This book raises general and specific questions by documenting stories dealing with some of the most extreme examples of the complex medical problems involved in severe developmental disabilities. What do people want and need to help them cope with these circumstances? What can be done to help people learn to live productively, while maintaining their self-respect and dignity—with and despite their illnesses?

I would maintain that we as medical professionals, and we as a society, are failing to help enough or comprehensively enough. I believe this argument relates not only to the severely and multiply ill, but also to people and families living with less complex chronic illnesses. We must remember that our failure to help adequately may actually cause further harm. As a consequence, many may not be able to live as satisfying or as productive lives as they otherwise might, if given appropriate help at the appropriate time.

Bernard Lown, M.D., the world famous cardiologist, writes in the preface to his book, *The Lost Art of Healing,* that "medicine has lost its way, if not its soul. An unwritten covenant between doctor and patient, hallowed over several millennia is being broken." Dr. Lown writes that this represents a "profound crisis" in the practice of medicine. He clarifies this view: "Healing is replaced with treating, caring is supplanted by managing, and the act of listening is taken over by technological procedures. Doctors no longer minister to a distinctive person but concern themselves with fragmented, malfunctioning biological parts." Later in the preface he writes that "healing is best accomplished when art and science are conjoined, when body and spirit are probed together." [6]

In his several books, Dr. Oliver Sacks presents his patients in three dimensions—actually four dimensions, including time—as he follows his patients over a number of years. He sees and portrays his patients as fellow human beings, without compromising his incisive clinical evaluations and comprehensive neurologic diagnostic and therapeutic approach. In perhaps his most emotionally insightful book, *A Leg to Stand On,* he tells in great detail the story of how a severe injury to his leg and its treatment dramatically changed his approach to his patients. He suffered and weathered the physical and emotional storms caused by his injury, including difficulties communicating with his physicians. He came out of the experience with a more profound understanding of the psychological, emotional, and spiritual aspects of what it means to be a patient. [7]

In *Migraine: Revised and Expanded,* Dr. Sacks writes: "medicine cannot be reduced to coherent and logically consistent terms—it is dependent on innumerable variables and intangibles, in 'magic' and above all on the trusting relationship between physicians and patients." [8] He explains that "the physician must function first as diagnostician, then as healer or advisor." He concludes that "whatever he elects to do, his relationship to the patient is pre-eminent." Dr. Sacks bluntly writes: "His authority, his sympathy, and the countless intangibles and largely unconscious bonds which are forged in an effective doctor-patient relationship are as important as the sense or otherwise of anything he says or does." He believes that the answer in patients with migraine lies in "a sensitive feeling for suffering and nature, a deep sense of the healing power of nature itself…and the humility which seeks to woo nature, but never to bully it." [9]

Dr. Sacks is not only obviously very intelligent, but has humility, a trait unfortunately not very common to physicians as a group, in my opinion. Physicians are, in fact, educated not to have humility in the face of patients with serious and disastrous illnesses, injuries, and disabilities. We are admonished in our medical school and specialty training to always project an authoritative image. We are also encouraged not to identify with our patients in a human way, nor to use our human emotions and reactions to our patients as part of our therapeutic relationship with them. This is my experience. This is the experience of many of the physicians whose books I have read over many years.

In many of the stories of patients and their families in *We Cry Out*, people did not find doctors who were prepared to attempt to help them in the humane, sensitive way that Dr. Lown or Dr. Sacks would have. They often did not have the benefit of a multidisciplinary team obviously beneficial in these complex situations. Social support systems were often lacking or insufficient. Some families and affected people did better than others, but all certainly could have been better served than they actually were.

In her books, Dr. Rachel Remen writes about many issues from her perspective as an experienced physician who, in mid career, began working with seriously and terminally ill patients. These patients and their families clearly need a psycho-social-spiritual, as well as a biomedical approach, as do the people chronicled in *We Cry Out*. Dr. Remen writes in *My Grandfather's Blessings: Stories of Strength, Refuge, and Belonging*: "We avoid suffering only at the great cost of distancing ourselves from life." She makes the even more dramatic assertion that "science is not a place of refuge. It cannot protect us from suffering. Hiding from suffering only makes us more afraid." [10] Later she states: "The denial of common vulnerability is the ultimate barrier to compassion." [11] In her book *Kitchen Table: Stories that Heal* she writes: "the expectation that we can be immersed in suffering and loss daily and not be touched by it is as unrealistic as expecting to walk through water without getting wet." [12]

Dr. Remen, like the authors of some of the most insightful books I have read by physicians about living with chronic illness, has a serious chronic illness herself. The traditionally taught physician is told to be totally objective in her/his interactions with patients. We are told that it is important not to allow ourselves human feelings for our patients. Dr. Remen, Dr. Sacks, Dr. Lown, and other author-physicians persuasively argue that this attitude is a disservice to their patients. Dr. Remen maintains that physicians who do not allow themselves human feelings such as empathy and sympathy are more likely to be emotionally distressed than physicians who do allow themselves to feel these emotions. Their burnout is fueled by using more energy suppressing and/or avoiding their feelings than they would by allowing themselves to experience these feelings as a fellow human being. They also have more trouble being *healers* who encourage their patients to improve the control of their illnesses and/or live better with their illnesses.

Equally valuable insights can be found in books by non-physicians with chronic illness. From their experiences with the health care system and its providers, they express strong opinions about their need for a caring attitude. Reynolds Price, a well-known novelist, speaks to the issue in a small non-fiction book published in 1994—*A Whole New Life: An Illness and a Healing*. He writes movingly about his long-time struggle with a severely painful neurologically-handicapping, life-threatening, spinal cord tumor. He describes one of his physicians as a "freeze-dried physician" and writes poignantly of his yearning for the "humane doctors of my childhood and youth—the depths of understanding that they gained by submitting themselves to the lives of their patients—those are merely the skills of human sympathy, the skills of letting another creature know that his or her concern is honored and valued and that, whether a cure is likely or not, all possible effort will be expended to achieve that cure or to ease incurable agony toward its welcome end...." What he got, with some notable exceptions, was good technological care, but not enough caring by his doctors. [13]

Several of the books I studied were written by psychologists, psychiatrists, and other therapists. What I considered the best of these books—those showing the most depth of understanding of the psychosocial, family, and spiritual issues—were written by professionals who suffered chronic illnesses themselves. The strength of these books is that they clearly see the patient's perspective in dealing with the complex health care system. They also discuss issues often avoided or skirted by other books, such as the functional fluctuations characteristic of many chronic illnesses and stigmatization and marginalization of the chronically ill and neurologically impaired. This is true of the general public, but also of some professionals who should know better. Some of these attitudes may be sub-conscious, but none-the-less painful for the ill and their families.

No one "deserves" to be ill. Does this seem obvious? Sadly, this blaming attitude is all too common even from health professionals. Subtle, and occasionally blatant, blame for being ill is experienced by ill people. They almost universally feel some guilt about being ill—presumably based on the underlying assumption that if a person takes good care of herself/himself, eats a healthy diet, has a good life-style including exercise, takes vitamins, gets check-ups, then he/she will be healthy. Moral and religious beliefs enter this perspective unconsciously, and occasionally consciously. The belief that a moral and/or religious life guarantees good health, and that ill health implies punishment for bad thoughts or behaviors is certainly misguided. Susan Sontag, in *Illness as Metaphor*, [14], and Reynolds Price, in *A Whole New Life*, [15] deal extensively with moral and spiritual aspects which ill people often face in other people's social attitudes. In *Equal Partners: A Physician's Call for a New Spirit of Medicine*, Jody Heymann calls for a major overhaul of attitudes of physicians toward their patients. She specifically asks for sensitivity to patients' human needs. Dr. Heymann movingly emphasizes the essential need to overcome the stigma of having a chronic, incurable illness. She personally has had to deal with these issues as a physician with epilepsy. [16] Health and illness relate to a complex interaction between genetic factors, environmental factors, and bad or good luck.

Perhaps this relates to the lens of so-called scientific medicine through which we, as a culture, have learned to view issues related to health and illness. Many people have habits, environmental exposures, and genetics which can predispose them to illnesses, but only some people with these factors in their lives become ill. Our culture needs to re-introduce *bad luck* into our vocabulary, as well as *good luck* to explain the really inexplicable—that some people become ill and others in similar life circumstances do not. There truly may be no way to understand why.

The vocabulary of our culture also needs to include the concepts of grieving, healing, life transitions, and living one day at a time. In the West, we tend to believe that we can plan our lives and expect the future to unfold as we have planned it. The reality, of course, is that life is unpredictable. We often experience fortuitous or tragic unplanned events which change the trajectory of our existence. We really know this deep down, but many people remain in denial. We, as a culture, need to discuss these issues more freely. Eastern philosophies are more accepting of life's cyclic nature, the ups and downs characteristic of natural events. Books I read about Chinese and Indian healing traditions reflect these concepts.

The sudden appearance of illness or accident resulting in severe injury is truly no more predictable than natural disasters such as tornadoes, hurricanes, droughts, earthquakes, and forest fires. Predictions are based on probabilities that cannot be used to accurately predict what will, in fact, happen in any specific instance. Medical science deals with statistics from groups of people. Statistics are not directly applicable to specific patients in complex circumstances.

The chronically ill and disabled still can *heal* enough to live meaningful, dignified lives with some happiness and fulfillment. They may be able to help others, and be productive during their lives. The traditional definition of productivity likely needs to be changed to allow the ill and disabled to work in their own time frame. This is especially true of those with illnesses with fluctuating symptoms over days, weeks, or months. The productivity of family members is also impacted by not providing adequate social support systems to assist in the care of disabled family members. Much talent, life experience, and insight are lost by not allowing useful opportunities for contributions to other people and to our culture.

In reading the narratives in this book, please consider how helping these individuals and families effectively would help them live happier, more fulfilling, less guilt-filled lives. There are prominent examples of people with significant disabilities who were still able to make very important contributions to our national life. Such well-known people as Franklin D. Roosevelt, John F. Kennedy, Michael J. Fox, and Christopher Reeve all faced serious medical problems and/or handicaps. They have in common other key advantages including wealth, excellent health care, and family and social support systems. They all were, or have been, able to accomplish much and to live amazingly full lives with and despite their disabilities.

Obviously, people disabled from birth or during childhood or adolescence may not have the potential these famous people had, but what might they have accomplished if given adequate medical, family, and social support and encouragement? Helen Keller is an example of a person severely disabled by blindness and deafness at a very young age who was nevertheless able to make almost unimaginable contributions during her lifetime. Furthermore, the entire family of these affected people is often negatively impacted, directly or indirectly, by the stress of attempting to deal with the complex illnesses and disabilities of their family members without adequate support. The potential for a happy and productive life for these family members often is disrupted. Society is the poorer for this loss.

One fascinating example of what family support can accomplish is the story documented in the book *The Music of Light: The Extraordinary Story of Hikari and Kenzaburo Oe* by Lindsley Cameron. A significantly developmentally disabled child with extraordinary musical ability was able, with the intense loving support and active involvement of his musically-gifted father to develop his musical talent. He became a composer of his own unique music. Without the support of his father and mother this severely disabled child would never have been recognized as having musical genius or been able to become a noted composer. [17]

A less well-known author, Barbara Newborn, writes in a small book published in 1997 of her amazing story in *Return to Ithaca: A Woman's Triumph Over the Disabilities of a Severe Stroke*. This book, written in a moving and poetic way, describes the devastating effects of a stroke when she was 21 years old. She writes about her struggle to re-invent her life, despite her difficulty speaking and writing, using her remaining talents and developing new ones. She ultimately became a therapist herself for people with neurological disabilities. She fortunately had the love of her parents and friends, as well as the help of her therapists in her recovery and healing. She writes: "People defeat themselves when they are too afraid to even try." [18] She emphasizes that physical suffering and disablement need not destroy the human spirit, but may lead to resilience.

Ms. Newborn writes about her own devastating illness: "Despite the physical destruction caused by paralysis and aphasia, I was determined more than ever that nothing should prevent my healing. I knew that the inspiration for recovery was within me. My reasons for living would come from the heart. It was the onset of my metamorphosis." [19] It is clear from her narrative that without the consistent love of her family and friends and the assistance of the rehabilitation therapists, she would not have arrived at her metamorphosis. Unfortunately, not all of her physicians were encouraging. They focused on her statistically poor prognosis rather than letting her know that there is no way to predict any individual patient's rehabilitation potential, as her dramatic recovery illustrates.

Oliver Sacks' book, *Seeing Voices, A Journey Into the World of the Deaf,* documents similar stories of the essential need for family education, and for educational institutions specifically for the deaf, especially the congenitally deaf. Without their comprehensive assistance and encouragement, deaf people are not able to develop their intellectual talents. They often live sad, isolated lives without these interventions. [20]

Our colleague and friend, the late Susan Dahl, co-investigator with John DeFrain of the narratives in *We Cry Out*, was able to accomplish much in her life with encouragement from her family, her friends, her physicians. Her great determination and intelligence were other necessary ingredients in what she made of her life.

Please remember that all of us, professionals and non-professionals alike, need to be aware of our own biases and points-of-view so that we do not impose them on our interpretation of these stories. We, at a minimum, need to understand that we view things through the perspective of our own life experiences. Listening, really listening, requires remembering this truth. Only by self-awareness can we even come close to creatively helping our clients, family, and friends to live with the losses and traumas every life contains.

In the final chapter of the book, John DeFrain and I, taking into account what Susan Dahl's views likely would be if she were alive today, will try to summarize the threads common to these stories to weave a fabric of conclusions attempting to interpret their implications. We will also suggest how professionals and society can better help prevent the loss of the contributions these people would have likely made, and to promote the happiness they could have had.

WHO WE HOPE WILL READ THIS BOOK

We hope many people of all backgrounds read this book. Primary care physicians provide much of the care for even these challenging patients because there are not enough specialists available to provide all the needed long-term care. They should read this book. Other health care professionals and student health care professionals, mental health professionals, and students should read this book. Disabled and chronically ill people, their families, and friends should read and evaluate this book to see if it reflects their experiences. We encourage you to take your time as you read these narratives. They are emotionally charged and moving. Allow yourselves to feel the emotions. We welcome your feedback and comments.

INTRODUCTION

How does a developmental disability affect an individual throughout the course of life? What impact does the disability have on the individual's family? What strengths do families use to cope with these disabilities? What do they do that works? And, what doesn't work? These are the kinds of questions we have been asking individuals and families in our research over the past 15 years. This book was written to report their stories, and to honor these people who have shared their lives and their cries from the heart with us. It is both a positive book and a realistic book: full of love and grief and tenderness and anger and kindness and sorrow and courage. It is as real as the people who gave us the gift of their lives.

"Disability." A word that means something different to each person who uses it. Some people don't like it. Some people do. Others prefer to use the word "handicap" or "handicapped." And then some like to use "physically challenged." It is also becoming more common to use the phrase "a person who experiences a disability," the focus being on the "person" first, rather than the disability. Actually, it is somewhat difficult to keep up with the current fashions in terminology. Some of us are even old enough to have suffered under such descriptions as "feeble-minded," "deaf and dumb," and "the lame and the halt." Unfortunately, all too frequently, "crippled" still creeps into daily conversation and media productions. Today there simply is not "one word" that works for everyone. There may never be.

Irregardless of what word or words we use to describe a person's physical or mental status, when we use "disability" or another word, we are recognizing that the person has something "wrong" with them. To say that they have something "wrong" with them is in no way a value judgment as to their worth as a human being. It doesn't mean that something has to be "fixed" to make them a valid person in their own right. It simply means that they are dealing with some kind of physical or mental "problem" that is affecting their life in some way.

It would be safe to suggest that most people at one time in their life have had or will have a physical or mental difficulty that is, at least, temporary in nature.

While it presents a crisis at the moment, the occurrence of the problem isn't likely to impact their entire lives or the lives of their families or friends. And, of course, none of us who are fortunate to be able-bodied never know what may be "waiting around the corner" in the future. Life is a roller-coaster that is constantly twisting and turning, bringing new challenges to all of us.

For the purpose of this book, we have focused our research on the individuals and families in which the disability has occurred early in life, and is likely to be permanent. This decision created difficult challenges for us as researchers, because there are so many kinds of disabilities, and there is so much variance in the severity of the disability. Would some kinds of disabilities make more of an impact than other kinds of disabilities? And, how does one measure the impact of a disability? In the final analysis, we chose to be inclusive rather than exclusive. The variety of disabilities described in this book is enormous.

Our biggest question was whether or not to limit ourselves just to those disabilities that were physical in nature. If we added mental disabilities, would that just confound the issues? In some ways, we felt that the issues might be different. But yet, since we wanted to see how a disability affected the family, it seemed in the end that we should include both mental as well as physical disabilities. If what we wanted to see was how an individual or a family coped with a disability, then why not include them all in the study together? This proved to be a wise decision. As the reader will see, the disabilities may differ, but the challenges people face emotionally are remarkably similar.

We did need some limits for the study, however. Since we wanted to see how the individual and family dealt with the disability over a period of time, it made sense from a developmental perspective to pick families and individuals where the disability occurred early in the life of the person. While someone becoming disabled later in life certainly can be traumatic, it would not likely have the same effect on the family in terms of how they coped with it over the long-term.

Different categories of disabilities are legion. Some are very broad. Some are very specific. According to the most recent census, there are 48 million persons in the United States with severe physical or mental disabilities. But we felt that we needed to have a more specific focus for our research. After much debate, we finally decided to use the current "developmental disability" definition. Even the definition of a "developmental disability" varies from state to state, so nothing is crystal clear and exact, but at least it gave us a place to start.

The Developmental Disabilities and Bill of Rights Act of 1994 states that a "developmental disability" means a severe, chronic disability that is attributable to a mental or physical impairment or combination of mental and physical impairments. It has to have occurred before the individual attains age 22, and is likely to continue indefinitely. The disability must result in functional limitations in three or more of these areas of major life activity: self-care, receptive and expressive language, learning, mobility, self-direction, capacity for independent living, and economic self-sufficiency. Obviously, this can mean different things in each individual situation, but it accomplished our desire to limit ourselves to individuals or families that have been dealing with a disability for a period of time starting in childhood, adolescence, or young adulthood. Figures from recent studies by the Arc of the United States indicate that approximately three percent of the population have developmental disabilities. The Arc has also found that one out of every ten extended families in our country has a member with a developmental disability (this figure includes not only the nuclear family but the extended family as well—parents, children, grandparents, aunts and uncles, cousins).

Now that we had decided upon our "population," we needed to decide what we wanted to know about them, their disabilities and how they deal with life. We developed two 80-question forms, one designed for the individual with the disability and one designed for family members. We also added a few questions to the family member's forms for young children with developmental disabilities and their young siblings. We felt their input was a necessary part of the total picture. Parents were asked to interview their young children and write down the responses. The questions were predominantly open-ended in nature, giving the person the opportunity to share as little or as much as they wished. We were not particularly interested in a great deal of statistical data, but more in the individual stories of their experiences.

With the questionnaires done and ready to go, we needed to find the people. Of course, this was an entirely volunteer option for them. We were asking for them to share their personal lives with us, and that had to be their decision. We sent 500 press releases to newspapers in all 50 states, asking for volunteers to fill out our questionnaires. We also sent notices to all of the developmental disability state offices, and as many disability-related groups as we could find. We merely asked for individuals to write to us indicating their willingness to participate in the study.

The response was overwhelming. We received letters from 354 persons in 39 states, and ultimately received completed questionnaires from 245 adults and children. We suddenly found ourselves with about 5,000 pages of personal testimony of life with a developmental disability. It was very exciting. Another step was completed.

Now, what to do with those 5,000 pages of life stories? First we thought perhaps we should examine all of the different issues that had surfaced on the questionnaires, and we did work in that direction for awhile. But as we continued to read one questionnaire after another, it became obvious that each one represented a story in itself. It felt like we were destroying the "whole picture" to focus on issues rather than people. We wanted these individuals' stories to be intact and speak for themselves. The issues became less important. The stories individuals and families shared became uppermost in our minds.

We began the process of choosing the most representative stories to share. This was difficult. Each one had something important and unique to say. But we did have to choose. All of the stories in the book are actual stories taken directly from the questionnaires. We have only added an occasional "editorial" word to put the stories in a narrative form. We personally prefer the term "developmental disability," or the phrase "individuals or families who have experienced a developmental disability." But within each story, we have left the descriptive terms exactly as the person has written them. It was important to us to maintain the integrity and perspective of each individual.

We chose to organize the stories beginning with people who have lived with a developmental disability for a long time—fifty years or more—and moving inexorably decade by decade toward those who are just beginning the journey. We felt this approach would help the reader put the experience of coping with a developmental disability into a life-long, one-day-at-a-time perspective. The book, then, moves steadily from the past to the present, and ends with thoughts about how to create a better future. There is a sense of tension the book conveys to the reader: Will these families relatively new to the experience face the same desperate challenges of those families who came before? Will these families today be able, somehow, to do better in the face of adversity? Will our society become more sensitive and caring in regard to these families? Can anyone know, for sure, what the future will bring?

Our final decision was to keep "professional stuff" out of the book as much as possible. "Professor talk" has its place in life, but frankly, the individuals and families who have experienced these disabilities are the true "experts." We have found in previous research projects that what readers generally focus on is how real people deal with their problems on a daily basis. What researchers have to say about all this is relatively unimportant to most individuals and families striving desperately to understand this difficult challenge they face. So, we will be relatively unobtrusive in these pages. Our words in the concluding chapter offer a modest synthesis of what we believe we have learned. We hope that the experiences of these people will offer guidance and hope to others who are dealing with similar situations in their lives. That is what we are offering to you in this book, then: the gift of these families' lives, honestly and movingly presented. Listen, and gain strength from what they have to say to you.

FIFTY YEARS

Stories told by individuals and family members who have been challenged by a disability for at least five decades.

I'D LOVE TO BE NORMAL.
I WOULD GO TO SCHOOL AND TEACH OTHERS

Cerebral palsy has affected this 66-year-old woman's life since birth:

I have cerebral palsy, my speech is affected and coordination is poor. It was caused by a birth injury.

When I was seven and my brother went to school, I told my mother she didn't love me because I couldn't do like the rest of the kids.

I lived at an institution from age five for 18 months, and then I went back at age ten after my mother died. At age 35 I went to a school in Kansas but they told me I was too old.

When I was in my early 20's and people got married—that was the hardest.

I like it when people encourage me, and most people are patient when I try to talk. It's difficult when we go out to eat and they ask someone else what I want.

I have never known anything else. I know I have missed something by not being married, but I don't know what I missed.

I'd love to be normal. I would go to school and teach others.

My favorite dream is I'm all right and driving a car.

My dad disappeared when I was little and I believe I had something to do with it. It was hard for my mother to have a handicapped child with no husband and no relatives. My family has been gone since I was ten.

Sometimes people get upset when I eat. Sometimes they say I talk too loud.

I wish I could have been married.

If I had not been disabled, maybe I would have been a teacher, or a mother...who knows. I feel my thinking would be different.

I wonder why I was born this way.

The hardest thing about being disabled is I can't do things I would like to do. Can't do normal things, like own my own home.

My knee is giving out. It's hard to get up from the davenport. Makes me wonder how long I can take care of myself. I know the future will bring death and eternal life.

I'm not afraid.

IN THESE LATTER YEARS SHE HAS ALSO BEEN A BLESSING

Sixty-five years ago this woman, age six at the time, became the big sister to a baby girl who subsequently was diagnosed as speech handicapped with mild cerebral palsy:

My sister, Aldine, is speech handicapped and has a mild case of cerebral palsy. As a baby she had a fall. She cried very hard. The doctor determined that she injured a part of her brain which controls speech. At first, when she would normally begin to talk, she would try to make sounds and roll her tongue. Her first real words weren't sounded until two-and-a-half to three years old. She didn't form sentences until five, and then very few people could understand her. Her words were taught to her through repetition. At the age now of 65, through additional speech therapy, she is able to communicate quite well. At first she is hard to understand, but as you grow accustomed to her speech, in time most people can understand what she says.

I remember when she was born at home, she appeared to be a normal baby. I was six when she was born and I remember being disappointed when she could not talk to me as a normal child would. I remember when she was taken as a small child to chiropractors and child specialists to determine the root of her speech problem and being finally told to take her home and love and care for her. She would probably not be the child who would give them problems, but rather me, her normal older sister.

It was very hard to finally realize that she would never be able to speak normally.

It is easier to be with her as an adult, because she has come to terms with her disability and is no longer envious or jealous of me because I am normal.

Grade school was difficult. When my parents enrolled her in the public school, I was six years older and my classmates would ask me about my "funny little sister." When I had girlfriends as overnight guests she would take an article of their clothing, like a belt, and run outside and throw it away. This was very embarrassing to me.

She attended first grade in the public school and repeated the next year for a few months. It wasn't possible for her to continue as the teacher couldn't give her individual attention. Then my parents enrolled her in the State School for the Deaf. This was a bad decision because she tried to talk less, and began to use sign language. They took her out, and at the age of ten enrolled her at the State School for the Feebleminded where she was for ten years. They educated her as much as possible. She returned home in 1989, after the death of both parents, and she became a client of a residential center.

A few people commented about how terrible it was when I enrolled her in the residential center and that she no longer had a home. The truth of the matter is that she has never been happier or felt more independent.

My sister understands our need to talk things out. My parents were very supportive of my feelings and concerns. My husband was wonderful and a great help. When my parents died we had decisions to make regarding my sister's future and welfare. A professional therapist helped when my mother died and Aldine was very upset.

When we were children, I felt embarrassed and a little ashamed of my little sister. Also, I was afraid that when I brought dates home to meet my family that they would think less of me because I had a handicapped little sister and wouldn't ask me out again. Now as an adult, I accept her, love her, and am emotionally secure.

I feel my parents and I did all we could to teach her to talk and provide other means for her to cope and learn with her handicap.

At this stage in life, as a widow, I would like to move to another state to be nearer to my three children, but hesitate to leave my sister here far from my family and me. She and I are the only children my parents had, so she depends upon me.

My three children coped with her well, except our youngest son who often was blamed for things my sister did, i.e., eating cookies from the freezer, etc. My husband was very understanding of her until he lost his health. At that time he became frustrated when he couldn't understand what she was saying or she talked too much when he had visitors.

My parents paid for her expenses. She is now on Medicare and Title 19. She has a paid-up insurance policy in the event of her death, a paid cemetery lot, and a tombstone in place.

My husband knew that as her only sibling, I felt responsible for her well-being after our parents died. He also knew how I was concerned about how my friends' boyfriends felt about her when I was young.

When my mother was ill with cancer at age 88 and she knew she was going to die, I said, "Mother, my sister has been a burden to you, hasn't she? You have had a cross to bear." She replied, "Yes, but in these latter years she has also been a blessing."

My sister: Sarah, I am sorry that I was jealous and envious of you and sometimes I showed it.

Me: I knew you felt jealous of me and I understood. I just hope that now you don't feel that way because you have a happy independent life now.

As a whole, she gets along well with people. She really likes her supervisors, anyone who teaches or works with her. She has some problems with other clients. Some are boisterous and noisy and this irritates her. I just fear that if I die before she does that she would have a hard time living without my support.

THE FATHER OF MY RETARDED SON COMMITTED SUICIDE. WHAT WOULD HAPPEN TO MY FAMILY IF I DID THE SAME THING?

A 69-year-old sister talks about her 65-year-old mentally-retarded brother:
Adolescence was the most difficult for me, because I loved him so. When he was taken to live at the state school, I was devastated. My heart actually felt like it was physically broken in two. That was when I learned life sometimes brings you things worse than death. I would have given or done anything to make him able to live normally and be home.

My brother has profound mental retardation because of the Fragile X Syndrome. He learned only limited speech, and is unable to make decisions or live on his own. We do not know where the Fragile X originated; we know of no people on either side of the family with this disability.

You feel acceptance from those who have gone through similar situations and have chosen the method of help (institutionalization) that you did. When you are hearing from society about those who were described as retarded, and later turned out to be intelligent, or presuming all retarded can be trained or taught to be self-sufficient or live in a group home, it's comforting to know others chose the option you did.

Some comments are not helpful: "He's not retarded. He's normal. He looks normal. He just needs training." (Fragile X children are normal at birth and they do look normal until their walk and mannerisms betray that.) It's been painful for me and my family to hear institutions always spoken of in disparaging terms. I know there have been gross abuses, but I feel he is happier there than any other situation we could have planned for him.

[I felt] Great, great grief when he went to live at the state school. I can't begin to explain the deep sorrow and grief. It caused concern regarding my dating. When, how soon in the relationship, do I reveal I have a mentally-retarded brother? And concern when I was pregnant that my child might be retarded.

I am glad my parents realized that my sister and I had a right to our life. Thus they made plans for him so we girls could choose our life. If my parents would have left him to remain at home (and I cried and begged that they would), I would have renounced marriage, family, etc., and become his helper. I'm glad and so thankful they had the love and foresight re: us. Also when my parents died, his life continued on an even keel. Knowing his needs are met and he's happy gives me peace.

Father: grief, a shattering of his dreams (I believe), although I didn't realize it until lately. My brother was named with the initials of his paternal grandfather.

He was the one to carry on the family name for my father. I know he had dreams for him when my brother was little. In fairness to my father, my sister nor I never heard my father complain about these matters or indicate he would rather have a normal son than daughters.

Mother: grief.

Sister: some grief but not to the extent of my parents. She had concern about telling her husband during their dating.

I spent so much time with my brother when he was home. I really tended him much of the time. He and I developed a very close relationship. He loved my father and mother dearly, but I was his favorite in the family.

We discussed our grief. Mother shared how she wanted to bring him home from the school and have him live at home, but my father reasoned with her it was not what they had thought was best for my brother, my sister and me in the years ahead. When I had my own retarded son, we often talked about how they felt and went through when he was with them. My parents chose no more children. They did not want to bring another mentally-retarded child into the world.

If he had not been disabled, he could have attended school, college. He could have had a career, a livelihood. He could have married, had a home, a family. He would be able to reason, make decisions, maintain social relationships. I would be able to relate, communicate with a brother and his family. I would be able to make use of travel and volunteer opportunities from our church. Since I feel I don't want to be gone more than three weeks (to visit him and my son) I need to refuse these privileges.

I had thought of killing him, my son and myself to deliver us into a glorious eternity (according to my belief). I never felt God "caused" it. I believe suicide for me is a sin. God will give me the grace and strength to carry on. Suicide solves nothing; it only leaves the problem (and adds more problems) to the survivors. The father of my retarded son committed suicide. What would happen to my family if I did the same thing?

It's been hard to accept that I had no brother to communicate with as a child. Today the hardest thing to accept is to realize the very serious loss and pain it must have meant to my father to have his only son so terribly disabled.

I'm afraid the push will be to put him in a group home.

I THINK MY DAD BLAMED ME FOR MY MOTHER DYING

Now 63, this woman describes how cerebral palsy has affected her life:

I have cerebral palsy and am in a wheelchair, unable to walk. My mother had uremic poisoning, something to do with the kidney. She was in the basement when the phone or doorbell went off. They think she ran up the stairs and tripped and fell down the steps. She laid for a long time before she was found. She was taken to the hospital where I was born. They told my dad they could lose me. My mother never regained consciousness and died two weeks later. At about six years old, I noticed I couldn't stand up without falling.

I was put in a state institution when I was 11. I remained there for 20 years and during that time I went through a living hell. Example: People were strapped down and put in straight jackets.

I never went to any school. What I know I taught myself. I would like to be able to read.

For awhile I was upset about being disabled but as I got older I figured it was meant to be.

I'm not around my family, we were separated when we were young. I wish they would pay more attention to me, they only see me twice a year. No one has ever expressed their feelings about me. Father remarried after mother died and my step-mother did not like his kids.

I think my faith has grown. If it wasn't for my belief in God…he is always there for me when others aren't. Sometimes I think he was punishing me for something.

I think my dad blamed me for my mother dying.

During my stay at the institution, I thought about suicide.

The hardest is not being able to walk.

I don't think anybody can really know how it feels to be disabled unless they are.

SHOT ABOVE THE EARTH, I TUMBLED
AMONG THE JUMBLE OF SOUNDS

A 63-year-old woman, deaf from birth, comments on her disability and her loved ones:

I have nerve loss deafness. It wasn't diagnosed until age 13. I was the "cute" little kid who said everything in a strange way. I was in a nursery class at our small church. I was always with normal children. At the start I was babied and enjoyed. Thus, I was always in the midst of a group. This is not usual. It encouraged me to feel accepted and lovable. We had many kids in the family so Mama had help from them and I never lacked for individual care, including reading aloud. Perhaps the imitations of a reader put unusual expressions into my speech. Whatever happened, I certainly profited from my escape from the social services that are now available for our deaf. I was accepted and felt free to find my own way.

I have loud tintinitus; the jumbled, mixed rhythm was frightening. I knew the fears of being "shot" sky high by sounds only I could hear. Once shot above the earth I tumbled among the jumble of sounds. I still dislike high places! Years later, I was to know a child with deafness. He knew and loved and accepted me. I once dared to say to four-year-old Duane, "Do you hear the noises?" Startled, he paled and whispered, "Can you hear them?" I said, "Not yours, but mine." Since he remained very scared, I put an arm around him and in a storytelling voice, I said, "When I was little I was afraid of the loud noises I was sure only I heard." He looked startled and after a bit said, "Aren't you scared now?" I replied, "Why ever would I be afraid of just a noise. It doesn't hurt me any. It is just a noise. I think maybe when you are big enough to have your corrective surgery they might go away." After a bit he sat upright and said to me, "I am never scared of just a noise."

I hated my hearing tests because it made everyone else scared of my deafness. (Most did not know I had it.) I spent ages 13-18 scared of me. Then I quit fearing me...Ah, well, one tries.

Always at home someone loved me. That helped.

Mama was 41 at my birth...Was that it? Well, at age 13 a hearing aid was tried. It was discarded by mutual agreement of teachers, parents, doctors and me. Thank heavens! At age 13 the hearing tests were scary. I never pleased anyone who worked with me. They couldn't understand my one-of-a-kind hearing loss. It was all too new in 1942.

It's very difficult accepting the reality, perhaps of the size of the loss. This is a devastating handicap but I do not feel handicapped by it. I think I hear, but I hear with my ears no words at all. No pain. But whatever does silence sound like? How I'd love to hear it. [Is it] Peaceful?

Early grade school teachers sometimes puzzled me, like when I misunderstood them. I have usually had good relationships with school teachers and great friends of some. Because reading and family interest was always a part of my life, that helped encourage me on through. The schools discouraged my college dreams. I studied photo-retouching and worked at it.

In high school almost the whole class were close friends. At lunch one day someone complained about an assignment due next period. I said, "What chart?"

"Oh," Carol wailed, "about three or four. You have a chart due for next period."

Well, someone had some art paper and someone else was leafing through a new *Seventeen*, and in a few minutes my chart was together, but we didn't have any paste or tape.

"Oh, what to do?"

Edna was "off on her clouds of thoughts," and absent-mindedly cracked her illegal gum. In a few minutes my chart was together to the joy of the whole table. I complained it would never be accepted. It smelled like Tutti Fruiti gum.

But it was accepted!

People can be so "unhelpful": "Well, I can't see how you can fit in. You see, we expect you to get some work done here!" and "Tell me what you didn't hear and I'll repeat."

I have survived by staying in touch with myself. That has been painful/tearful/time-consuming, but very good. I hope I am open to see another's pain. This is not the "easy" way to live, but it is a lot easier than being closed and uptight.

Feeling disabled is noisy, jumpy, being afraid of me, unsure of how I will react, scared, and always wrong.

I wish I could telephone my kids. TDD just is not human warmth.

Conversations with my parents said I was a joy to them, and vice versa. We could get angry and get over it quickly. An example of how Mama handled me: Excursion boats to a picnic/amusement area are available in our city. We went two or so times a summer and she always invited a playmate or two to go along. As the boat steamed down the river, Mama would point out the docked boats and tell us where they were from or where they were bound out to, what they brought and what they loaded to take where. I assumed everyone knew this. Sometime perhaps in my 40s I realized she memorized the shipping news from the morning newspaper. What a geography lesson! What a vocabulary lesson! How my playmates loved Mama!

My siblings say: "Ellen, of course you were spoiled rotten, that's what saved you!"

My disability has affected other people, good and bad. I've been a great help to some. A real bother to others. Oh, life!

Life knocks us all down.

[Sex?] I guess I must admit my husband is it: my only sexual relationship. Some boyfriends kissed better! We've lived a tough life and done a big job. Sex has been important to both of us and we know that.

The Lord our God loves with an unconditional love. My deafness is loved as a part of my condition. My deafness is usable to Him. Now that's where I think He's really a puzzle! But it's true.

Suicide? Well, something always is just too interesting to let go of, and I sigh and go onward. The hardest thing is when my disability hurts others and deafness does. I feel crazy when deafness is considered "dumb," you know.

The future, don't bother to think about it, except to plan where to live and on what, etc.

WHEN I LOOK TOWARD THE FUTURE I JUST SEE "WORSE"

This 62-year-old man has dealt with polio since he was a baby:
When I was nine months old, I contracted infantile paralysis and was affected from the waist down. Around five years old I was put in braces. At age eight I was operated on and regained the use of my left leg. My right leg is mostly deformed to the hip, and I walk with a limp. I remember being afraid in the hospital and wanting to see my relatives. Also, I remember the itching inside the casts, and the pain when they removed them.

The worst has been not being able to perform like everyone else.

During the hurricane of '38 or '39 I was in casts up to my hips. My brother put me in the window to watch the action. One real tall elm started swaying in my direction and I started hollering for my brother. The tree eventually fell in the opposite direction.

Most of the time the pain doesn't go away.

They should have made me exercise more after my operation at age eight or nine.

The disability has made me more bashful, more bitter. Conspicuous, incompetent. I wish I could run and play more sports.

The bad part for my parents was that they had to bring up a handicapped child. My children had to do more around the house. All of them had to spend time around a handicapped person.

I don't make such a big hit with the opposite sex, but some adjust. I don't think my disability has made any difference after we become acquainted. Some of the women I meet aren't very adventurous.

Why am I being punished if there is a god?

I've thought about suicide, but not about my handicap, but about getting older with more diseases to contend with. I am experiencing post-polio syndrome. I don't want to lose any more maneuverability.

My biggest fears are financial collapse and having to live in a nursing home. When I look toward the future I just see "worse".

AS A TEENAGER I WISHED I WOULD DIE MANY TIMES, BECAUSE EVERYTHING GOOD ENDED AND NOTHING NEW HAPPENED AND I WAS VERY LONELY

Life has been very difficult for this 53-year-old woman with cerebral palsy, though she now enjoys her job and works with happy people. Her younger sister's story follows:

I can't walk. I can't use my hands. My mouth falls out of shape when I try to talk. I have cerebral palsy. After an operation to straighten my legs when I was 13, I couldn't sit up anymore without pushing my arm around the back of my chair. Now I have a twisted back.

I almost died when I was born. My mother was anemic while carrying me. My face was bruised and I had seizures when I was born. I remember when I was five or six, I was afraid to be alone, so I would roll off the sofa, roll over to the door and cry until mother came in. When I was two or three I was afraid of baths, afraid of drowning. I was afraid to roll over onto my stomach in the water.

The braces were the worst, then therapy. It was wasted. I didn't get better. I was disappointed with the operation, too.

During adolescence I hated everybody and I hated myself. I wanted to walk so bad and do things by myself.

I don't know if it's just my age, but I enjoy things more now than I used to. I work with happy people. We all work together. I like it when people don't think of me as disabled or treat me that way, when they are friendly and not shy about talking to me. When they ask me what I want. It's hard when people don't even know me but they don't like me because I'm disabled. When they treat me as if I were mentally retarded or deaf. When people let me know that it's not all right to move around, but I have to.

I wish I had been on medicine when I was young so I wasn't so nervous.

When I move my arms and legs, I feel like I bother people. I feel uncomfortable. Sometimes when people are sick and dying, I get awfully upset. Sometimes I feel real sad inside that I can't walk or use my hands or feed myself. I would rather be paralyzed from the waist down because then I could use my hands.

I was the first child. I didn't want anybody but Mother to take care of me. It was hard for her. She had to stay home a lot. It was hard for her to lift me all of the time. Dad had to work hard to pay for doctors and therapy. He couldn't serve in WWII because he had to take care of Mom and me. My brothers teased me a lot. My younger brother didn't want me around when his friends came over. My sister was like a second mother to me. She was the one who could understand me best.

Mother took care of me 24 hours a day. Everyone else went out during the day. Also, when I was born and so sick, it was awful for her. Mother kept it inside and got ulcers. Dad had a bad temper and yelled a lot.

My siblings didn't know how to deal with me. They felt sorry for me but they were embarrassed with their friends. I told them I was sorry I made their growing up hard for them.

When I was little I was afraid to be around other people. I was nervous and moved around a lot and bothered them. Sometimes I hit people accidentally and I felt ashamed. It's hard to talk and get people to understand me.

I believe everybody has a disability in one way or another.

I didn't know about sex until I moved into nursing home when I was 29. Another patient touched me and the nurse suggested my sister tell me about why I shouldn't let that happen. She explained all about sex.

God allowed me to live because he has a purpose for me here on earth this way, but I don't know what it is. I blame God first. Sometimes I blame Mom and Dad. I blame the doctors who didn't help, but made me worse.

As a teenager I wished I would die many times, because everything good ended and nothing new happened and I was very lonely.

I can cope better when you don't feel sorry for me. I don't feel sorry for myself. Other people are a lot worse than I am.

I want to go to school again to learn how to read and spell better. I'm afraid to get my hopes up too high about going to school. Sometimes I worry that I won't be able to go to work or have my apartment if I get sick.

When I'm feeling bad about myself, I think about others who are worse off than me and then I don't feel so bad. I teach people how to take care of handicapped people. My disability makes other people act better and be more caring.

IF THIS IS HER ONLY CHANCE AT LIVING, IT'S JUST NOT FAIR

This 47-year-old woman gives her perspective on the life of her sister, whose personal story was told directly before this narrative:

My sister has severe athetoid cerebral palsy. She uses a manual wheelchair, has little control of her arms, and her speech is very much affected. She is unable to sit up without propping her arm around the back of her chair, which has resulted in a twisted spine.

The disability was caused during a long and difficult birth. When my parents first saw her, one side of her face was bruised. She had a seizure after birth.

I remember taking her for walks around the neighborhood and teaching her what I learned in school. Talking together after we went to bed. I must have been at least six years old.

As a child I was overwhelmed with sadness and the need to make her life more satisfying. She had a teacher come to our home for 11 years for approximately ten hours a month. She got the basics in reading and math. I informally taught her myself as a child, and about ten years ago in a formal educational program for about one year. As an adolescent, I felt embarrassed when she was around my friends.

When she was young there were no training programs or jobs for severely-disabled persons. Today there aren't any for people of her age. She paints landscapes and sells them. Her sense of accomplishment is great. She loves being with friends, special events, going and doing things. Sometimes she just sits, waiting for others to come.

People are helpful when they let her do what she can, treat her with respect and as an intelligent adult, give her their complete attention, and invite her to go places and include her in their lives.

People are not helpful when they are condescending, treating her as if she were retarded, deaf, or completely helpless. They are not helpful when they won't give her their complete attention, especially when she is talking to them.

Psychotherapy helped me to understand the childhood difficulties I experienced as a sibling of a disabled person. Also, to discuss the ongoing and lifelong responsibilities that I have with her. Also, the reason I am a graduate student in special education.

I needed psychological help as a child and didn't get it. My parents needed it and didn't get it.

I grew up feeling responsible for my sister's happiness, trying to placate my father's anger, trying to be a perfect daughter, overly sensitive to shame, and disturbed about body image and functioning.

I love her. I pity her. I do what I can for her. I feel so much responsibility for her now and for the future. It's demanding, stressful, and it never ends. I wish I were free to live in another state. I wish I were free to make other arrangements for holidays than providing a place for my sister to come to. I wish I had not been so impacted by it in my childhood. I would have had to been born with a different temperament.

I wish our family could have been more emotionally open, discussing problems, brothers sharing responsibility with me for our sister.

My sister has had her horizons dimmed by her disability and lack of interventions. My parents were devastated by their first-born's disability. There was confusion, bitterness. Father's anger and negativity. Mother's emotional distancing and frustration. Brothers rebelled, were embarrassed with friends, escaped the enmeshment. I was the second girl, third child, enmeshed in the family tragedy which created self-esteem problems in my life.

Until she moved at age 29 into a nursing home, my parents were responsible for my disabled sister's total care, feeding, dressing, bathing, toileting. When she visits me, I take care of those needs. She was well cared for at home until the last years when her need became very taxing on her aging parents. Mother, especially, felt some anger and frustration at the lack of freedom and the time and physical strength necessary for her care.

My parents did not wish to rely on financial help from organizations. My father was critical and impatient with them. After she left home, however, SSA and SSI have taken care of her financial needs. My parents have bought a funeral/ burial plan for her.

I have talked with my parents about the disability only to sympathize with them over their hardships and their accomplishments in her happiness today. I guess I did this so I could hear them sympathize with me. They also talk to me about how they wish I didn't have the responsibility after they die. I matter of factly tell them that I do have it. It made them survivors, but I think it embittered them and made them sadder and angrier than they might have been.

For me, her disability has made me compassionate, tenacious, responsible. I care about the world. I care about people. I'm a better mother. I'm working with special needs children. But her disability also brought too much responsibility, anger, fear, frustration at too early an age. My life has been harder to live.

At my instigation because of psychotherapy, my sister and I have talked about the plusses and the minuses of our relationship. We know what we have meant to each other.

She is open, joyous, and delighted to be around other people. She feels a mission to teach others about herself. Other people respond to her warmth and openness. She makes people feel good.

I told her the facts of life complete with drawings when I was in my 20s and she in her 30s. [And sexuality?] What sexuality? Prior to our talk she had been touched sexually by a nursing home aide and she didn't understand what had happened.

I used to think God had a purpose for making this happen to my sister, but I lost my religious faith when my husband died and my feeling of personal connection with a God that cared. I don't get mad at God anymore. I think that's why I lost my faith in religion. Feeling mad at God is so futile, such a fantasy.

The cause? An old doctor using archaic delivery methods. Either the forceps slipped or my sister was dropped or the delivery was so long and traumatic, injury was inevitable. No one in the family knows for sure exactly what happened.

If this is her only chance at living, it's just not fair.

As a child I used to pray that my sister and I could switch bodies. Did I do this to take her pain or get the attention? Probably both. I have arthritis and bursitis in my knees. I had to get a temporary handicapped parking sticker for my car once because walking became too difficult. I felt like such a fraud doing it, though. I have always felt that I had little or no control over my body. I'm sure this feeling comes from relating to my sister and her lack of control over her body.

I don't look forward to the future. I really think her life will be much more difficult then.

If I have learned nothing else from my relationship with my sister, I have learned that caring and doing what you can to make life better is what life is all about. It's a late career, but I am training in the pre-school education and early intervention with infants and toddlers program to work with children with disabilities.

FORTY YEARS

Stories told by by individuals and family members who have been challenged with a disability for four to five decades.

IT'S DIFFICULT TO KEEP UP A PLEASANT
AND POSITIVE PERSONALITY WHEN YOU'RE BLEEDING TO DEATH

Since birth, this 47-year-old man has been challenged by hemophilia:
My earliest memory was wondering why I looked "different"—everyone else was circumcised. I had frequent sore joints, and I was treated very carefully, protected. I have hemophilia, an inherited genetic disease that is carried through the female to the male offspring. Clotting factor in the blood is low or missing. I bruise easily, get internal bleeding and have problems with external bleeds. With age, joints deteriorate and lose motion. This also gets painful. Activity is limited by ability to move and to endure pain.

The news media proclaims that all hemophiliacs must be HIV positive. They're wrong.

There can be several serious problems. You really don't lose a lot of blood before things happen. The one that scared me the most was a hemorrhage of the jaw just caused by a dentist shooting Novocain into the nerve. As I bled, I swelled and couldn't swallow. Breathing became hard and I got symptoms of a stroke. I really thought it was all over.

Things are different and better than 30 to 40 years ago. Back then, I recall there were lots of home remedies and doctors who just didn't know what to do. Then, there were hundreds of transfusions, ever-changing treatments, and many long drives to university hospitals because only they could treat it. No one understood it, but every doctor thought he was right. I endured weeks of transfusions, traction, surgery, braces, rehabilitation, strange diets, etc. I learned a lesson I still believe today: No one listens to a kid!

By the 60s I enjoyed free run of the local small town hospital, self check-in, self dismissal and self treatment. Most doctors were scared of trying to treat it. I nearly bled to death driving 300 miles looking for someone to sew up a half-inch cut. By the 70s a platelet concentrate was developed and totally changed my life. This allowed home treatment. It also confused doctors who didn't stay up on the treatment. And it was about this time that insurance became more of a problem than the disease.

During the elementary school years, I hadn't lost joint motion yet. I lived on a farm and didn't miss activity I might have not been able to have with friends in town. Farm kids in those days spent time alone, healthy or not. I missed a lot of class in high school. I'm sure my grades suffered. Also, I didn't follow my interests in college because of the limits I knew I had. I knew I couldn't farm, couldn't be a mechanic, and couldn't work for any large company. Currently, I'm a salesman. The good side is that I'm free to do my own thing as I see fit. The bad part is trying to keep up a pleasant and positive personality while I'm bleeding to death.

Pain is the most prominent thing in my life. I work everything else around it: work, food, sleep, etc. There are days it gets out of control and you don't know where you are headed. The average person may not see this situation, may not understand it, and may not care. To help, a person has to let me be the judge of what I can or cannot do. I know my limits. I don't want to be expected to do more, or held back if I can do it.

The most difficult question is, "Do you have AIDS?"

No, I don't.

I'm real sure I am pessimistic, doubting and negative because of this and have a problem trusting anyone. I'm a lot more conservative than most people and sort of anti-social. Some things I do are so stupid and hurtful to others. Why can't I see ahead more clearly? I take risks that are bound to catch up with me. I feel kind of like extra baggage—I hold too many people back in one way or another.

The sexual aspect of my marriage is not good. We are totally opposite on needs and desires. We have both strayed, but my wife just pushes away any thoughts of anything related to sexuality. I'm in a relationship now with a married friend, but it is not sexual and probably never will be. Right now she is my only link to sanity. We are very close friends. I judge myself too old to have the sexual need I seem to have, but the needs are met mostly by doing things I know I shouldn't.

My two daughters are grown and gone. They think the problem is very serious and at this point don't want to risk having children who may have it. After watching the pain I have experienced and the disappointments, they are waiting for gene engineering. They are totally aware of all aspects of the disease, but don't discuss it very often.

I think all of us have some kind of load to carry at some time in life. This is just a test to see how each of us did it. As a child, I asked myself, "Why me?" But by age 12 or so, I quit feeling sorry for myself.

IF I WASN'T GOING TO DIE, THEN DIDN'T I NEED
TO "DO SOMETHING" WITH MY LIFE?

Susan Dahl, the co-author of this book, tells a small part of her life story here. When she was four years old, Susan began to be affected by steady and relentless spinal muscular atrophy. Susan died February 12, 1995. Only two weeks worth of work remained on this book, which she never saw in final form:

I think it was his eyes that got to me. They were so blue and clear, but they scared me. They seemed so pain-filled. He was trying valiantly to get me to calm down, to get me to go to sleep. My brother was a comrade during my stay in the pain prison. I, a captive of sorts, was being held beyond my control in an ICU unit. I was there by choice, but not by choice. Or so it seemed. The beauty or terror of morphine had separated me from much consciousness. Where, when, or what I was had blended into a nightmare and my battered body could not cope. Pounded by the tools of a surgeon and filled with what felt like yards of unyielding steel, I was catapulted viciously back on a tenuous voyage to the living, wondering whether it was worth it.

Medical treatment was not new to me. My initial diagnosis of a neuromuscular disease came when I was four years old. An unusual foot reflex was a seemingly minor indication of what was to become a progressively weakening disease. I found myself an unwilling participant in a lifelong drama. I had freedom to make choices. But the choice whether or not to be disabled was not mine to make.

My earliest memories are those of going to school. Like many of my fellow kindergartners, I shed tears of separation from my mother and father at the classroom door. Medical knowledge at that time did not predict a long life for me, so my parents had to make many decisions about me. I loved school, but I do remember being sad and confused about what was happening to me and my body. I went to school in a special education unit that was self-contained. We had minimal interaction with able-bodied students.

In this group, I became rapidly aware of braces, leg and back braces—and lots of kinds of wheelchairs. I experienced many varieties of braces and chairs. I could walk until I was about seven, and then needed to be in a wheelchair most of the time. My introduction into the world of braces was painful. The measuring and adaptation of equipment was not always a comfortable experience. I got poked and prodded and moved about a great deal. And frequently, the bracing attempts weren't very successful.

I knew within myself that the braces and other equipment made me different. It was obvious to me that I couldn't walk like I wanted to; my muscles were too weak. My spine was also beginning to curve. Back braces were a new addition to my life. I didn't understand it all, but I knew I was different. I didn't feel perfect like I thought I should feel.

I was "mainstreamed" into a regular junior high school. Entrance into a new school brought excitement. But it also brought me pain. Junior and senior high school is a time when you want to be like everyone else, look like everyone else, just be the same. I knew I wasn't the same. I didn't really understand why I had to wear a back brace. I somehow knew it wasn't going to make me better, but I still had to wear it. I was pretty frustrated with life. But the dreaded back brace was discarded and actually put into the family garbage can.

Even though my physical and emotional status was uncertain at the end of high school, I chose to begin an undergraduate program at a local liberal arts college. My physical involvement on an inaccessible campus was difficult, but as I became more involved in campus activities, my physical and emotional health improved significantly. No one really expected me to complete my degree. The medical expectation continued to be a short life for me. This was not discussed openly, but lay in the backs of many minds, including my own. But I did get a degree—in psychology—which didn't prepare me for work. Now that school was over, I missed intensely the camaraderie of the campus. It was a lonely time for me. I lived with my parents and younger brother.

My brother and I combined our talents and opened a gift shop, an enjoyable venture. But there was a growing unrest in me. Something about me did not feel right. I was unsettled. I did know that I was unhappy. I don't remember wanting perfection, but I wanted more. The growing thorn in my side seemed to be the uncertainty of my health. Was I going to become gradually worse? Was I going to stay the same? Was I going to die soon? These questions plagued me. I rarely talked about them, but I thought about them constantly. I wanted to find out about my future. At least, I thought I did. I had a medical evaluation at a state-wide medical center. After a confusing and painful three days, I was glibly told that my disease was very unusual. "But plan on kicking around for awhile" was the neurologist's comment.

My initial reaction was elation. I wasn't going to die. Yet, anyway. But if I wasn't going to die, then didn't I need to "do something" with my life? I began to consider the possibility that I would outlive my parents. Where would I live? Could I take care of myself? I felt a profound sense of urgency. I had to choose a new direction, or choose the old routine life. I fought the decision, like I do any decision. It made me angry. I was tired of adjusting to new things. Even though I wasn't happy in the old way, the new way scared me. I knew I had a choice, but it felt like I didn't. I had to do it. I guess. And I did it. But very slowly. With the assistance of a rehabilitation counselor, I decided to go back to school for a graduate degree in counseling. I chose to move out from home into a dorm. In order to be more independent, I ordered my first power wheelchair. For the first time, I really could go somewhere by myself. It just felt so good to be free. At least, I thought I was free.

But another decision had to be made. A new neurologist told me that my breath was shallow. My spinal curvature had become so marked that my respiration was being affected. My spine needed to be stabilized with steel rods—or I would have to be on a respirator in two years. My feelings were mixed. The thought that I might even be better after the surgery was almost too good to be true. But the thought of being worse haunted me. I was angry that I even had to make the choice. A choice, but somehow, not a choice.

I did have the surgery. I still ask myself how I made the decision. Would I have had it if I would have known the intensity of the pain? Would I have had the surgery if I had known I wouldn't be as straight as I wanted? That I would totally have to relearn how to dress myself, transfer into the shower, sit up? What if I had known that making a seating support brace would be a desparate event? That I would feel the hooks each time the weather changed? That I would want to scream a lot. That I would want to cry a lot. That I would wonder a million times whether it was worth it. That I would know that even the surgery didn't make me perfect. That I would still get angry, frustrated. That I would still have to make choices, decisions forever.

It seems like such a long time ago—actually 14 years since the surgery. I can say more than three words without taking a breath. I can sit upright enough to drive a van. I have worked for several years as a family counselor, and later for the state special education department finding services needed by families with children with disabilities. I live independently in my own apartment, and until 1993 when I was hit as a pedestrian by a Handivan transporting persons with disabilities (ironic, yes?), I was still working. Now I have additional back injuries and a head injury that has resulted in some subtle, but very disconcerting problems for me. I frankly don't know what will come next. Right now, I don't feel like I have too many choices. Many things seem totally out of my control. But the decisions still keep forcing their way into my life. I still get angry and frustrated about being disabled. I don't like it. I don't expect I ever will. I get tired of having to adjust to it, to live with it. Sometimes I think I can't make one more decision. But I continue to make them. I hope they're right.

From foot drop to leg braces to body braces to crutches to wheelchair, all in a few short years. Then college, craft shop, trip to Holland, graduate school, independent living, a motorized chair, back surgery, a job, and a specially-equipped van. Yes, you might say that all that shows a spirit of independence to the nth degree. What is it like to live with such independence for 47 years? It means that there is always a new challenge and new experiences that I never dreamed would happen. It means lots of patience, working together, helping each other in a family to feel that each member has an equal place in it. And it means putting our trust in God to help us at all times.

MANY PEOPLE SAY I'M A ROLE MODEL.
IT'S NOT HELPFUL TO BE CONSIDERED A "ROLE MODEL"

This 46-year-old man describes the path he has taken in coming to terms with his disabilities:

I have spina bifida, clubfeet with leg braces, crossed eyes, and incontinence. It is a congenital anomaly, possibly from my father's family in Sweden. It was hard to be made fun of in school for my orthopedic problems and incontinence.

My mom was told not to give me the regular "shots" any child would receive, due to the doctor's belief in my anticipated death.

After years of psychotherapy, I've come to accept the disability.

Many people say I'm a role model. It's not helpful to be considered a "role model."

Emotionally I've been affected by depression, low self-esteem, confidence problems, and sexual concerns. As a child, being disabled felt "yucky," and I was miserable as an adolescent and adult until I began working in therapy.

If I could pick another disability I would pick a minor one so I wouldn't have stood out like a "sore thumb."

My brother was upset. Mother was upset but spurred me on to meet my potential. Dad was always emotionally warm and supportive.

I remember Mom yelling about my incontinence because she thought it was intentional.

My sister-in-law is very angry for my brother, who she said was "abandoned" by our parents when I was born.

At 46 years I have not had a sexual experience with another person.

I have learned that God is good.

MANY PEOPLE TEND TO SEE ME AS A BLIND PERSON, INSTEAD OF A PERSON WHO HAPPENS TO BE BLIND

This woman has dealt with blindness for nearly 50 years:

Optic nerve atrophy, physical cause unknown. No pain. My first memory was when I was around six when glasses were tried. My sighted peers drifted away during adolescence. That was difficult.

Anyone would like to wake up after the pain is over. Though I'm not plagued by any more than headaches, psychological pain gives me enough insomnia that I don't care to sleep until I resolve the problem.

I can't work, mainly because of unresolved dizziness that is associated with occasional small panic attacks.

What helps the most is when people make me feel like a capable person—not rushing to help when I've asked for none, or asking me to help with something. On the other hand, I like someone to be perceptive enough to realize I need verbal cues to compensate for my lack of sight. I realize this is not easy because it is hard for people to know how much I can see, and hard for me to describe how much I can't see. Problems come when people beep to say "hi". I don't know that it isn't an alert. I don't like for people to tell me when to cross the street or call to me when I am crossing. People that move things and don't put them back also cause me problems.

I think my disability has helped me to solve problems and meet challenges; sometimes these get to be overwhelming, so I feel weakened. Being disabled is feeling not like others, though I do like people to acknowledge my individuality, the way I think, feel, and act. I often feel people look at my disability as the cause of my thinking, etc.

I wish I had done the practical work to finish my M.A. in counseling. I knew when I decided not to continue that I would regret it later, but it was the best choice at the time under the circumstances. I also wish I could drive. I wouldn't be hesitant to visit friends one-to-six-hours away. I could also take in workshops and exhibits that are far away.

My favorite dream is playing the piano better than I do. I think I even create music and lyrics in my dreams. Flying is another. This gives freedom I don't usually have. I can touch things I can't see.

As a child, I was expected to do chores like anyone else. I never felt siblings were ashamed to be with me in public. I didn't feel overprotected. I'm glad my education wasn't delayed or didn't suffer due to my blindness. I feel more capable and accepted as a person than I would have if I'd been excused from chores or been left at home when my siblings went somewhere.

Recently my father gave me the feeling that he may think I'm less capable than I feel I am. I think Mom may echo Dad's opinion, but she probably suffered more when I left home to start school: not able to mother me and to do for me like she did the others. Even though I am the oldest, my other sister looked after me when we were in public, and babysat when my parents were gone. Since we "made friends" before I went away to school, she missed me the most. My other three siblings hardly knew me. If they were jealous of the special treatment over the weekends when I was home, or by visiting relatives who came annually, I never knew it. Aside from my older sister, I neither argued with nor played with my other siblings.

My grandfather wanted to sue the doctor after learning about my eye condition.

Mom washed and rolled my hair through high school. She also shaved my underarms when I was going to wear an evening gown. The only thing I remember about how well the tasks were done is that my sister consistently rolled the curlers so tight that the hair felt pulled and would give me a headache. Maybe she did this because she was angry.

Many people tend to see me as a blind person instead of a person who happens to be blind. The latter viewpoint obviously fosters a better relationship. Those who can't seem to get beyond the blindness, I try to educate, but in that process I may call more attention to the very thing I'd like to have them ignore. I am, therefore, responsible for perpetuating my own problem. Yet education is important. I feel more accepted as a person and not as a blind person. Disabled people appreciate the struggles I have when dealing with the non-disabled, and don't think I'm a miracle worker when I accomplish things that anyone else would.

The school for the blind only allowed holding hands while walking. Obviously, we snuck kisses. Passing notes was also done on the sly. In hindsight, I'm sure we hid a lot less than we thought, but we weren't reprimanded because where there's a will, there's a way. No formal instruction was given. This resulted in some wanting to learn through experimentation.

In high school, the man I thought I was going to marry was curious, or so he said. I masturbated him and he, me. I did this out of duty. When I was in my late 20s, I took birth control for about a year [in preparation] to have sex with another man. I saw this, again, as an accomplishment. I was particularly interested in gaining a man's approval. Going through with it, however, made me feel dirty, and I couldn't seem to wear enough clothes. I wanted to hide. The shame of that one-time act, only hours later, has remained through life.

Many disabled people go to great lengths to be accepted. I fear I paid dearly for that. I, therefore, could care less about my sexuality. Maybe I care more about my sexuality than I think. It probably affects my grooming neglect. Maybe I care more about my sexuality than I think because I've written so much. Maybe it's just guilt and anger at the system that failed to give me a decent outlook on sex. It suddenly occurred to me that gender identification may affect this. I have felt that I might have a problem here, too. I'm not interested in sex with other women, but think I wish I had a penis. I don't blame the system only, for some responsibility is mine. Sex was "dirty". This influenced how sexual you were to be. I have discouraged sexual attraction, had sex to please my companion, and had sex simply for accomplishing something. I've had men "leave me" because I wouldn't give them sex. I have no desire to attract men.

I get mad at God when I feel betrayed by others, or am allowing myself to stew rather than deal with or face a challenge. I have thought about suicide but not related to my blindness but almost feeling death would let me rest from the effort to accomplish anything from self-care to my job. It's never been that bad. I don't like to feel defeated and I would be, if I killed myself. I don't want to be a loser, I don't want to give up.

The hardest thing is not being able to drive or read. Never having seen birds, insects, wild animals, things beyond my touch....

I have learned to appreciate sounds and texture. Most people don't have that. People are kind and funny. Life is more than many seem to absorb and live.

ONCE HE LEFT HIS GROUP HOME AND CAME HOME
50 MILES IN A SNOWSTORM AND IN 12 DEGREE WEATHER

Now age 61, this mother looks back on 43 years of living with a son challenged by mental retardation and epilepsy:

Ben would run away and still does if he does not understand anything or feels he is trapped in a situation. But he always comes home; he has a good sense of direction. Once he left his group home and came home 50 miles in a snowstorm and in 12 degree weather.

We placed him in a school for ten years. This took the pressure off all of us, saved our sanity and marriage, and helped give the other three children a normal life. However, we brought Ben home on holidays and all summer. He never was dumped or forgotten like a lot of children. We loved him, but needed rest.

Because we could not find any help for him except by a regular doctor, we didn't find out what his problem was for four years. Then we could not find anything much in our libraries, doctors' offices, for us to deal with a mentally-handicapped person. Our doctor even told us to put him in a home and forget him. This blew our minds. We loved our son. No way.

At first the younger children wouldn't bring their friends home from school because they would make fun of their "dumb brother." They denied him. Our son nearly burned down our home once, ran away numerous times, and tried to choke the baby once. Once I had to put silverware around his bed because he would get up during the night and leave the house. This way I could hear him get up. Our younger life was always in turmoil.

ISN'T IT A SHAME, WHEN SHE'S SO PRETTY?

This young woman, a freelance writer, tells about coping with polio:

I got polio at age two, caused by a virus. I need help with transferring [from and to a wheelchair], hygiene, etc.

The most difficult part has been medical personnel who won't understand that ultimately I know what's best for me. Two years ago I almost died when a doctor ordered oxygen but failed to direct that my carbon dioxide be monitored.

The preschool years were the easiest because I didn't know about ignorance and discrimination. Adolescence was the worst because of social isolation.

I had home teaching first to tenth grade, when I dropped out. After a few years of reading romance novels, I passed my GED and I began at a community college. Then I transferred to a Big Ten university from which I graduated.

I am a free-lance journalist. I can choose my own hours, subjects, and there's no discrimination because editors seldom see me. The bad part is I'm limited in traveling for assignments because I need personal assistance.

My earliest memory is people saying to my mother, "Isn't it a shame, when she's so pretty."

IF WE DIDN'T ACCEPT HER, WE COULD NOT HAVE LIVED WITH HER

Forty-two years ago this mother gave birth to a daughter who is mentally retarded. She worries today at age 72 about who will take care of the daughter when she and her husband are no longer capable:

The most agonizing part was finding a diagnosis. During the first few years we went from doctor to doctor, clinic to clinic. A doctor in Miami finally diagnosed her as mentally retarded with a brain that was half scar tissue. He suggested placing her in an institution before we got too attached to her. She was two-and-a-half-years old at the time, couldn't sit up alone, couldn't hold a feeding bottle. We couldn't afford a private hospital so they put her in a county hospital for an encephalogram that pointed out the brain damage. While in the hospital she was tied in a crib and fed intravenously. We felt we couldn't put her some place where such treatment would continue.

When we finally got a diagnosis we decided to do our best for her and celebrate each of her accomplishments. We did our best for Jane. She has rewarded us with many actions and her improvement has been a joy. I don't ever say that she can't do this or that. She usually can. We accepted her from the start. If we didn't accept her, we could not have lived with her.

At age five she started at a parents-sponsored day care where she learned much until age 13 when they could no longer control her and requested she be removed. She has been in several institutions and group homes since then. This happened against my husband's wishes, but he agreed when I explained that I would have to be at a mental facility if she remained at home. The State Department of Human Services agreed, but appeared to do only what they had to do and not pleasantly. The judge who declared her "incompetent" was horrible.

We all helped exercise her feet, although I did the bulk of it. Her brother "babysat" when I had to leave the home on brief errands. When Jane left the home without escort, whoever was home went looking for her. She had an uncanny ability to exit doors and gates inadvertently left unlocked. Her father "babysat" evenings while I worked. It was a break for me to be relieved of the responsibility for short periods and gave me a chance to talk to other adults.

Her brother, as an adolescent, just once, punched her in the stomach. I piled both kids in the car and drove to the school for "bad" boys. We talked to some man and it never happened again. I always wondered if my son's revolt as an adolescent was because he was concerned about having children who might also be disabled. I may have been angry about all the wet beds, clothes, feces messes, menstrual mess, etc., but I never did more than grouch and clean it up.

Once as an infant, before we knew her problem, I dropped her in our ancient family bassinet and the mattress fell through and I had to pick her up off the floor. We had gone to visit my mother and Jane screamed all through the visit and half-hour drive home. Those days she cried all night and slept all day. I have felt guilty about my loss of temper ever since.

I think I have become more patient and understanding. Sometimes I wonder why me (us)? But my faith in God's actions has made me accept. As I become older and have physical disabilities myself, I have less patience and it is harder to fulfill my role.

My greatest fear is what happens when her father and I are no longer able to support her. Will she get what she needs from others? Will her brother support her like we have? If he does not, who will?

I SAW THE LIGHT, BUT I REFUSED TO GO TO THE LIGHT, BECAUSE I WAS NEEDED BY HER AND WE ARE MAKING IT FINE

This 62-year-old mother has ten children. She talks about her 42-year-old daughter who has cerebral palsy:

My earliest memories are of coming home without a baby in my arms. She was in the hospital for about three months. When she came home, seizures were about every 10-to-15 minutes apart. At times she turned blue, and had to go back to emergency several times.

I do everything for her. She was at a sitter in 1990 and fell out of bed between the side rails. Broke her hip. The first time I had to sign papers for surgery, and waiting for the final results of the surgery was plain hell on earth. She has two permanent pins inside the hip line now. We go to the doctor's office once a year for a yearly checkup. She is very healthy. At the dentist it takes three of us to hold her down and she likes to bite the dentist's finger. She has never had a cavity.

The last seizure was in the bathtub, and it was very difficult to get her out because of the stiff body.

When my husband was in the hospital, I was working three jobs. We had other children at home. My father was ill, and my mother watched her but forgot to lock the door when she left to take care of my dad, and our daughter was raped.

We didn't know about this because her periods were very irregular. Her stomach was sticking out one day. The next day my husband and I took her to the hospital thinking maybe a tumor, but she was six months pregnant. They sent us across the state line for an abortion. Six weeks later she had a hysterectomy.

Being the parent of ten children, all nine said "Mom" at one time or another. I pray someday God will let her say "Mom".

Her father could not accept her.

I hope that in the future, when God calls her, she will go straight to Heaven and look down on us, not crippled, able to talk, walk, etc. She will be as she is today with no pain.

I had a stroke in 1985 and as they say, there is a light at the end of the tunnel. I saw the light, but I refused to go to the light, because I was needed by her and we are making it fine. I have had several surgeries over the years, and my doctor knows about her. When I have to go to the hospital, he lets me know about two weeks ahead so I can get respite help for her.

WE ALL ARE DISABLED.
IT'S JUST A MATTER OF DEGREE

Coping with cerebral palsy since birth, this 42-year-old man has gone through a divorce and would like to develop a meaningful relationship with a woman, but is not obsessed by this desire:

I was born with spastic/athetoid cerebral palsy, quadraplegia, with a moderate speech impairment. Four years ago I developed an unexplained numb feeling in my lower limbs, hands, and around my waist. Stress from a poor marriage, or possibly a fall, are possible reasons. I've always needed help in feeding and fine-motor activities, but the new condition has affected my balance, sitting up from a prone position, and getting in and out of bed.

I've been told that while my mother was in labor and not fully conscious, she was given medication orally. As a result, her lungs collapsed and I was without oxygen for about ten minutes. I was also a breach birth with a prolapsed cord. I know, also, that I was a twin. Both my mother and brother were unaffected.

My parents always recognized my disability but treated me like my two brothers and sister. I think I always knew I was disabled, but perhaps first felt handicapped when my brothers started going to play with neighbors and I was forbidden to cross the street.

As a child I wore leg braces, used a walker and practiced using crutches, and learned to use an electric typewriter with a spastic keyboard. I've used wheelchairs, both manual and electric, and I use a computer.

Both my immediate and extended families have always been very supportive. No one ever told me, "You can't do this or that." Within the boundaries of safety, they let me find out for myself what I could and couldn't do. When I was young I wanted to be a carpenter. My parents bought me hand tools, even though I was limited in using them.

My schooling began early at age three. I attended special kindergarten until age seven, then attended a special elementary school until 14. This was before a high school education was mandatory. I tried attending a regular junior high. The teachers and students were great, but the administrators refused to accept that I wasn't retarded, and refused to let me take a full load or even keep any records. I applied for a residential state hospital school, but still had to fight and use political pressure to get in. Once there, I knew what I wanted and excelled.

I look at it from the perspective that we all are disabled. Basically, it's just a matter of degree. You realize that you do have limitations, you may be slower at doing some things, finding alternative ways of doing things, or have someone do things for you, but you have to weigh your disabilities against your abilities. I wish I could speak more clearly so that everyone could understand me. It would, I'm sure, open more job opportunities for me.

Other than having a vasectomy, since my ex-wife would have great difficulty bearing children, I can perform and have the same sexual drive and desires as any other man. Expression is the problem.

I can't say as I really had any sexual relationships. When my ex-wife and I were going together, we used to "get naked," but that was about all. I thought we were sharing intimate moments, but guess not....

Dating has always been a problem. I grew up in a rural area and depended on my parents for transportation. My ex-wife and I were, more or less, childhood sweethearts. We really didn't start dating until around 1980. We'd see each other once a month; she'd either stay at my apartment, or I'd go visit her and her family for the weekend. Her folks were, and still are, good friends. We'd also talk on the phone once or twice a week.

I'm not actively dating. Settling my financial situation is more important right now. I'm always looking, hoping to find a compatible mate, but I'm not obsessed with it. If it happens, it happens. I've always found masturbation to be a safe release of sexual frustration. I'm told, however, that sex is highly overrated. Perhaps what I want more is a deep relationship where there is committment and mutual sharing and caring.

Anyone answering "no" to being mad at God is lying. We are finite, imperfect beings. I want to trust God, just as I always wanted to trust and obey my early father, but I still got mad when he punished me or wouldn't always let me do what I wanted to do.

Coping should be seen as a continuum. It is something we all must do to some degree.

I AM IN THE PROCESS OF BREAKING UP MY HOUSEHOLD. I KNOW HE IS GOING TO SUFFER MORE THAN ANYONE IN MY HOUSEHOLD

A 78-year-old father talks about his 40-year-old son, whom he adopted at ten days old. The father is grieving as he writes, for the family is breaking up:

Our son was born with PKU, damage to the brain due to feeding, milk, etc. In his case high protein cannot be processed by the body and eventually causes brain damage if left untreated. His coordination is very poor, attention span is nil, very shifty.

At that time doctors kept telling me, "He will grow out of it," whatever it is, since PKU was unknown. When it was time to enroll him in school I could not find a place for him so I quit my job and moved and enrolled him in a private school. Frustrating!

He was to have an operation on his nose. (He had breathing problems.) At that time the doctor explained that this was the first PKU case being operated on and they had no idea of the effect. So it was an experience for both doctors and family.

Had to teach him the facts of life—all of them!

He learned to read well. Because a retired doctor had the patience to hold his head, point to the letter, pronounce it, and give him time off (two or three minutes later he would start all over again and again). Till he read a line at a time. It probably took two years to get him to the point he could read well.

People he works with keep praising him. The man he works for asked me, "How do you slow him down?" My reply was it took 40 years to get him going, don't try to slow him down.

Transportation to his job is bad. He gets up at 3:30 a.m. to start at 7:00 a.m. But for three months he got up with a wrist watch I had given him for Christmas. When time was changed to daylight savings, he called me up at 4:40 a.m. and started to cry. Then I discovered what it was. I purchased a radio alarm, showed him how to set it, and told him not to change the station!

Just show them "how". Show them you care. Warn them to be careful or they'll get hurt.

Our family was no help! We just faced facts as they arose.

[What is the hardest thing to accept about the disability?] The only thing is that I have to die and not know what will happen to him. I can't make people understand that if he goes off his diet he will end up in the nut house. Yet his disability is visible since the tremor in his hand will get worse with age. Attempting to train him in measuring, say, a teaspoon in making bread, is impossible. Yet the world believes he should be on his own!

He appreciates all the things I do for him and is not afraid to show it. He's grand.

God gave me a head to use, not to hang a hat. Since I could not father a child, I should have lived without.

[What do you wish you could do but can't because of the disability?] I had hoped to leave the keys to the house and all that is in it and say, "It's all yours." But I can't. I know he couldn't handle it.

I am in the process of breaking up my household. I know he is going to suffer more than anyone in my household.

Would life have been different? The answer is yes. I could have made certain moves which I could not accomplish under the circumstances. Is it the disability that has driven the family apart?

Why blame God? That happened when two people were experimenting with the facts of life.

The future is bleak! I have no answer, but hope. I've learned you have to live with what you're born with.

I AM NORMAL IN MY DREAMS. FLYING. I FEEL SO AT PEACE

When she was a child this middle-aged woman was severely injured in an accident and has never fully recovered. She talks of the crushing loneliness of being different:

I fell from my grandmother's high porch when I was ten. My right side is affected. Right hand has limited use. My walk is "different". I have panic attacks, mostly controlled now by drugs. This has been difficult. My voice was hard to understand, somewhat better now.

My earliest memory was that my right hand closed into a tight fist. I used my left hand to pry it open, and to keep it open I leaned on my arm.

I went to school, had friends. Even though I missed four months of school in fifth grade, I was not behind. But during adolescence, I no longer fit in. I was alone. I did not talk plainly. I had panic attacks. I was unable to walk or talk. I graduated from grade school, went to boarding school and regular high school. I had little self-esteem, was unhappy, alone all the time.

Jobs are hard to find because I can't use my hands or speak very well. A State Voc Rehab counselor told me to "go home or get on welfare." Being disabled feels lonely, awkward, different. I am uneasy when a child asks, "Why do you walk like that? Why don't you walk normal?" I wish I would have been encouraged to leave home sooner. I would have had a fuller life.

I am normal in my dreams. Flying. I feel so at peace.

My family was very kind, caring and sharing. My mother had two babies for me because she thought I'd never have any.

I'm the outsider. It's so difficult to explain me. It's embarrassing. I was not interested in boys or men. I felt unattractive. I did have a long-term friend. Allan and I were a couple. He came often to see me. He was younger than I was. And he had a serious mental problem. He said, "Don't you think I'm better? It's because I have a friend."

Dalton and I were a couple for 17 years. We saw a great deal of each other—went many places together. He taught me how to dance. He was ten years older than I was, divorced. I loved him. He gave me an engagement ring. The sex was very satisfying. Now I have no one.

If I had not been disabled, I would have been married and had children.

Do I blame anyone for my disability? No, no one pushed me (off the porch).

In unhappy times, lonely days, I wish for death.

I am losing my sense of balance. Afraid. Fear of falling. I am fearful of complete disability.

I have learned, though, that many people are kind.

THIRTY YEARS

Stories told by individuals and family members who have been challenged by a disability for three to four decades.

THE PAIN IS NOT PHYSICAL BUT EMOTIONAL

A 48-year-old mother talks about the epilepsy she has been dealing with for many years:

I have psychomotor epileptic seizures. They hit with a tightening in my throat. Then they break all conscious thought processes, plus erasing my memory for the previous ten-to-thirty minutes. Usually, the only outward signs of my seizures are that the eyes set, a slight drawing of lip muscles, and at times I clench my fists, drawing them to my mouth. They have always become more frequent at times of ovulation. No medication will totally control the seizures, so no employment or driver's license.

There is scar tissue in the left temporal lobe of my brain. Doctors feel this is probably a result of a head injury at the age of ten. A swing struck my upper head and face, resulting in much torn flesh, an injury to my left eye and lid, and unconsciousness. Neurologists feel the extreme turn around of hormones at the time of pregnancy caused the seizures to surface and stay surfaced.

Counseling sessions were traumatic at times, as I expressed my true feelings toward the epilepsy becoming a part of my world. Feeling a lot of hate toward God for taking away my great life, but realizing later through the help of a minister that God didn't turn me aside. Some doctors seem to try to "medicate away" the emotional problems that come with the physical problems of life. Other doctors stay aware of the emotional side of the person's health and help the patient through them with personal counseling as a part of each visit.

The main risk to my life and other lives was continuing to drive. I finally had to just say no to driving and adjust my way of life to either walk or depend on others more.

The pain is not physical but emotional. When the seizures become extremely frequent they alter my abilities to do even ordinary things, because of the interruptions to my train of thought. When people treat me as though I'm retarded, it really causes my temper to flare within me.

During the first years, suicidal thoughts ran through my mind often. Now I find myself in depression at times during a three-or four-day stretch of seizures. But with love from my husband and turning with more trust to God, I bring these under control.

I don't feel like a full, complete person. I'm afraid to try different things. I feel more secure in my regular, daily routine. At times, I feel as though I'm odd. It's as though people are inspecting me; anticipating they can see something.

My first husband (the man I was married to at the time the seizures became part of my life) refused to accept me in any way. A divorce resulted six years later. My present husband has accepted all things well. My daughter of the first marriage had some of her father's lack of acceptance, and yet has grown very accepting and understanding of the situation. I feel mainly this was due to her true understanding of the epilepsy and emotional problems associated with it.

My first date with my present husband I expressed to him about the epilepsy and what it was and how it affected all sides of me. He listened and asked merely to learn. He says the seizures don't worry him as he knows "I live!" and that all that can be done is being done, so let's live with what we have.

Daddy just accepted the seizures and expressed that he loved me anyway, "Let's go on from here." Mom will not accept the seizures just being a part of me. Instead, she feels and says that she may have done something wrong to cause them. And even though it doesn't help anyway, she always mentions the seizures for no reason.

Things just happen but God gives us strength to deal with them. Others have learned a great deal from my seizure disorder as to how they can cope with their own lives. It's influenced some away from drugs and into a better life for themselves. At times I get mad at God, but not very often. Once in awhile, when I get into a day or two of five to ten seizures a day, it keeps my mind from clear thought. I thought about suicide years ago before I had learned what epilepsy was and how it affected me and others. The hardest thing is the fact that it gets in my way at times and I can't do as I want. Many people just automatically think that all seizures are controlled by medication.

Once when a fine neurologist put me into the psychiatric ward of a hospital, I asked myself many times if I was "going crazy," but after thinking through the situation and verbally opening up to him and my minister, I realized that I wasn't "crazy."

My fear is that my legs will lessen their ability to do all the walking I do, and we don't have any transportation services in town. Finances and old age worry me, too.

I REALIZE THE PROBLEM IS THERE
AND WE HAVE TO LIVE WITH IT

A 55-year-old man talks about his wife's disability:

My wife has epilepsy. I first knew about it when we started dating in 1976. One doctor told us that we didn't know what we were talking about concerning my wife's epilepsy.

I guess her life was most at risk when she continued to drive after the epilepsy surfaced. She had a couple of accidents before she quit driving.

I realize the problem is there and we have to live with it. It didn't affect me much because I knew the problem was there before we married. It bothered my wife's daughter quite a lot, she didn't like the epilepsy at all. My wife's mother does not understand the problem and refuses to believe it was there.

We are holding our own financially.

I WONDER WHY GOD PICKED MY FAMILY TO SCREW UP

A 23-year-old daughter talks about her mother's chronic seizures:

My mother has psychomotor seizures occurring every day—sometimes more than once a day. Each episode lasts between one and two minutes. The seizures wipe out short-term memory, creating confusion as to past and present. The seizures consist of lip-smacking and repetitive hand motions. They cannot be controlled with Rx, and surgery is too risky.

[Why?] My mom was hit in the forehead by a wooden swing at age eight. This caused damage to her temporal lobes.

When I was about three, my mom would blank-out and I couldn't make her "wake" up.

My mom drove a car until I was about ten years old. I've been in three major accidents with her because she had a seizure while driving. She did not get hurt during those accidents because she wore her seat belt. I fear she will have a seizure while cooking and burn herself, but so far she has not. She smokes which creates a problem as she crushes the cigarette or turns it around backwards in her mouth during a seizure.

The seizures limit her life so much and have made her an emotional mess. I want a "normal" mom.

When I was a teenager, I would get embarrassed if my mom would have a seizure in the presence of my friends. Also, I couldn't go a lot of places because she didn't drive.

It helps when you treat them "mentally" as you would anyone else. A disability does not make you stupid. Do not pity them. Try to be patient with them. I hate it when people say "I know how you feel." It helps when people just listen and reassure you that you are not a bad person for having negative thoughts about the disabled person.

I wish I could have seen a good counselor during my adolescence. Also a support group for families.

My mom's disability has made me grow up in a hurry. I'm only 23 but I feel like I'm 40 because I've been caring for someone else since about six. My counselor says my family is dysfunctional and I am co-dependent. The anger I feel about the disability and how it's disrupted my life will always be with me no matter how much counseling I get.

I am afraid to discuss anything controversial with my mother because it always puts her in a seizure. When I was younger, my mom's family blamed me for causing her to seizure because I argued with her.

If I could live my life over, I would have been more open about my feelings concerning the epilepsy with my mom. I wish I could just ask her to stay away so I won't feel any pain, but she's my mom and always will be.

God is a strong part of what keeps hope alive with my mom and dad. They attend church regularly. We pray to God to give us strangth to cope with each day. I wish the family would stop babying my mom. She needs to learn how to care for herself because my dad will not be around forever.

My biological father couldn't deal with it and left. My step-dad doesn't seem to get emotional about the situation.

I have had my life rearranged because of it. Everything I do is somehow affected by having grown up with a disabled parent. I am more sensitive to people with disabilities.

My mom has become dependent upon others.

My father used the disability as grounds for divorce.

My grandma refuses to accept the situation and gets upset when my mom has a seizure. My mom's oldest brother has been supportive over the years when she needs to talk.

If she had not been disabled, I think I would have been more emotionally stable. I would have had the chance to be a kid.

I wonder why God picked my family to screw up.

As I grew up I prayed to have a normal family. I wasn't allowed to be a kid because I had to be strong for my mom.

I cut my wrists because I didn't know how else to get help. No one listened otherwise! Once as a child I pretended to have a seizure to get some of the attention my mom was always receiving.

It's so hard because I have no control over when my mom "blanks out." Often it happens when I need her to be strong for me. Arguments usually put her in a seizure.

I fear I will have to take care of her again in the future.

What doesn't destroy us makes us stronger.

I KEEP FROM SUICIDE BECAUSE OF THE COMMITMENT
TO MY PARENTS (AND OTHERS) TO PUT AS MUCH EFFORT
INTO MY OWN LIFE AS THEY HAVE PUT INTO KEEPING ME ALIVE

A 40-year-old woman with spina bifida and scoliosis talks about her life and her family:

My primary disability is spina bifida (open spine). Paralysis has also resulted in numerous skeletal deformities, including scoliosis (curvature of the spine). I have congenital osteoporosis, a weakness of bones resulting in predisposition to falls and fractures. I also have congenital cataracts resulting in inability to drive at night and read small print.

The exact cause is currently unknown. Latest research suggests predisposition triggered by unknown environmental factors. Low levels of folic acid in women prior to pregnancy are currently suspected.

I remember asking my mother why other children didn't have crutches and braces. Her answer, "God made you with sick legs." Terrified of venipunctures (blood drawings), three or four technicians needed to restrain me. Terrified of loud noises, such as dentist's drill. I generalized fear of male doctors to my father; I remember asking for female technicians, not allowing my father near me. I remember being angry at nurses for waking me up so much at night.

When I had physical therapy sessions grades one through three, I remember going up and down steps until therapist left on "coffee break," then rested until she returned. I remember the therapist "drawing pictures" on my back, then taking pictures of me semi-nude; I felt very degraded. I was upset at hospitalizations where parents were allowed to visit only every other day. I would cry, scream, think my parents had abandoned me.

The most difficult has been realizing the life-threatening nature of my condition, and the reality that my condition will gradually worsen over time; knowing there is no medical treatment for many of the symptoms.

Preschool was the easiest because young children don't have enough life experience to realize how difficult a situation is; you're also not old enough to have learned about prejudice. Adolescence was the worst. I left special school to be mainstreamed in a "normal" junior high school. Students at that age and during that period in our history were not ready to accept anyone who was "different," plus I came in during the middle of junior high and friends were already established.

I'm not employed because strict licensure requirements went into effect before I could find employment as a counselor. I can't take the second or third shift required in most entry-level jobs, can't travel, ruling out outreach requirements on most jobs. I have had several part-time jobs over the last seven years, most of which were not in my field. SSI restricts the number of hours I can work, the salary I can earn. There is no incentive to work part-time, knowing medical benefits will cease.

It's not helpful when people say, "Everyone has a disability."

"It's not important that you're not employed."

"You'll probably never get a job."

"Do you really think you can work?"

"You're such an inspiration."

"I don't think I could handle it."

My junior and senior high counselors and college advisors could have provided more guidance in choosing an appropriate vocation. I could have been paired with a potential role model in the field, a mentor. Since so many others have doubted my abilities (including my parents), it has been very difficult to overcome shyness and low self-esteem.

Being disabled is being trapped inside a body that doesn't work as well as I would like. It has been easier to be disabled from birth because I've not had my world turned upside down acquiring a disabling condition, which prevented me from doing those things I had become accustomed to; you don't feel bitter since you can't miss what you've never had.

In my dreams I see myself as a disabled RN working alongside non-disabled healthcare professionals, working in a hospital setting. Sometimes I don't picture myself at all; I just hear myself talking!

As an only child, I have always felt very close to my parents. Even though we now live in separate states, I think about them often. Since the death of my last grandparent in 1989, I have probably been drawn even closer to them, at least emotionally. My parents have always "been there" for me. Knowing that I could count on my parents to help has made the transition to independent living much easier. (I have had to call on them since during times of illness/surgery and a move.)

Just before leaving for college, my parents told me that no matter what happened, they would always be proud of me. That has stuck with me ever since. I wish my parents could better let go of their "little girl." In earlier times, my mother found this harder. Today my father seems to have more of a need to offer unsolicited advice. Other family members have been extremely supportive of me and my parents over the years. Some, however, had great difficulty accepting my going off to college, living independently.

Mothers usually "take the rap" for producing a baby with birth defects, since they're the ones who carry the child for nine months. I suspect this may have been the case in our family, although my parents don't like to talk about those first few years very much, so I don't ask many questions. Most men have difficulty talking about their feelings and my father is no exception.

The most that either of them has said is when I was preparing for serious ostomy surgery. At that time, they told me the story of my first operation and how the odds were stacked against me. Then they noticed a tiny baby being wheeled towards the recovery room. They knew I had survived! At that point they both broke down, my father saying he didn't think he could ever go through anything like that again. To that extent, I think he has even been more deeply affected than my mother. An aunt (mother's sister) lived on the other side of the duplex during my mother's pregnancy. At the time of my birth, she was with my parents. She rode with my father, with me on her lap, on a two-hour trip to the nearest major city for specialized medical care. I've always had a special relationship with her.

I'm sure both parents blamed themselves and each other in the beginning. Now I think they both suspect a genetic cause for my birth defect, although none has been found to date.

Occasionally my mother who is a compulsive cleaner would express anger at my not being able to perform bathing or other personal care to her satisfaction, especially when I was ill.

Caring for any chronically ill or handicapped member is bound to be a financial strain for the whole family. For us, my parents were able to bear the burden for me while I was not working until 1983 when I applied for SSI (while I was still in school, I was covered under my father's health insurance). This was supplemented by limited part-time work and parental support until 1991 when my father began to receive Social Security retirement. At first my application for SSI was rejected, but following an appeal, I received my first check in September, 1991. My ability to work part-time even is severely restricted due to regulations. My doctors all agree that my physical condition allows me to work full-time, but to date no work opportunities have presented themselves. Although I get enough from SSI to live on, I lack the ability to improve my lot in life unless I am able to find suitable employment.

I think my parents have come to realize that their problems in raising a handicapped child have been no worse than others with non-disabled children (drugs, pregnancies, etc.) They've tended to get into a habit of feeling sorry for themselves because they've had to raise a handicapped child. This trend has gotten a little worse as I've gotten older.

It usually takes a while for people to be able to look beyond the disability and see the person inside. I like to "break the ice" by laughing at myself, joking about some aspect of my disability (usually my short stature). I also like to mention some part of my day which is likely to parallel their day, e.g., stopping at the grocery store. This usually reinforces the idea that I'm more like them then they thought I would be.

My sexual organs have been affected by extensive paralysis from the waist down on the right side. They are also affected by scoliosis in that abdominal organs have been/are being squeezed by pressure from the spinal curvature.

I have had "crushes" on guys in school, but have had no serious relationships. I do not consider myself to be sexually attractive, especially in light of urine incontinence. I do not feel it would be fair to "lead a guy" on in light of the seriousness of my medical condition. I have always known (although not formally told by doctors) that I could not have children. I would feel badly that I could not give a "normal" man what he would certainly deserve—a normal, active sex life.

I feel that as a society, we tend to place entirely too much value on the physical aspect of marriage. While I would not rule marriage out of my life entirely, I am living proof that one can live a perfectly healthy happy life without the benefit of sex. I also believe that intimacy can take many forms. Persons with other debilitating illnesses have managed to maintain a close relationship with a spouse, and I believe that there are many ways for the disabled individual to assert her/his sexuality without actually completing the act itself. We are all sexual beings; how we express our sexuality can be as different as the people who express it.

I believe that God has created everyone, including those with disabilities, in His image. I also believe that everyone has a purpose for living. While none of us can understand why anything happens to us, I believe that everything happens for a reason. I also believe that everyone, no matter how severely disabled, has talents to share with the world. Some day (after our deaths) we will all understand and the reasons for our disabilities will not only make sense to us, but will more than compensate for our losses.

I do get mad at God. Sometimes it's hard to understand why God would not allow me to have a job.

My disability is no one's fault; no parent wishes a birth defect (or any other medical problem) on their baby. I see spina bifida as simply a random occurrence in nature. I was one of about 11,000 babies who are born with spina bifida per year.

When I thought my kidneys were failing (they weren't), I thought it might be easier on my parents if I were to die quickly (and not have a long-term burden of a daughter on dialysis). I keep from suicide because of the committment to my parents (and others) to put as much effort into my own life as they have put into keeping me alive; and my conviction that a higher power gives and takes away life.

The hardest thing to accept is that it will probably get progressively worse over time (at least the complications of the spina bifida will). My vision is deteriorating due to cataracts. I also have experienced loss of physical stamina in recent years (not able to walk as far, climb as many stairs as before. It makes me feel depressed, afraid I'll lose my independence.

If the economy improves, maybe the future will bring a job in human services. If not, I will stay on disability for the remainder of my life. My fear is I will have to give up independent living to move in with my parents or go to a nursing home.

I've learned that life is worth living, no matter how disabled you are, and that all life is precious, no matter what form it takes.

THE HARDEST THING

Now 39, this woman has been struggling with arthritis since she was an adolescent:

The hardest thing to accept? Readjustment. Over, and over, and over, and over…again.

I NEEDED TO KNOW WHY EVERYONE WAS SO SAD ALL THE TIME

A younger sister talks about her 39-year-old sister's polio and how the disease affected the whole family:

My sister got polio and she started out paralyzed from the neck down. Following multiple surgeries and treatment she regained the ability to walk short distances and some use of her right hand. She has no use of either arm.

I remember my sister being gone for long periods of time. I was quite young during the most intensive treatment. My mother was pregnant with me when my sister became ill. However, as a small child I remember her having to sit in her wheelchair in traction with the headstrap around her head and chin, with weights pulling down to stretch her back straight. It appeared quite painful and I remember how much I hated seeing her like this. I remember saying good-bye to her and my parents many times as they would leave for weeks at a time to go for treatment. I remember her homebound teacher coming to bring schoolwork to her. I remember getting to go on one trip, meeting lots of doctors and nurses and being fascinated with the people and things in the brace shop.

I hated seeing her in pain. I hated watching her cry. I would wake up in the morning and hope that this never would have happened.

It took me a long time to understand that other people weren't experiencing similar things and that her disability was the cause of all the underlying sadness that was prevalent in our home. At some age, about eight I think, I remember feeling responsible for her disability. If I prayed more or had more faith, she would be healed. It hasn't been until the last ten years that I've really dealt with the impact of her disability on my life…and this has been a very difficult process.

A homebound teacher came to our house for years. Then at some point we got an intercom system that sat on the end of her bed that she could push with her toe when she wanted to talk. Otherwise the sounds of the classroom were heard for the rest of the time. Her junior year of high school she attended school half day, and all day as a senior.

People are always saying stupid things that just show lack of understanding on their part. Likewise, some people are just generally more sensitive than others and are more aware of the impact of comments they might make. People need to be educated, but it isn't useful to judge them on their ignorance.

My hardest lesson has been to get over the feeling that I'm somehow responsible. The most helpful interactions have helped me to look at this and process why this has been such a strong feeling in me. It was absolutely off-limits to talk with either parent. They just couldn't handle it. As a child I always spoke with my sister herself and often still do. However, more often as an adult, I'm more apt to talk with a professional counselor as it is my work to be done today.

As a child I needed things explained to me. I needed to know why everyone was so sad all the time. I needed someone to tell me that it was okay that I wanted some attention, too.

I think I'm a better person, but I've had to work through a lot of shit. Like dealing with my own body image. Deciding it was okay for me to enjoy my body even if my sister couldn't. Acknowledging that I had needs that weren't met because of her disability and that it's okay to ask for some things for me. Learning that I don't help her in any way when I deny parts of myself.

We've always been very honest and open with each other. It's our parents who have lived their lives in denial. I wish I could have open discussions with my parents. They just aren't able to do this and I don't anticipate that they ever will.

Honesty. I'd like us all to be able to really talk about the multiple issues affecting our family system that were directly related to my sister's disability.

Dad was the strong one. He was responsible for all of the initial care during the crisis time due to Mom being pregnant. He developed a strong bond and a great loyalty to my sister.

Mom. She was always sad but never dealt with it.

My brother was eight when my sister got sick. His response was to be the troublemaker, to rebel against his change of status. This continued for years.

Me. I became the peacemaker, caretaker, my job was to keep everyone happy and never complain.

Mom was affected most, but all were affected. However, I think Mom and Dad's response has continued to affect all of us throughout our lives. I always felt that Mom must have resented some of these responsibilities, but it was not acceptable to express any of that. I've tried to talk with my parents. I can get some of the basic facts, but they refuse to express or deal with any of the emotion.

I used to get mad at God. As a child I thought for sure He could heal her, but for some reason (probably having to do with me) didn't.

Life is messy, but good; there's always hope; it's worth the fight; people are basically good.

This woman's two children share their feelings about their aunt's disability. The 10-year-old nephew:

Sometimes I'm sad because she's the only one in the family that has a disability. I've wondered how she got it. Sometimes I'm afraid of [her] future, but it helps to talk about it.

And his 12-year-old brother:

She got polio when she was a kid. I feel sorry for her and wonder how she can live with it so well. She's always really happy. When I think about my aunt, I just think about her and not her disability. [But I do] worry about if she's gonna get sick sometimes. [It helps if you] talk to me about it.

LIFE IS GOOD, EVEN THOUGH AT TIMES I STRUGGLE
AND STRUGGLE DEEPLY

A 37-year-old woman who has been challenged by her disability from birth talks about her life and her family:

I have congenital cerebral palsy. I was a breach delivery and I weighed two-and-a-half pounds at birth and was about three months premature. My weight from birth went down to about a pound and a half. I couldn't swallow at birth. Forceps were also used on me in the breach delivery (by the OB physician). I was in an incubator for a long time and didn't leave the hospital until I weighed five pounds and was fed by a nasogastric tube. Even upon leaving the hospital the doctors told my parents I was not going to live.

I remember the daily floor exercises that were very painful, and realized no one else in the neighborhood or my family had to do them—with my mother's help or without her. I took dance lessons, and also realized at about age five how uncoordinated I was. I fell and tripped frequently, drug my foot. My mother was always telling me to "pick up my feet."

As a young child, doctors as far back as I can remember didn't communicate with me about my cerebral palsy. Until my mother told our family doctor, no one told me until I was 14 or 15 that I had cerebral palsy. I knew inside something was really wrong with me, already, but I finally found out what when I sat down with her and said I wanted to know what it was. It was painful for her to tell me. The family doctor's comment was, "I think she is old enough to know now!" Even with that, he didn't talk to me about it. I had an Achilles extension surgery at age nine. No one explained why I had to have surgery. My parents just told me I had to have it done, so it was. My neighbor asked me why I had to have it and I said my parents just said it had to be done.

The hospital didn't do any pre-op teaching with me. The doctor only said to me, I would have a cast, be on crutches, and have stitches after that first surgery. I also took swimming lessons to help me learn to swim and exercise. To add to early childhood struggles, the specialist I was sent to said I needed a metal leg brace. My parents refused the brace and until about age 15, I always had to wear orthopedic saddle shoes with a shoe lift. Then I decided I didn't want to wear them anymore and wore tennis shoes without a lift. My left leg is one inch shorter than the right leg.

In the early 1980s I was put in an AFO brace and started using a cane just before that. I had many cortisone injections in the hip and groin area. And I was told I would have the brace as long as I had the hip and leg problem. One of the medical professors wanted to talk me into doing a hip surgery repair to muscles and tendons, but he couldn't promise/assure me it would relieve the pain. He, in front of the medical student, said he did not want to put me on muscle relaxants. The med student had suggested it. I suggested physical therapy, and they said since I was an LPN I could do my own (no offer of what to do, or instruction)! "I could swim" was their reply.

Not until I moved to a different state did I meet a wonderful doctor who tried various muscle relaxants and intensive physical therapy. I responded well and my muscles totally changed for the better. My foot continued to turn inward gradually and I was sent to another specialist who recommended a tendon transfer and another Achilles extension on my left lower leg. I had that in March 1991. It did straighten out my foot. The spasticity is better in my calf most of the time, but the hip problem and pain remains. And muscle fatigue. I still have definite heel pain, it did help some, but from my point of view, not as much as I thought it would. Physical therapists have been good.

I do not like to be a patient in a hospital and prefer to get out of there ASAP. I feel doctors leave a lot of the decision-making, as far as how much I can do, up to me. And many times they are at a loss as to know what to say. Except, "Slow down, don't do so much." Additionally, with the exception of the one doctor above, they are very blunt and say I just have to learn to live with it and offer no "practical how-to." Usually.

There are many ways to say the same thing in a much nicer, not as blunt or hard way. That makes it easier for the patient to take. (That comes from my LPN experience and also from my "patient" point of view.) Taking time to listen is important for doctors to do, instead of just saying things like "Your foot is straightened out." One surgeon made that statement from across the room with my clothes on and not even looking at my hip. He said that I didn't need a hip release. As a nurse, I was surprised he made that diagnosis without checking me over.

Another doctor after tests suggested another hip release operation. I had said no further surgery/tests, but I agreed. After surgery they could see what wasn't correctable, and my doctor put me on a new medication to which I have responded very well. However, it is very expensive. I had hoped for a lot less spasticity/pain after surgery. Hoped to cut back on some anti-inflammatories and muscle relaxants, after the surgery in 1991. It has helped to some extent, but I had higher hopes for it though.

It would be nice to just go to sleep and wake up after the pain has gone away, but I'm fortunate that my physical pain level varies day to day depending on distance walked and amount of time I'm up on my feet, etc. Realistically speaking, it will never completely go away—especially after all these years, after the surgery, after losing weight (to my knowledge hasn't helped). I have lost about 25 pounds. The doctors said it would help my hip but it really hasn't. So, I need to deal with it.

Before age five, I don't remember the other children teasing me, so that was easier. Later, it was "duck feet" and being chosen last for teams. Adulthood is easier I guess because I now realize I have done everything I can do and I will live with it the rest of my life. Fortunately, I have good days like everyone else. Not all days are "bad."

My parents always encouraged me to do whatever I wanted, participate in sports, etc. I went to regular elementary school, then on to junior high. After high school I received a partial scholarship to a junior college where I was accepted after applying to vocational nursing school. I did graduate, however, the nursing school director did say I was too slow, and there was "something wrong with me." Interestingly, my parents told me to never admit to anyone that I had CP.

Years ago, I worked as an LPN in a hospital, but my leg worsened and I did voluntary missionary work. I was "relieved" of my duties as a voluntary missionary as my leg worsened and because of the demands of walking, etc. There seemed to me to be a lack of understanding about CP/disability in those with whom I worked.

The best question someone ever asked me was, "What have I learned about God through all this?" And I like it when people leave the decision of when I need help up to me.

People will often pat me on the head. Then there are those who don't listen to me, i.e., pushing me in a wheelchair down a hill. One time I told a nurse/friend that it was too steep and she insisted she could handle it. She lost control of it and I tumbled out of the chair.

As far as what people say, the most exasperating are: "You don't have it as bad as some/a lot of people!" and "You are too slow," and "I would just stay at home rather than go out in a wheelchair."

I wish there could have been better open communication with me at a much earlier age, and the admission that I did have CP. The doctor could have told me instead of waiting until the young teenage years, that aren't easy anyway, for anyone. Especially as it seemed my mother found it so difficult to admit. She cried and cried, etc.

Stress definitely increases my CP symptoms. I have good days of feeling good about myself and other days where I find it frustrating when I really realize and recognize "head/on" what my limitations are, and that's not easy. If I don't get enough rest it is worse, as well as it is very hard when I don't get breaks at work. But I am pushed to my physical limits, and beyond, on some days, which increases stress, pain level, and decreases my ability to cope. Feeling disabled many times means not being accepted by others. People do not know what to say, how to approach me, so I usually take the initiative. I feel like I'm different and never totally fit into a crowd, except in the support/social group.

[What if you could trade in your disability…What would you trade it for?] I don't think I could pick a disability…even if it is mild, pain is pain, whether it's emotional, physical or a combination, none is easy.

I wish I could be able to walk as much as I want and for as long as I want, especially without the pain and muscle spasms. Freedom from limitations!

I cope by not giving up. I stand up for what I believe to be right. My independence has helped me, to keep pursuing goals. I usually question doctors until I get an answer, or if I can't get an answer I will sometimes say, "You are not going to give me an answer are you?"

I believe underneath it all my mother feels guilty or somehow responsible and is in somewhat of a "state of denial." I definitely to this day pick up feelings of her being ashamed and not willing to be open with me about it. She says, "I've given up so much for you, I took you to the doctors, paid for your medical bills as a child. And that kept her, she feels, from doing what she wanted to do.

With the high cost of medication and post-surgery check-ups, my money situation is poor. Having my car in good running order to make sure I get to the doctor visits, I need to work as many hours as possible to keep up with the bills. I have no retirement or health benefits through work.

My mother does not seem to understand yet. My father has over the last two or three years, especially, been more supportive. Through the help of the local independent living center, their resources as well as one-on-one counseling has helped me to communicate more effectively and to bring a better understanding of CP to me and to pass that along to my father and step-mother. It's hard for my dad and step-mom to know how I struggle financially because of it.

I've tried to discuss my first surgery with my father and it wasn't easy. I believe my family quite possibly feels that the first and now the second surgery for CP would solve all the problems with it, and I just have to push myself harder and it will "all go away and be fine." Sometimes I wonder if they are still in the denial stage, mother, brother, etc. Although as I said, my father is more open than he used to be about it. Financially my first surgery as a child was hard on my father as he was the sole breadwinner and didn't make much money.

My brother (in his teenage years) at a restaurant stated loudly and clearly that he didn't want to be around me as I ate out in public. He was embarrassed, as frequently there is food in my water glass and that bothered him. My parents stated, "She is your sister," and we would go out occasionally and eat together whether he liked it or not. It hurt me but I didn't quite understand it, as he is four years older than me. Recently, soon after my surgery, he felt I was lazy and needed to push myself "like everyone else." He tried to compare me to a former classmate of his who has polio and went on for her master's degree and has always been in a wheelchair.

Sometimes I feel there is a lack of understanding of CP and its effects on people: tiredness, muscle fatigue, speech impairment. Sometimes people do not know how to approach me and avoid me and talk with someone else, or I try to make them more comfortable and approach them with an introduction of my name and ask about them, etc.

I'm comfortable around most people, but sometimes it's nice being around my friends who have a disability, because then my disability doesn't matter. We tend to see each other as people first and the disability doesn't get in the way (that I'm aware of), and I am free to be just me and not worry about what others think, say, or how I can help them feel comfortable being around me.

I believe God allowed my disability but He did not "cause it." Nevertheless, I believe God loves me and cares about me just the same as a "whole-bodied" person. Sometimes I wonder, "Why me?" But then life is not fair for anyone, disabled/able-bodied alike. As a former OB labor and delivery nurse, I wonder why the OB physician allowed a breech delivery and used forceps on top of that! Even though my mother told me it hurt too much, apparently he told her that the baby (me) was too small to hurt that much. Then again, I am not familiar with the labor and delivery policies of 1950s. They know a lot more now.

For a split second, I have thought about suicide, but I feel that it is not an option and in a sense it is really running away instead of facing life, no matter what circumstance I might find myself in. I could not take my own life. I have meaning and purpose in life, although life is not always easy for anyone. I would deeply hurt my family and friends and I wouldn't want intentionally ever to do that, plus I feel I could cut short God's plan for my life, and the good I can do to help others.

The hardest thing about the disability is that it won't be going away. The muscle/skeletal problems associated with it, I have been told will gradually, very slowly grow worse as I get older. My doctor told me that years ago, and I have seen some of that occur.

In the future, hopefully, I will be able to get a scooter, work more hours and get some benefits. (Not just vacation, as I am now.) Pay off medical bills faster. Give my muscles a rest and have more physical freedom to do and go as I like. Possibly a new job.

My fear is what will happen to me financially? I never expected to go through the surgery or the crutches...what will happen to me physically?

Life is good. My joy/happiness isn't dependent upon my circum-stances—good/bad. I like to try to make the best of it, even though at times, I struggle and struggle deeply.

THE MOST DIFFICULT PART HAS BEEN, ACTUALLY, MY SENSE OF EMBARRASSMENT, I'M SORRY TO SAY

A 35-year-old woman, the caretaker for her 37-year-old sister with cerebral palsy, talks about their lives:
She has cerebral palsy due to a head injury at birth. Being unprepared for delivery of her first child, my mother never made it up a flight of steps to the delivery room and she had the baby on the steps. I first remember my sister's inability to verbalize competently, to skip, and her over-anxiety.

No equipment has been developed to compensate for an inability to comprehend the written word, or understand cause and effect, or not comprehend time passing.

My sister has no major physical medical problems. Professional people, and others in general, usually interact only when absolutely forced to. If they can speak with another nondisabled person, they do, even to the extent of being rude.

The most difficult part has been, actually, my sense of embarrassment, I'm sorry to say.

Being a support/enabler for a mentally-retarded person has a daily risk involved. Fortunately, we live in a small town with caring neighbors. Will she know what to do if she cuts herself, or burns, or smells smoke or gas? Even putting a street address on an ID card causes me concern. Phone solicitations worry me, door-to-door salesmen…you name it. With crime what it is, you never know.

The easiest time for me was when she was in elementary school. My sister had to go to another town to attend school and came home once a month. It was like being an only child with all the attention.

With our father gone and mother diagnosed with Alzheimer's, my sister's condition has placed a great deal of responsibility on my shoulders. If anything it has made me stronger and I thank God that is all I have to worry about. I am very blessed.

[It's] Sometimes burdensome. I wish I could be away from home for longer periods. I have a six-year-old who often doesn't understand my role of caregiver/provider.

Our family works hard and we have the ability to find out the truth in a situation. Less driven people could not do what I do. We strive for a normal lifestyle for all. This is what keeps me sane and from becoming bitter. We need more tolerance, patience to set a good example for the community.

I don't think my mother understood the long-term commitment and dedication needed to raise a mentally-retarded child. I'm sure my father felt helpless and disappointed. Future concerns were probably foremost. I never considered my sister's future to be my concern until I was probably 29 or 30.

She has a trust fund for the future. I don't think the level of care my sister required kept my very frugal parents from attaining what they worked for.

It's like having another child. My sister's mental age is about that of an adolescent. Dealing with the body of a woman must be very difficult.

It may take our whole lives but I'm sure some good will come of all this. But it's hard to accept that mentally-retarded people never get better. Also, it is true that "This, too, shall pass."

I TAKE TIME TO BE. THAT IS THE SECRET
THAT MARTIN HAS ALWAYS KNOWN, BUT I HAD TO LEARN

The adult sister of a 34-year-old man with Down's Syndrome talks about her younger brother's life:

My brother is severely mentally retarded and has some autistic characteristics. Down's Syndrome Trisomy 23, no family history prior to or since. I remember him as a newborn who slept a lot and was often ill. When he got the "usual" childhood illnesses, he always seemed to get sicker than his younger brother. Yet the doctor didn't seem interested in caring for him. My younger brother appeared to get better treatment even though he didn't seem to be as ill. As a child I wished it was all a bad dream and I would wake up and everyone would be okay and life would be normal.

There was no medical intervention while he lived at home. During a flu epidemic in 1959 he became very ill. The family doctor refused to admit him to the hospital, telling my parents to do the best they could and reminding them that Martin would die in childhood anyway. I believe that his first full-scale evaluation for medical reasons occurred after he became a resident of a state school in 1968. He began school at age eight in a self-contained classroom. At age ten he was moved to a state institution where he spent part of each day in an educational setting.

He is now working in a sheltered workshop situation, washing cars for a local auto dealer. He appears to enjoy it and is always very eager to get started. Once he masters a task, he is able to do it very well. He needs some reminding to keep going.

It is hard when people who believe they are being sympathetic say things like, "It must have been terrible growing up with people like that"—making the family a freak show rather than an ordinary family.

I feel uncomfortable around people with disabilities whom I don't know. I see, too often, people caged within a disability for which no one, myself included, has a key.

My youngest brother and sister have had very little contact with Martin over the years. They do not even think of him as part of the family for purposes of large gatherings, weddings, and holidays. Making inclusion happen is difficult, but the thought at least would be nice. Talking about him was something seldom done in our immediate or extended family. For myself as a sibling, I see people with disabilities as people who can accomplish things, though it may take a long time. They are not quitters in nearly the numbers that able-bodied people are.

God created a perfect world. Man chose to sin and brought error into the world. God never promised to fix the world, only open the next to us. We still get to decide about a lot of things in our lives. We can give up and get mad at God or we can get mad and get going. It's our choice.

I just wish Martin could talk to me. I wish I knew exactly how he felt about things instead of inferring how he feels. I have periodically suffered from depression that, however, is the cumulative effect of years in a family overwhelmed by disability, my own inadequate coping skills, my own problems. His disability can be construed as a factor, but not the primary cause.

It may feel like it at times, but it's not the end of the world. I've learned how to survive. I even have fun at it. And, I take time to be. That is the secret that Martin has always known, but I had to learn.

THE DISABILITY. THERE IS NO END TO IT.
AND NO RELIEF FROM IT. I FEEL TIRED AND DISCOURAGED.

A 42-year-old sister of a 34-year-old woman with Down's Syndrome speaks eloquently of the stress and strain:

For the last 12 years, I have taken her to most of her medical appointments, including doctor, dentist, hospital, and psychiatric care. Some people are caring, helpful professionals, others are not. More than one doctor (all male) have told me a specific procedure (example: mammogram) was not necessary based on their definition of her "quality of life." Each of these doctors, upon questioning, each admitted to me that they recommend that same procedure as regular care for their "normal" patients. The most difficult part is continually having to be one step ahead of the doctor and insisting on adequate care, i.e. lab tests, mammograms, and referrals to specialists (where I often must go through the same process of "insisting"); and reading the *PDR* myself, and not letting them get her in a category of care rather than as an individual. Because her medical coverage is Medicaid, many doctors will not accept her as a patient. About half of those who do provide substandard care as compared to what they do for their "regular" patients.

Her life has not been medically at risk because of her disability. The risk comes from things she does, like walking or running in front of cars.

I am often physically and emotionally exhausted. I am the only family member who is involved in her care and the only one who lives near her.

She is employed at a warehouse on a crew of disabled adults. She says she's very satisfied, but she'd rather be working at McDonald's, her previous job. She's occupied most of the day, likes her supervisor, and likes the paycheck even though she doesn't understand the value of money. Very low pay, and repetitive, boring tasks.

The most unhelpful people are most of her social workers who see themselves as "instant experts" and spend very little time with her or those who know her best, and yet insist they have all the answers (which means manipulating her to fit their programs, needs, slots, and biases).

It helps when people don't patronize or expect too little, or make decisions for her which she can make herself. It is difficult not to be caught in the disabled person's manipulation games (I know!), and see "them" as a category rather than as individuals with specific needs.

My friend listens to me without advising or judging, often she helps me think how to deal with social services. My sister's "foster mom" is also my friend. We are able to "de-tox" each other during high-stress episodes and to work together to resolve issues and advocate for my sister.

My sister is 34 years old. I've survived the ups and downs over the years and have usually landed on my feet, but the last two years have been difficult. Sometimes I am not happy with the choices I have made regarding my life and her disability. Sometimes I am angry because I think I have spent my life working extremely hard to make other people's lives happier and better and have not done that for myself. As my sister's behavior becomes more difficult, I find myself not wanting to be around her and then, of course, I feel guilty. Through the years I have often felt "pulled apart" between my sister's needs and those of my own family.

If I could just be her sister and take her out to lunch or shopping occasionally or see her during a vacation (like the rest of my family does), it would feel fine. But since I have had to be advocate, trainer, counselor, job support, tailor, chauffeur, legal representative, negotiator, nurse, etc., not only for her, but often for those who have worked with her over the years, it is draining.

My mother had most of the responsibility and was the driving force behind my sister's growth and development. My father was resentful toward mother (blamed her), and was not involved in my sister's care, by his choice. Siblings as adults have expressed resentment about the extra care and time my sister was given because they think it took away time and care which "belonged" to them. Me…during the time I lived at home, my sister was my "responsibility" much more often than any other sibling. While I was not aware of resenting that then, I have since thought it an extremely unfair distribution of her care, but I also understand the reasons it happened that way.

When my sister was a child, my mother had primary care of my sister, but also of the entire family of seven children and two adults. She also worked full-time outside the home. Since the disability is primarily mental, physical care was mostly what was usual for a "normal" child, it just took more time, much more time. The care was provided by me and my mother mostly. I was not aware that siblings were angry about providing care, but they did avoid it whenever possible.

It is difficult for my husband to understand since he wasn't there! Now he sees the results of the stress, but I still don't think he understands my feelings because I don't express them well.

My mother is honest and direct about how the disability affected her, believes that she did what she had to do, thought there was only one way to do things (now knows there were other choices, but still thinks she would have done the same). My father has never been willing to discuss his thoughts or feelings.

My family was dysfunctional in a number of respects and while the disability was not the cause of the dysfunction, I believe it was a major contributing factor. The disability also added a lot of stress for family members. My sister doesn't have the ability to understand how the disability affects her, but she denies any subject that is uncomfortable, so it would be unlikely that she would be willing to talk about it. She has only one disabled person she defines as a friend, and she chooses to do activities with one disabled roommate. All of her other activities (other than work-related) are, by her choice, with the "regular" population.

The disability. There is no end to it and no relief from it. Current medical information indicates that it will become much more difficult as she becomes older. My mother is not able to care for her anymore and my siblings choose not to, so as long as I care about what happens to her, she will always be "my job." Sometimes I think I'm going crazy when I let her provoke me to the point that I yell at her. I know that yelling doesn't help her or me. She refuses to accept the fact that my yelling has anything to do with her behavior and it certainly doesn't change the behavior, only stops it for awhile. And my yelling means that I have lost my patience and control. In self-defense I have to say that I have only yelled at her five times in the last 12 years (yes, I remember them), and that they were each times when she was deliberately destructive, abusive, or deceitful.

Her cognitive abilities are decreasing. She is becoming more rigid in behavior and more demanding, chooses to be less active, yells and swears more often, is more manipulative. It is unclear whether the changes are by choice or are biological in origin. I feel tired and discouraged. I don't see anything to look forward to.

The good thing I have learned is that there are some people who truly care about others and are willing to "buck the system" to make a difference.

I TALKED ABOUT SUICIDE WHEN SHE WAS FIRST BORN

Thirty-four years ago this 72-year-old man became the father to a baby with Down's Syndrome. He describes the journey he and his family have been on:

My daughter was diagnosed at birth with Down's Syndrome. Her doctors gave sympathy and were very supportive. The most difficult for me has been having to be with her all the time and seeing her hurt by playmates. During adolescence she didn't have any close friends to go places, and she didn't have a boyfriend.

It's made me more caring. The family all accepts her as she is, and will all help her all they can. We've talked about what will happen after we are gone. It's made us stronger people.

I talked about suicide when she was first born. We were deep in the middle of the night and she was so disturbed. We felt so sorry for her.

We are not the first people this happened to, nor will we be the last.

My hope for the future is a cure for Down's Syndrome.

AFTER 34 YEARS IT IS AS MUCH A PART OF ME
AS THE COLOR OF MY EYES

This 68-year-old mother once considered killing herself and her daughter, who was diagnosed with Down's Syndrome. But today she has grown comfortable with the disability and sees her child's life as being as valuable as the life of any other child, disabled or not.

In the beginning it was devastating, but I accepted it as a challenge to me as a mother. As she has grown and blossomed into a lovely young woman, I am very proud of her. Her Down's Syndrome was diagnosed at birth. Trisomy 21. Confirmed by genetic counseling at age six.

I can't think of any disability I would be more comfortable with. Given the circumstances as they were presented to us we did the very best we could. It would be nice if we could be more independent. We also have a daughter who is divorced and a single mother. She needs us almost as much as the disabled daughter. We would like to see our "birds flying from the nest" at our age.

We have too much responsibility for our child. There is not a sheltered apartment program in our community but that is what she needs. She is our financial responsibility forever. She will never be self-supporting. She will receive SSI and share in any inheritance with her two sisters.

The most difficult aspect, when receiving help from strangers, is to convey to them the value of this child, and to insure that she receive as much as would any other child. My daughter and son-in-law are professionals in the field of education and psychology. They have good information and give me the emotional support I need most. The hardest thing to accept is to see her in emotional pain. I guess after 34 years it is as much a part of me as the color of my eyes. The hurtful years are over. I hope.

When she was very young, I did think of staging an automobile accident with her in the car.

MY DISABILITY IS A PART OF ME,
LIKE THE COLOR OF MY EYES, MY TEMPERAMENT

This 33-year-old minister tells how cerebral palsy has affected his life. He has been in love three times, and hopes some day to marry and have a family, but wonders if this is realistic:

I have cerebral palsy, cause unknown. I don't remember noticing a difference until high school when my friends drove off, and I didn't.

I was a strong-willed child. Disliked doctors, therapists, etc. I didn't like the exercises they wanted me to do. I remember crying when the doctor told me I would never walk. When I was 12 my right hip went out of place. They couldn't hold it back so they were going to cut some nerves to ease the pain. I chose not to because I would lose what use of the leg I had. The most frustrating is doctors who don't understand my disability.

Adolescence was when I really noticed the differences. Afraid of girls. Poor self-image. I'm determined, yet I've battled with a poor self-image. I wish I would have had more information as to what adulthood would be like.

I currently direct a ministry to the church and the disabled. Lots of variety, travel, interaction with others.

My disability is a part of me, like the color of my eyes, my temperament.

My family was supportive of each other. They have a sense of humor, but they had to choose between me getting braces and having vacations. The disability has brought them closer to the Lord.

I have been "in love" three times in my life. The first was with a fellow student in college. It lasted about a month. I think my disability had something to do with our breakup. The second time was also while I was a college student. She was a divorced woman in my home church. We were friends and served together in ministry. She wasn't really ready for a relationship and swore she'd never remarry. I never really told her how I felt. We've since drifted apart and she has remarried. She's about five years older than me. The last time was with a co-worker about five years ago. She was a college student and a summer intern. She's also the younger sister of a friend of mine. She seemed to really love and accept me. Our friendship really grew over the summer. We started dating at the end of the summer. It lasted about six weeks. We were close physically. Lots of heavy kissing. I think our age difference did us in. I'm about ten years older.

I don't have any real prospects for female companionship. I have engaged in telephone sex which is only momentarily satisfying and produces guilt as it violates my morals. I'm trying to quit.

I believe God creates us as individuals and that He creates within us all the characteristics we need to do His will. He doesn't make mistakes in creating us. I do get mad at God. I sometimes think he owes me because I'm in the ministry.

I hate how long it takes me to do things—four hours to get ready for work in the morning. What will I be able to do as I get older? Will I ever marry and have a family? How will my cerebral palsy slow me down?

I WANT TO CRY OR SCREAM OR CHANGE THINGS
SO THAT SHE COULD BE MORE "NORMAL"

For 33 years this mother has cared for her mentally-retarded daughter, Beth. Now at age 58, the mother looks back on their lives:

Our daughter has cerebral palsy and is mentally retarded. We were told that some type of "accident" in the womb soon after conception was the probable cause. Beth was born in November. The previous March I had a severe case of Asian flu. I have attributed it to that.

We had no idea that she was disabled until about the age of six months. Before that she cried a lot. We got very little sleep. Nothing seemed to comfort her. But we just assumed that she was a "difficult" baby. Our doctor gave no indication of severe problems. At six months when we expected her to begin to sit alone, I realized that something was wrong.

I remember being very frustrated that the doctors were not able to tell us what was wrong until she was two years old. At about eight months she was put on a waiting list for a complete evaluation. The eval started at about age one, consisting of several appointments. My memories are of a compassionate staff. Physical therapists motivated her to begin walking at about age five by distancing her from "water play" which she loved.

The most difficult was waiting—and the insensitive reactions from some of the public we came in contact with.

At approximately the age of 28 years, she had back surgery for severe scoliosis. She came out of surgery okay, but when the surgeon tested her legs, one was paralyzed so they took her back in and opened her up again to remove the steel rod that was pressing on a nerve. For several days we didn't know if she would walk again. But she did—and does. That was when her life was at most risk.

I want to cry or scream or change things so that she could be more "normal". Beth lived with us for 20 years. We learned so much from the experience. But in terms of difficulty those years were all difficult. At the time I took it one day at a time, but looking back, I see how hard it all was.

Her need for total care has always been a challenge—at times an overwhelming one. As I grow older I have less and less energy to deal with her visits. Three or four hours seem to be the best solution now.

I feel an obligation or duty to support and take care of her. I am now realizing that I need to do things for me and to pull back, since my energy level is slowly decreasing. It's hard for me to set limits on how much time to spend with her since she has such an attachment to the family. I have to accept that we are all constantly changing and that even though Beth can't understand this, my first priority now is me.

I sometimes think that if it had been possible for us to know before her birth that she was severely retarded, we would have been wise to have an abortion. Then I wonder if I would have been emotionally able to do that. And looking back and seeing how we often failed our other children while dealing with her, I wonder if we should have institutionalized her sooner. (We actually placed her in a group home.)

It was hard when Beth was growing up at home, the feeling of isolation from other families, because of her lack of development. Now we still have the responsibility of making decisions for her.

In retrospect, our other children are sharing some negative feelings about ways we handled the situation when they were growing up. We are all talking and working with this.

Her grandmothers were both very supportive—took care of her when we needed them, accepted her. I'm sure they worried about all of us but did not interfere with our decisions.

When I had feelings of wanting more freedom and a life of my own, I would sometimes spank or hit her when she didn't "use the toilet properly," etc. That made me feel "crazy".

I believe that she misses never having experienced a boy/girl relationship.

Life is too good to miss out on it!

I'm afraid that she will live longer than my husband and I and our other children will be responsible for decisions about her.

IT IS THE JENNYS OF THIS WORLD THAT TETHER THE REST OF US TO REALITY. OTHERWISE, WHY WOULD ANY OF US BE NEEDED?

Thirty-two years ago, Jenny was born. This 58-year-old mother cannot imagine what life would be like without her:

Jenny was diagnosed at age five with unexplained mental retardation—"mildly retarded"—IQ 50-60. Essentially autistic until age five, she didn't really respond much to learning until age nine and then proceeded steadily with special education.

Worst were the first speech therapy sessions when I watched through a mirror window and she was like a caged animal. The kindness and patience of the therapist was inspiring. I couldn't imagine that services would begin. First hearing about Jenny's diagnosis was traumatic. I do think it was more effective to have "someone else" tell us, than had it initially been the doctor whom we met with more often. He could then serve as the comforter rather than the bearer of bad news, even though he had to confirm the diagnosis to us.

At age three we'd submitted to an in-hospital diagnostic, and I felt it cruel to not visit her, but my doctor husband wanted her to be separate from us for a clearer diagnosis. That didn't mesh with my mother instincts, but doctors' ways have brought good enough results with our kids through the years to help them to an independence while still knowing we're constantly available to be depended upon.

But were the authorities correct?

Sometimes when she was 0-16 years I would cry in the shower because of the unknown, but now I repeatedly thank God for this gift in my life, especially the days when she is my legs or I don't feel like cooking. At young adulthood, I have finally accepted that Jenny's abilities fit just fine according to God's design for her.

The early school years…fear of the unknown can be traumatic! What should our role be? What are the options? Who can care enough to help? Heartache at seeing failure and unwillingness to try. Nursery school in a few weeks. Hundreds of individual speech therapy sessions. Three years of kindergarten. Then special education until graduation at age 20. Formal education beyond age 20 would very likely have much benefited Jenny. She didn't really start learning until age nine and was just getting a head of steam when others went on to college.

The best is when people give unconditional love. They listen to Jenny without interrupting. Physical assistance when indicated.

The worst: One man in particular seemed to act afraid of Jenny when she gave cookies to the new neighbor. One priest treated her and a deaf adult in context with a small child group. A disability does NOT keep a person a child all their life. Calling normal people "retards". My priest could have read the book I wrote about Jenny.

The disability made me stronger. Brought me to write, and sometimes lubricated the tear ducts. Makes me never cease to be awed that bodies and minds work in most people even if slightly flawed. I certainly would not ask that she be normal, because I see more people react to Jenny in ways that most normal people aren't privileged with.

I'll never know what I might have been like had Jenny progressed normally through life. Or how would all of this family be? Probably no better, but it's just something to wonder. Did she maybe save us from something? Or for something?

We periodically decide we should have Jenny on SSI to help ready the future, but then we hesitate because others need it worse. Even with it I suppose there are no guarantees. It truly seems that welfare patients are as well cared for as those with borderline income, and Jenny does not comprehend finances easily at all. Of course we realize the government won't realize this family has saved them untold amounts by self care. There are no easy answers in this financially crazed world.

The future. I do wonder. It will depend on the children's mates, if any. Auntie Lee won't last forever, nor will Ken and I. I can easily see her living in a nursing home setting, but I rebel at the thought of a group home if they are all mentally handicapped, though Jenny could be an asset in helping. My fear is sexual molestation that could destroy the wonderful trust that Jenny places in most people.

It is the Jennys of this world that tether the rest of us to reality. Otherwise, why would any of us be needed?

IF HE'S NOT PROTECTED 24 HOURS A DAY, HE'LL KILL HIMSELF

This 73-year-old mother describes vividly the challenges of caring for a profoundly-retarded son for nearly 40 years:

Robert has an unusual chromosomal abnormality, diagnosed at age 20-22 months. He started head banging against anything hard, or against us, beginning suddenly at about age two. He does not walk well, actually not at all now because he is kept in a wheelchair at a center where I had to place him in September. He says a few words, is not toilet-trained. He does nothing for himself. He is diagnosed as profoundly retarded.

He can yell for a week, almost 24 hours a day, but he can also go for months where he is very easy to manage and in such a happy mood. I can't imagine why I ever considered giving him a Valium tablet. He didn't hold his head up or manage his body like other babies his age, or try to do anything for himself. The pediatrician never had anything good to say about him.

In August of 1986, a few months before his father died, Robert went on one of his "fighting sleep, fighting food" spells. It was terribly hot and instead of snapping out of it as usual he became so dehydrated we had to rush him to ICU where they kept him for over a week. He seemed his normal self when they discharged him, but we were warned that if he should go two days without eating or drinking we should bring him to emergency immediately. They were in favor of putting in a stoma tube, but with Robert that would never work. He's a fighter and you can't get near enough to him to feed him when he's having one of his spells.

I used to dream that I walked him into his pediatrician's office and said, "Look, see how wrong you were!" I think a doctor or a teacher could have advised us how to get Robert doing things for himself.

I've had a sick child for almost 40 years, so we never had a normal family life, if there is such a thing. We worked around it somehow. However, I have been depressed this last year because I don't feel he is getting what I want him to have.

I feel I have options now that I can do just about what I want, but nobody listens to my feelings about Robert and I'm feeling useless. I think my husband felt he was not as far along in his work as he would have been if we didn't have Robert. I don't know. We didn't talk enough, I regret. My daughter took it very hard and it probably affected her social life. We are friends now but as she said the other day, "At one time we weren't."

My husband was a good man. There are none better. I think he worried more about Jill and me than about Robert, if that's possible, because of the care Robert needed. Much of the time the care wasn't all that hard and truly I don't know if I could have kept up with an active normal child.

I don't blame anyone or anything, not really. One can't be sure, but I believe there was some genetic defect triggered by some sample drug the doctor took out of his desk drawer at just the wrong time for me. There is no way to know now.

I believe in life, not suicide.

My biggest fear is if Robert is not protected 24 hours per day, he'll kill himself.

TREAT HIM AS A PERSON WITH A "CONDITION," NOT AS A "CONDITION"

Thirty-one years ago this 58-year-old mother gave birth to a baby boy who was later diagnosed as mentally retarded and autistic:

My son is autistic, mute, and mentally retarded, caused by anoxia at birth. He was a normal baby, though there were some periods of high-pitched crying.

We had some counseling, but the focus was mostly on what we as parents do wrong. It was a very difficult period in our lives. We came to see that the counseling served no purpose other than perhaps as documentation that could prove valuable later. Ironically, when they were asked to forward records, he [the counselor] was very uncooperative.

The adult years have been easier since he has been living outside our home and after the guilt of placing him somewhat subsided. Adolescence was worst, as he seemed to become increasingly aware that he was different, and began resisting leaving the house.

I didn't share my feelings and fears with my husband enough. Rather, I feel I "protected" him. I've often felt resentment toward my husband. We have a strong marriage and family bond, but I should have not taken all the responsibility on myself. I realized later in my life that my husband was saddened and hurt by the disability as much as I, only from a dad's aspect.

He's always been my little boy.

My faith has strengthened. I feel strongly that God has watched over our son better than we have and I rely on Him in the years ahead. I got mad at God very much during the early years, but I'm no longer angry.

I did think about suicide several years ago when there were no answers, schools or understanding.

The hardest think to accept has been the lack of knowledge about autism.

I feel his condition is deteriorating, or perhaps he's aging. I pray that the Lord takes him while we're still around and able-bodied.

Just interact with him. Treat him as a person with a "condition," not as a "condition".

HIS LIFE HAS NOT BEEN AT RISK,
BUT HIS DIGNITY HAS LOTS OF TIMES

A 38-year-old woman talks about her 31-year-old brother who has been diagnosed with cerebral palsy and mental retardation:

He was initially diagnosed as having cerebral palsy and severe mental retardation, affecting fine motor skills and speech. Probably caused by anoxia briefly during the final months of pregnancy. I was seven when James was born. I remember him as a happy, beautiful blonde-haired, blue-eyed younger brother who smiled a lot and was very well-behaved and quiet. It was not until he was about six months old that he didn't develop as the rest of us did. His life has not been at risk but probably his dignity has lots of times.

Currently, I am assisting my mother in defending and protecting James' rights.

The disability has made me stronger at times. I can cope with a lot of life's nastiness. On the other hand, it has made me cynical, and I laugh at cruelty as a form of escape.

Our family is very functional, very verbal, well-liked in the community. We have many economic resources, and are close and supportive of each other. I think we're comfortable in our roles and don't need to change them soon. My older brothers who were 12 and 13 at the time James was born seem to stay on the fringes. My sister who is a nurse is very active in James' life. She monitors his medical needs. Mom is the facilitator of all of James' life and is his legal guardian. She continues to carry an enormous amount of guilt and confusion. She will admit to wishing that he had died early, has a tough time seeing his worthwhileness sometimes.

James provides a unique perspective on life. He has a good sense of humor and provides joy. But on the other hand, he requires constant attention and focus: he has a different kind of energy to interact with.

[We have had] Lots of tears, lots of resistance to change. They (Mom is the only parent alive) were informed of his disability in many cruel ways by physicians and have been equally confused by care providers. But, they generally coped well.

It made us closer. I am in spec ed, my sister-in-law is in spec ed. My brother-in-law is a psychiatrist in dual diagnosis. We have lots to talk about.

The disability is harder now that we are older. James remains a young child, we can't include him in activities we do without someone taking charge.

Probably a busy schedule is what keeps me from suicide.

It is hardest to accept that it will always be there and the fairy godmother will not make it disappear.

I went through a doctoral program in spec ed to find the ultimate answers.

I think we are changing from viewing disability as negative to simply being a part of life. We are learning the importance of accepting people for themselves. But governments in charge of funding many programs get more insane with budget cuts. I wonder who will care for and train James? Does the community feel any sense of responsibility?

I think in the final analysis you are responsible for your own happiness. There is a big picture to all this, and sometimes the little parts will get you down if you let them. Lots of people whose lives seem tougher than mine are full of persistence and happiness.

SHE WAS PROBABLY ONE OF THE FEW HANDICAPPED PERSONS WHO GOT TO THE TOP OF JOHN MUIR TRAIL

A 64-year-old woman describes life with her daughter, who was born with cerebral palsy 31 years ago:

[What caused the disability?] I'm met with silence on this. One doctor said damage during the third month of pregnancy. A doctor gave me Dexedrine during pregnancy. Those were the days you were not to gain 25 pounds and I did.

[My earliest memory is of] Chris lying on her tummy at the doctor's office and him saying, "What a beautiful child," which was very out of character for him. A sweet, soft little girl, either loving or a bit "dopey." Increasingly very hyperactive. "Terrified crying, glassy-eyed at times, pale." All, I later learned, were seizure activity. The doctor said "temper tantrum." She was my fifth. I wasn't that stupid. They said "spoiled," and I knew I wasn't that kind of mother.

The most difficult time was having to make a decision when my doctor and school doctor differed on whether surgery was necessary. The decision was "No." Also, arguing over over-dosage of anticonvulsant meds. After two horrible weeks, he admitted I was right. And waiting long hours with a hyperactive child in the doctor's office (one-and-one-half to two hours).

Once she was vomiting and having seizures at the same time. The doctor never did tell me what I should do if it happened again. To be honest, I didn't panic, and I did everything I knew to do. I've always felt if she goes, she goes. Her gain.

When she was small our two junior high and high school daughters played with her a lot. It was better for me than help in the house. When school started in the fall her teacher would often say, "What have you done with this child? She has improved so much." Any new teacher was usually convinced that, "This child has never been reached or challenged," and was excited about having her in class. But before the year was over, the new teacher would be thoroughly frustrated. I feel instead of struggling with reading and math, they should work on what she can and wants to do.

[How might it have been different?] It's hard to say since I only went the one route. Basically I'm a high-energy, practical, serious but with a good sense of humor sort of person. I think I may have a higher stress level with the years of such intense watching and listening. I've been far more isolated and limited for years in what I was able to do. Right now, I am somewhat frustrated because I do not feel her care (a group home) is adequate.

I think the four children now are more compassionate and less materialistic than others their age, but then I'll never know if Chris was the reason. I sent a picture of her to our adult son while he was in college, it was a sorrowful, rather pathetic shot. I told him he could put it under his underwear in the drawer. He wrote back and said he had it on his tack board over his desk. He said, "Actually I think I can study better when I see it."

The oldest son carried her a lot. She was probably one of the few handicapped persons who got to the top of the John Muir Trail, and went through a lot of caves, too. The kids played with her in the front yard after school. It was the better time of day for her and they seemed to enjoy it. It was very much like playing with the family dog, which we didn't have. Very relaxing after the stress of the school day. Chris was fun, very cooperative, and giving, so there was no conflict. She would be awake all night after a morning seizure and sleeping all day, so I would hire the older daughter to sit with her at night until she went to sleep (during the summer). I don't think there was ever anger over her care and I never forced the care.

Chris came home once with a ring. She said she was getting married. I asked her why. She countered, "Why did you and Dad get married?" I told her if she were getting married she couldn't come home every weekend. On this she promptly took off the ring and said she changed her mind.

Talking is quite a difficult thing for her as the time spent on figuring out what she says is very detrimental to a conversation of any length. When I asked her about walking and talking in her dreams she said it didn't make her feel bad to wake up and find she couldn't, she's very happy and accepting, it seems.

Chris's speech puts a barrier between her and others. A number of people have said they'd love to be able to understand her because she'd probably have something interesting to say. I babysit daytimes just to have children in for her.

[Have you ever thought you were going crazy?] No, not about the disability, but the isolation and her dependency probably contributed to it, although I never felt she was at fault. I had an early period of depression when she was small where I felt if I ever "let go" I could never make it back alone, and I never felt there was anyone who could help. Three times since I've gotten in it again, and I've been able to verbalize enough to my husband so that he would withdraw less.

TWENTY YEARS

Stories told by individuals and family members who have been challenged by a disability for two to three decades.

THEY SEE HER AS NO ONE'S BURDEN BUT THEIR OWN

An 40-year-old woman talks about her 30-year-old sister and their family:
Caryl was born with cerebral palsy, epilepsy and mild mental retardation. I don't know what caused it. I remember my mother saying after Caryl was diagnosed at about one year old that she had suspicioned all along that something was different with her.

I remember waking up to Caryl having a grand mal. Our beds were positioned so my head was close to hers. It was quite frightening. I also remember being angry at the church people when she had a grand mal after church in the foyer and people clustered around clucking their tongues. I remember her asking me to read her a story after she recovered from a seizure—so relaxed and sweet.

We had to be careful she didn't follow us when we were kids. There were lots of places we went that she could get hurt in by losing her balance or by not knowing how to deal with the situation. Once when she had a *grand mal* seizure, she ran into a glass front door, slashing the muscle of her upper arm quite badly.

She went to a state school for handicapped children. The bus picked her up in the morning and brought her home in the afternoon. There was occupational therapy. Speech therapy. Physical therapy. Preschool plus 19 years. She moved to a group home after that, after my parents moved to another state.

We should have had some respite care, lovingly and carefully done. She was precious to us and we didn't really trust anyone to love and care for her like we could. Putting her back together was too difficult when people weren't careful.

I guess looking back I wish my parents had been more involved with my life. I wanted us to do family things—outings, but even then we didn't. Because of Caryl's disability or because Dad liked to stay home? I feel slightly jealous of their attention to her. My parents are the most wonderful people, but I wish they had the emotional wherewithal for me and my family.

[If I could choose a disability] I'd pick a disability that the person could compensate for, like blindness. At least one that didn't require such a tricky balance with medication. The guessing game of keeping tabs on her program was difficult for my parents. They found they could not trust the medical field to be in charge of her care. They had to monitor everything.

I wish I could be a better friend to her. Distance makes it difficult. Concepts are hard for her and she can't "see" me in a letter.

My father is an exceptional provider, my mother took her role as mother and homemaker seriously as a full-time job and selflessly gave up many interests so we could find ours. She never made us feel guilty about Caryl's care, nor did she become a martyr. I have faith and assurance that God will provide, even if it came to be my task to be her primary care giver. His strength would be sufficient. (It would not be a bed of roses, but it would be survivable.) I wish we all were in closer relationship to each other. Our problem-solving skills and communication skills could be better. Expressed anger or disagreement is not kosher. We don't actively build each other up. I think mother wanted so much for us to grow up normally that she shielded us from the realities of Caryl's constant care. She wanted us to have the freedom to do our own thing. Well, we did and we're miles apart and keep in touch very poorly. There are five living children. I'm the oldest girl and Caryl is the youngest. We did not operate as a family unit working together. She was our "parents' problem," not ours. They didn't want us to be burdened-encumbered with her limitations.

As a teenager I remember taking Caryl for walks, giving her a bath, fixing her a snack—nothing out of the ordinary for a substantially older sibling to do for a younger one. Just that the needed response lasted longer in years. She didn't out-grow the dependent preschool needs while I was at home. I don't think any of the siblings were angry at the care we had to give her. We did get very angry if anyone teased or tormented her from the neighborhood. She was sweet, trusting and was bewildered and crushed when other people laughed at her or hurt her (running over her with their bike). We expressed it by yelling, chasing them off and telling each other how cruel these children were.

I remember looking back on it, and how many things we didn't do as a family. There were many reasons for that, but I'm sure that Caryl's disability had a part to play in that because I believe my mother felt so isolated and trapped. (She had never gone to college and still does not have a driver's license. My father was financial director for a fair-sized city.)

I have an understanding of the "normalcy" of the disabled person. There really is a human soul locked up inside a twisted cage and but for God's design, it could've been me.

For me, probably the main issue is I've been married for over 21 years, and my parents have come to see me in my home only once. They came another time in conjunction with a business trip and they've paid our way to see them once (twice?). I just wish they had a greater desire to know me, even though I don't need their help. Caryl seems to require so much attention, there's not much left for me. They say they'd come see us but Caryl cries and cries when she can't come home on the weekend. They feel her poor life is miserable and no one will love and care for her like they can. They can't bring her with them as she'd have a seizure and be easily upset and it would be more work than it would be worth, so to speak. And I don't live anywhere near them to lend a hand. They see her as no one's burden but their own. I feel selfish in wanting to demand their attention and I understand their concern for her. My mother writes me once a month and I call every six weeks or so. I think I've grown up on the selfish independent side but I miss the companionship of some really great people. I wish my children could know their grandparents.

I've heard in later years that there might have been some mistake made at delivery. My mother remembers hearing the nurse say to the doctor in the room when Caryl was born, "I'm so sorry...I'm so sorry." What that referred to we'll never know.

I guess I never really thought that it would be any different, but it would be nice if she could be normal, and we'd just get on with it.

My fear is that my parents might spoil her so much as to make her very difficult to deal with when they're gone. After all these years, what if I became the primary caretaker? The dependency would be very difficult.

There are some things in life that really matter and a whole lot of things that don't.

PUT HIM IN AN INSTITUTION AND FORGET HE WAS EVER BORN

This 54-year-old mother tells the story of her son, age 29, who was diagnosed with severe mental retardation:

When he was three or four months of age, I noticed how differently he was developing from our other two babies. He insisted on being in only two rooms of the house—his bedroom and kitchen—and he would scream if taken into other rooms or outside. He did not like to be held or cuddled and could not be consoled or comforted if he became upset.

The diagnosis was not made until three years of age, despite our expression of concern about his development to the pediatrician. Later we learned that he shared our concern but was of the opinion nothing could be done and there was no need to "upset" us by revealing his concern.

He is minimally verbal, and was not toilet-trained until 14. He has no receptive language. He gets easily upset when his usual routine is disrupted. He is sensitive to noise and fearful of new environments and activities.

There are no physical characteristics to distinguish autism and no medical tests to indicate autism is present. Our doctor was unwilling to act on our concern until our child was 18 months old. We as parents insisted we be referred to a specialist. First a diagnosis of mental retardation was given and then rescinded later into autism. By then we had located a preschool willing to accept children with autism. The professionals were adamantly opposed to an educational program for the child and recommended psychotherapy for the parents and child. At that time, one school of thought concerning autism was that it was caused by cold, rejecting parents, faulty parenting, etc. We consider ourselves most fortunate that we did not have to encounter any professionals who held this view.

As our son grew older it became increasingly difficult to find any doctors who were willing to treat him, even for his yearly physical checkups. At age seven it became necessary to admit him to a residential care facility. He spent two months there, and then for the next 22 years he would spend weekends at the facility and be at home with his family during the week.

His life has not as yet ever been at risk, but certainly his well-being has. Too many staff members at programs he has attended refuse to treat him with gentleness, kindness, and patience. They often act as if he were in control of certain behaviors that we know he is not. They demand more of him than he is able to give. When he is in such an environment he withdraws, stands and rocks from foot to foot, refuses to eat, mostly wants to remain in his bed (a "safe" place), and will not risk doing anything at all that might cause others to yell at him or show displeasure. He is very fragile emotionally and vulnerable to others' reactions to him and what he does. He is always eager to please and when unable to do so, retreats from everything and everybody, even refuses to eat. Too many staff seem to feel all behavior problems should be dealt with by physical restraint. With our son, speaking slowly and calmly is always the best approach.

He is now 29 and the last several years have been quite difficult as it was only two years ago that we made the decision to have him enter an intermediate care facility in our community. This was a direct result of mismanagement on the part of the staff at his day treatment program, and the bus matron that transported him to this program. He retreated to the point that he refused to leave our house and go to the program each day. Now that he is not living at home, there is less stress in our lives simply because we are not dealing with problems on a daily basis. He is home every weekend, however.

On the one hand it feels good to know you are one of the two most important persons in your child's life (the other is his father). Yet it is excruciatingly painful to think of the future and know that one day you will be leaving a totally defenseless person at the mercy of others.

There has been a lot of stress in our lives: fighting for appropriate services, problems with bus drivers due to his behavior on the bus, some teachers who didn't seem to care or understand. Our family could have been more accepting and made us feel he was welcome at family gatherings. Our family could have helped by offering to provide child care on occasion. He, and consequently we, were ostracized by the family who advised us to put him in an institution and forget he was ever born. This, from my mother! On the plus side, this experience has made me more tolerant of differences in people.

I have no advice for others, each must find his/her own way.

I SUPPOSE THAT I "LOVE" MY BROTHER, BUT PRESENTLY I DON'T "LIKE" HIM

An adult sister talks about her 29-year-old brother and their family:

I remember having to support my brother during Christmas photos because he couldn't sit up by himself. He has spastic cerebral palsy. His birth was premature. He weighed three pounds, three ounces. They said it was caused by lack of oxygen to the brain.

I was mainly involved in my brother's physical therapy sessions. He was often stubborn and fought, or would not work during therapy and I would coax him or model for him. Exercises were also a daily routine at home and I remember helping my mother motivate and encourage my brother.

It was difficult for me because a lot of time was spent focused on my brother and all the special care he needed. As a young child I had to grow up quickly. I had many responsibilities and was a "good helper."

I feel like my brother's biggest disability is his attitude. He asks for advice and then doesn't make any changes in his life and then complains about his problems.

He is afraid to make changes, doesn't want the stress, applies for other jobs within the company, but has been passed over many times. Personally, I don't see any positive things about his current job situation. It is a demotion from his last position; it is a dead-end job that doesn't pay enough to live independently.

It helps when people smile, have direct eye contact, say something positive other than focus on the disability. Treat and talk to the person like they would anyone else. I hate it when they stare, say stupid things like "God must have chosen you to be such loving parents, sister," etc.

My spouse is the only one who provides helpful advice. Probably because he is not a blood relative and can sort out issues between the disability and family issues. I wish they would have paid more attention to me as a young adolescent.

Presently I would describe my emotional status with my brother as frustrating. Having no other siblings to compare to, I do not know if we have a normal brother/sister relationship. I suppose that I "love" my brother, but presently I don't "like" him.

I think that it is the person's attitude that makes adjusting easy or difficult. Not the type of disability.

Knowing the outcome of me and my parents' hard work of getting my brother as independent as possible today, and how I feel that he sabotages his successes, I don't think I would have put so much energy and devotion into his well-being if I had known in the future that he wouldn't care. Although I feel frustrated with my brother, I have not given up on the hope he will make changes with his life and once he does, I will be there to support and applaud him.

[Family dynamics?] Grandparents…doted, gave extra gifts and attention.

Father…worked

Mother…feels guily, overprotects, but yet gives my brother mixed messages.

Myself…initially I was the helper, then became angry and acted out to get attention. During my college years I pretty much stayed out of the picture. I presently offer advice, if asked, but am not invested. I have my life and family now.

My parents don't set limits on my brother. They are currently trying to get my brother to move out of their house as they get ready to move to a retirement home.

I don't get mad at God. Stuff happens. Most people are lucky.

I'm not sure about his future. It's going to depend on whatever my brother puts his mind to. The question is if he would just decide to do something. My fear is that he will end up in a wheelchair, living with my parents for the rest of their lives. I hope he will become independent from my parents.

I HAVE HUNDREDS OF SKIN TUMORS ALL OVER MY BODY

When she was ten years old, this 39-year-old mother of two children developed a disfiguring disease:

I have neurofibromatosis. I have hundreds of skin tumors all over my body. My internal involvement has not been as great as my external involvement. Internally I have had tumors removed from my carotid artery, knee cap, breasts, calves. It is a genetic disorder but no one else in the family has the disorder. I remember so early having the tumors and being embarrassed by them.

I have had numerous operations to remove tumors. I underwent psychological therapy with a psychiatrist, but that didn't last long after the doctor asked me if the tumors on my arms were heroin tracks. I had a plastic surgeon who performed numerous tumor removals, hundreds at a time. One time as I was outside the operating room waiting to be wheeled in, the plastic surgeon told a colleague laughingly that his next case was "the Elephant Girl."

I had an extremely rewarding psychologist, who, after a relationship of mine failed terribly, helped me realize that I was worth something and that my skin, as strange as it is, was not worth disrupting my whole life over. The most difficult has been coming to terms and living with tumors, more tumor growth, and not knowing what I can expect in tumor involvement in the future.

Adolescence is difficult enough being secure in the person you are. Having skin tumors and looking different didn't help.

What doesn't help is people who don't know me, or just met me. They look at me, and you know they are wondering about my skin but don't ask. I have had strangers ask me if I am contagious. Sometimes in stores cashiers will not put my change in my hand so they will not need to touch me. People who do not know what is wrong tend to look at me at times with disgust, as if I'm contagious and will harm them. Just listening to me and letting me get out my insecurities helps.

I wish I would have had more information when I was younger. I was in my 20s before I really knew the full impact of what could happen with me. It has made me an insecure, self-conscious person at times. It has made me stronger as I got older.

I wish I could go to a beach and wear a bathing suit without having people staring at me.

I grew up with three brothers, all with whom I have a close relationship. I was never treated special or different. I'm not sure, but sometimes I feel my parents have felt a little guilty.

It has made me more guarded and not as open in meeting new people. It has made me self-conscious, but I've never had a real good self-image. I have an extremely open and satisfying sexual relationship with my husband. He loves me and accepts me for myself.

I hate the stares from people, people who won't meet your eyes, but look away, people giggling or laughing at me. I wish people would ask me what is wrong. I would rather be questioned than ignored.

I'm looking forward to watching my children grow, sharing my life with my husband. But what if I get more tumors and I look even more "freaky"?

And from this woman's four-year-old daughter:

I want to have bumps just like my mom when I grow up. Touching [them] makes me laugh. Sometimes [the disability] makes me sad. Hold me when I'm sad.

I AM NO LONGER A WHOLE PERSON

This 34-year-old man developed arthritis as an adolescent:

My dream is to have two days in a row without pain. Before the disability I could do anything. Now I have to make plans and depend on other people. This is one part of the disability I really do not like. I'm not self-sufficient any more.

When I'm out taking a walk, and I have to stop to rest, I am told by people, "It can't be that bad, you are just giving in to it."

I am no longer a whole person. There are things I can't do at all, and things I have to think about and make plans to do.

I blame myself. If I had taken better care of myself, it would not have happened.

I GUESS SHE HAD ALWAYS THOUGHT IT WAS
A TEMPORARY CONDITION LIKE CHICKEN POX

A 32-year-old woman talks about her 28-year-old sister:

My sister is mentally retarded. She has a profound stutter and a distinctive speech pattern due to a flap in her windpipe that does not close completely, as it should, for certain consonants. Due to her brain damage, she is also very short. Because of her retardation and stutter she was misdiagnosed when she was suffering many ear infections and ended up with a slight hearing loss and almost constant tintinitus, that sometimes wakes her up from a deep sleep.

The disability was caused by my mother's drug abuse: barbiturates and tranquilizers. Two doctors prescribing drugs without the others' knowledge to alleviate symptoms of manic/depressive behavior. My mother wasn't an innocent victim, she knew what she was doing.

My earliest memories consist of my sister being different and of the neighborhood kids looking out for her. She was pretty much protected from discrimination because of this. In our society, people tend to be far more accepting of retarded children than they are of retarded adults. She was the "Honey Sunday" poster child when she was about six or seven. I remember my parents being very pleased about that.

She also had the opportunity to go to camp. No other children in my family ever had a camp experience because of the costs involved, but most of her fees were absorbed because we were so poor. I never resented this because I wouldn't have traded places with her for all the tea in China. I knew in my heart that such experiences for her would be few and far between as she grew up.

I remember when my sister started school. She was bussed out to the school where they used to lump all retarded children, regardless of ability. In the sixties parents were encouraged to put their retarded kids in institutions, forget about them, and "try again." It seems the ones who kept them were the poorest, most uneducated group.

The "retarded" child is considered cute, and the hard-won accomplishments are met with admiration and considerable praise. The adolescent is considered dumb and other adults either lose patience or choose to disregard the retarded individual altogether. My brother to this day has very little patience with our sister. It obviously makes him feel uncomfortable. People fear what they do not understand.

During early adolescence other kids used to beat her up on a daily basis, just for the fun of it. When my sister was about 12 and had been mainstreamed for a couple of years, I walked into the bedroom we shared and found her crying. I asked her what was wrong, thinking that someone was taunting her and I could give her a little talk on ignoring them. She caught me quite off-guard when she said, "When will I not be retarded anymore?" I could feel the tears start to form in my eyes and knew my answer would have to be brief or I would start to cry, and she would realize how agonized I was for her. As kindly as I could I told her she would always be retarded. I guess she had always thought it was a temporary condition like chicken pox. She cried even more, with wracking sobs that made her body shudder. And I couldn't make it any better. I said she would always have her family, and she did have some friends, and that her life would be filled with good times as well as bad times. Then I left because I knew in my heart that her life would never have the quality that my life would have, and this hurt me almost as much as it hurt her to know she would never be totally accepted.

She works at a laundry, her main social outlet. It is a small business and she is genuinely accepted.

I wish my family would consider future plans for her. I wish they were reasonable and rational about it. If I could have done things differently, I would have been more assertive on behalf of her when it came to friendships and independent living. Many evenings I've cried out of frustration because she is not being prepared for the future. My mother's inability to accept the retardation will eventually come raining down on me if my parents should die before my sister does. Any suggestion I make is met with scorn. If I could I would get my sister out of the family house. They all live in a make-believe world.

Kathy doesn't even realize that her siblings sacrificed for her. She was the one who had the camp experience. She was the one with the better clothes, so she wouldn't stand out so much.

More because of my mother than Kathy's disability, she doesn't socialize well. She's very self-absorbed. She expects people to jump for her, but thinks nothing of it to inadvertently hurt another's feelings. Mother doesn't like her to have disabled friends. My mother will forever feel guilty about the retardation and would like to believe she is normal.

If my sister had not been disabled, my energies could have gone elsewhere maybe. I could have gone to camp. Maybe college at 18 would have been a possibility. She is a continual problem that I will ultimately have to deal with in one way or another. I will forever be raising a child. I don't look forward to anything. I deal with things as they come along. I've learned how cruel people can be.

In this day and age of amniocentesis I would suggest that a woman think long and hard about bringing a retarded baby into this world, as it is now. The baby grows up and, unfortunately, even though the retarded are good and reliable manual labor workers, society shuns them. As far as the retarded individuals who have been born, I believe they deserve to live as full a life as they are capable of. I wish every anti-choice proponent would spend as much time, money, and energy concentrating on the life that is already here as opposed to "saving a life" that maybe was never meant to be....

PLEASE ACT NORMAL, OR NATURAL AROUND US. WE'RE STILL REGULAR OLD HUMAN BEINGS... NOT FROM ANOTHER PLANET

Though she sees her wheelchair to be a barrier between her and men, this 26-year-old woman with cerebral palsy hopes someday to marry and become a mother:

My first year of life my parents believed I was just slow in learning all of the activities that children learn to do. Then when they and others got curious, my parents took me to a school for the handicapped. They told my mom right away what I had. I then began physical therapy and going to school there. I was able to read at three-and-a-half years. I wore braces on my hips and legs to keep my legs from rotating outward. I walked in a walker and also had a wheelchair.

After years of therapy I only have some spasticity when I'm nervous or scared. When I got into high school I got an electric wheelchair. It was, and still is, a life-saver because once I got older and bigger, my parents couldn't carry me anymore, plus I could move around on my own then.

When my mother was in labor, I (my brain) was without oxygen and caused brain damage to my nervous system. I can't keep my balance at all.

I can't remember any therapy until I was three or four. Overall, I know that therapy was good for me but I did not like it when I was young. I had therapy on a fairly regular basis until I was 14 or 15. I have been very lucky—I have only been in hospitals a few times. I hated being there. I did not know anyone. I was far away from home. I was able to come home the weekends. That did help.

My life has never been at risk because of the cerebral palsy. I think I was most scared last summer when the seizures came up. I was not aware of having the grand mal seizures and being in the hospital when not being aware of what was going on was very scary for me.

The preschool years were easier because it had been that way since I could remember, and kids tend to accept things easier because of that reason. Adolescence was the worst because of what I could/could not do compared to others. And because of the lack of male/female relationships I've had, even so far, which is zero.

The academic part of it was as normal as possible at the handicapped school. It all seemed normal to me. I did get along with all my friends there. When I was 13 years old, I was transferred and mainstreamed into the public school. I was very scared at first about changing schools. I'd be in the "real world." But it all turned out better than I had feared. I made some terrific friends who are still my friends.

Technically I'm not employed, but I print labels for the owner of a florist on my printer in my home. The owner just gives me cash whenever I do it.

I like it when people love me and support my decisions. Also they help me make other decisions. They are able to help me out with physical things I can not do. They say that my spirits are great most of the time. I attribute that to my faith in God. When I pray, I get the feeling of calmness that everything will work out if I trust him. When I talk to my mom we have these heart-to-heart talks. We discuss the situation and then talk of alternative ways/solutions to handle the problems. It's basically the same when I talk to a friend.

As I've said, for the most part I am well-adjusted to it (the disability), but sometimes I do feel as if I've missed out on something, such as a relationship with a man, going out on dates, and sports, among other activities that anyone else could do, but a wheelchair-bound person can't do as easily. Although most things aren't limited physically, a wheelchair sometimes puts a wall between that person and others.

To feel disabled is for the most part to feel "normal"—normal as I know and feel life to be. But, again there's times when it is the pits when I come up against my limitations.

I just feel that what I've done and what's happened to me is what was meant for me. In my dreams, sometimes I'm disabled and other times I'm not. I have several dreams. But as of late, my favorite dream is I'm walking and I'm sitting, talking with a boyfriend.

My family—we all love each other and we have love for God/Jesus. We support each other and my family helps me in any way they can. And I support them. My father has a drinking problem and that is definitely a weak link for us all. All of us but him have gone to counseling to be strong. He has not gone for help and he doesn't feel he needs it.

I believe my parents were surprised at the news of my disability and of course they wished it wasn't there, but with God's help they soon adjusted. My sisters, since they are younger than me, knew me as handicapped all their life, so it was a way of life for them.

In terms of talking with my parents about how the disability has affected them, I have to say that the topic wasn't discussed in so many words, but I'm sure after the time they knew something was wrong, at first it did take some adjusting. But as I've mentioned before, with our family's faith in God, we (they) learned to adjust and it was all in God's plan for us.

Most people I know have no real problems with my disability. The people that can't handle it stay away, I'm sure. My first real exposure to the "real world" was when I went to a public school. I made and still have great friends from there.

I have had no sexual relationships as of yet. At times I think and feel that I can be sexy (i.e., when I dress up or I'm in my bikini at the beach), and other times I think the wheelchair is like a wall between me and the guys. I feel that men see the chair and they stay away. Although a part of it may be people are leery because of other reasons (for whatever reason). They may feel there's other problems besides physical. Or they just don't want to deal with anyone that isn't "normal."

Please act normal or natural around us. We're still regular old human beings…not from another planet.

I'm looking forward to a family of my own.

I REMEMBER ONCE BANGING MY HEAD ON THE BATHROOM WALL
BECAUSE TIM HAD SOILED HIS PANTS 14 DAYS IN A ROW

Twenty-six years ago this 48-year-old woman gave birth to a son who was subsequently diagnosed with autism:

I am constantly concerned that his life is not a good experience for him. I do well most of the time, then something, such as a close friend's child's wedding, opens up the hurt afresh and I am always surprised because of the acute pain I feel.

It was devastating at first. I remember trying to bargain with God once to let Tim and me change places and let him be non-disabled and me have his disability. I considered killing both of us in an automobile accident but I was afraid I would botch it and both of us end up with more problems. Sadness and despair are part of my life. Most of the time I do well though.

I still feel very frustrated. He does not show or does not feel the feelings I have for him. He responds variably to me but two days ago when I left, he kissed me which he has not done for several years.

His father was very good to hold, feed and care for him when he was small. After an evaluation of Tim when he was seven, we were told to put him away and forget we ever had him. My husband wept and grieved for him and let go a bit and put energy into a second son age nine months at this stage. I became the absolute caregiver. My husband wanted to place him outside of the home at this point.

My husband cared for our younger son. Everytime there was a problem with Tim, my husband and I would exchange a mean look. No words were exchanged but the stress was very high. I was angry when he messed his pants every day for weeks. I cried a lot. I remember once banging my head on the bathroom wall because he had soiled his pants 14 days in a row. He was 13 at the time. It was either to hurt me or him. I also had two other small children to care for with no assistance as my husband's job kept him out of town three days and two nights per week. When he started abusing himself, I struggled with wanting to hit him.

When Tim was very small it was hard to accept the fact of his limitations. As he grew older, acceptance was difficult. It is very hard with one's children to let them become persons in their own right and not the people that we planned and hoped for them to be. This was extremely hard with Tim. Now that he is grown it is easier most of the time. Once in awhile there is a fresh hurt because my main concern is that he is not happy and content in his life. I fear that his life is a fearsome jumble that makes no sense to him.

I hoped Tim's life would have been different as day is from night. He would be able to see the wonder of creation and really experience the world instead of simply travelling through it.

I remember talking to God about this and saying, "God, why are you punishing us for this. My husband and I have been good and love what is right, so why us?" I turned away from God for awhile, and then I realized what a foolish and rebellious child I was. I know that God gives me the strength each day to meet the things that come my way.

When Tim was four or five, I thought about getting both of us out of this world and its problems. I didn't believe I could face the future but I always knew that I must try and keep on trying.

Two siblings in this family share their feelings, also. First, a 20-year-old brother:

I'm sad because I grew up with a mentally-retarded brother and I was always teased and picked on by others because I was different. My mom told me all about it [what caused it]. Sometimes a child is just born that way and sometimes the parents cause it by using drugs. I just deal with it [the disability]. I enjoy talking to disabled people, that's just about it. I just live one day at a time. I don't worry about the future. Just let me be. I have my own way of dealing with it.

And a 16-year-old sister:

I don't really think about it much [the disability]. I mean I do, but it doesn't seem strange that my brother has autism. I guess because I'm just used to it and hearing about it. I feel sorry for him because he will never be able to marry and mentally grow up. I also am sad because I don't have him like I should have him and neither do my parents or brother—as a son or brother. My parents said he was born with it. That kind of bothers me because my parents weren't even "druggies" or anything like that. Yet people that drink and do drugs have normal children. I'm afraid of the future because I am growing up and enjoying life and it seems he has nothing to look forward to. [What helps?] I don't know, maybe talking, but mostly just telling myself that things happen and God has made things happen for a certain reason.

NEVER REACT TO THE FEELINGS, BUT BE AWARE OF THEM

This 47-year-old mother blames herself for her son's epilepsy:

He has epilepsy, grand mal seizures several times a day. He takes medication that isn't working and has bad side effects.

The cause of his disability was mother not being in touch with her feelings during pregnancy and most of the time during his upbringing. I look back and see that he was seizure-free, either with or without medication, if I was in touch with my feelings, thus setting an example for him.

Frustration? When doctors ask me what I was feeling. This was very frustrating for me because I wasn't in touch with my feelings, so I didn't understand what they were getting at or wanted. They should have shown me love/acceptance, and tried to focus in on me, and tried to encourage me to try to become aware of my feelings, and if I couldn't, they shouldn't have humiliated me this way.

His education was horrible and humiliating. They didn't zero in on his learning style, or my style of struggling with the difficulties, of having a style not understood by most people, and being a single parent working and not qualifying for welfare. Consequently, the father got away "Scot-free" of any obligation, but I now recognize that he, too, must have a learning style not fully understood by everyone. No one understands my son. They need to accept the positive and constantly affirm him and motivate him and help him stay in touch with his feelings.

He's been given too much medication, causing bad side effects. Giving him more burdens to carry on his shoulders. People don't understand epilepsy.

They should have encouraged my son to respect me and love me, instead of blaming me like so many relatives, school officials, and doctors did. This was very detrimental to our mother/son relationship.

The disability has helped me in my co-dependency and has held me back tremendously from my potential. I've detached from him for my own survival and I think his, too. He has drawn big walls between himself and other people.

Sexuality should only come after spirituality, and if he had that he wouldn't be epileptic.

[We asked several questions about children's feelings in our questionnaire, and she felt these questions were inappropriate.] I don't agree with this. It is not important for you to know their feelings. What is important is that you encourage them to be in touch with their own feelings and stay focused on themselves. Never react to the feelings, but be aware of them.

MY MIND KIND OF WANDERS TO AND FRO

This 25-year-old woman experienced a head injury in a traffic accident as a baby. We debated whether to present her story exactly as she wrote it, or to edit it extensively for the sake of clarity and to honor her dignity. We chose the latter approach:

When I was seven months old I went through the windshield, hit the dashboard and [had] glass all over the head.

I am totally disabled. From the waist down, but can do anything I can do.

I had surgery on my leg and arm. I can use my arm some of the time, but usually it just hangs.

Well, I had to have therapy on the left side of me because it was doing me a lot of good to have it done.

[It is difficult] Not remembering where I am at.

It was a scary life for this chump, because my great grandmother died the 15th of May, 1987 at 7:37 p.m. That's the only thing that's scary.

Yes, sometimes my legs hurts like pins and needles. Walking on both feet is just like falling down three flights, which I did at one time.

I can't think at what I'm doing most times.

[People say] Why don't you use your arm? Walking down the road [is hard]. People don't have any brains to tell everybody....

[It's difficult] Because I went through the windshield at seven months old. The feeling is not fun to feel to be handicapped.

[I would like to] Drive a car and go to Colorado for six months.

My mind kind of wanders to and fro.

I TELL HER SHE IS AN ANGEL

A 64-year-old grandmother talks about her daughter and her grandson, who has been diagnosed as having Down's Syndrome:
At first the doctors said this baby would never dress himself and gave my daughter and her husband little hope that the infant would be much more than a vegetable. This diagnosis was given at the hospital. He has Down's Syndrome, caused by an extra chromosome. The doctor said, after my grandson was delivered, "He looks mongoloid." My daughter's eyes, when she told me about this later, were red with tears. She had cried all the way home. He was the first born, and after much consideration, the last one in that family. It was difficult for me to see how my daughter suffered, and seeing Randy develop such a fear of doctors.

Pain teaches us. Those who would leave pain out of their life must face it some day. I wish people wouldn't label these kids as "retards." We all have disabilities. Ours may not show, Randy's does.

Our holidays are not the same. Some in-laws seem to see him as a dangerous influence. They grumble about him, and think he should be locked up in an institution. I would not change him. God gives us many gifts in disguises sometimes. I wish we could go to restaurants or stores without worrying where he is going to wander off to.

Randy's mother handles all the problems well. It was hard at first, but she is, and always has been, an excellent mother. My husband (Randy's real grandfather died before he was born) does not like to be around any handicapped people. He does not care to have him here for a meal. He says they laugh too loud. My husband's sons seem to resent Randy. They much prefer an avoidance rather than an acceptance. We can no longer have family get-togethers. He does not eat the best. He has to put his tongue out to swallow. It makes my youngest daughter sick. She rarely ever visits here, and never visits Randy.

I wonder who would care for him if his mother should become ill. He thrives on the things he knows will always be there…his chair, his room, his pool table. He does not like changes that upset him. No one should sit in his chair at the table unless he is not present. He likes life to stay the same.

His mother milks morning and evening. They have a small dairy set-up. It is hard, no days off, not a vacation in over 20 years. Randy's father is not a good worker, he doesn't have the energy maybe? Sort of lazy, would rather sit and watch others work.

My husband does not speak of things he disapproves of, or cannot face. He says Randy makes him nervous. We dread to see Christmas come. Due to my husband's inability to accept Randy, we can only visit over the phone, or at a relative's home. Sometimes we go to the restaurant to visit with each other. Then my husband joins us. We have to be careful what we say. We feel like we are not free to be ourselves. Someday we want to be together again for the holidays.

[What are other people's reactions to him?] It runs the gamut. Most people who have worked with him care about him. A few do not. It is hard sometimes to be with him. He wants to be a man, and that does not lend itself to "minding" Mom. Randy likes to feel he is as anyone his age. He is not aware of his disability.

To me, we are all on earth for a reason. Randy may have come as he is for a reason we do not know.

[Have you ever felt like you're "going crazy"?] Oh, that's a good one. I am sure his mom has thought that every day. She calls me, I tell her she is an angel. She sees me through my emotional upsets. We can talk about anything. We are there for each other.

My husband's daughter-in-law, who turns her nose up at Randy, teaches handicapped children. I was told that she says Down's Syndrome kids are a result of one or both parents being on drugs. Do you have any idea how this makes me feel? I am outraged. How can a teacher with such a poor understanding of a child's illness or disability be allowed in a classroom? Do the very people that are entrusted to help our children with special needs, sometimes turn out to be the ones who are most in need of enlightenment? Being a teacher should bring out the desire to help others. It does not always work out that way.

IT HAS BEEN DESCRIBED TO US AS 100 TIMES THE PAIN
OF A MIGRAINE HEADACHE

A 60-year-old mother talks about her 23-year-old son:

Donald was misdiagnosed as an infant. He should have had a shunt immediately following birth for Dandy Walker Syndrome, caused by hydrocephalus. He was diagnosed at 17 months. The pressure by then had incurred enough brain damage to cause mental retardation. Donald has no cerebellum. He is quite high functioning.

When his shunt was originally implanted, he was in a life-threatening situation. The intercranial pressure had caused seizures and he was in great respiratory distress. He has had many hospitalizations through the years for pneumonia, hernia repair, crossed-eyes repair, and replacements of his shunt. The times that the shunt would occlude, Donald was rife with pain. Nothing helped. It has been described to us as 100 times the pain of a migraine headache. This pain was caused by his ventricles collapsing. We always had fantastic medical care. One time Donald's pain lasted for several days before they could replace the shunt. He was in terrible agony, screaming with pain which could be heard all over the neighborhood.

The most difficult aspect was trying to be brave and not frighten him with our tears and concern. And getting the doctors to talk about his condition.

We have feared for Donald's life many times with his brain surgeries. We are deeply religious and prayer definitely helps. His life was most fragile when his shunt would malfunction. We fear for his life on a daily basis now that he is in a semi-independent living situation with very little supervision.

Sometimes things get so overwhelming and you need to think about other things. Your mind can only handle so much.

Preschool was the easiest, because I could protect him from the teasing and subsequent pressures put on the disabled child through mainstreaming. I do not like the idea of mainstreaming. Adolescence was the most difficult because of the prejudices against the disabled. As he is growing older, I find that the mentally retarded have very few "rights."

Donald now works at a recycling facility. He has often expressed his desire to work at something more challenging. His wishes in this regard are largely ignored. He tries hard, is a "people" person, but he gets overly tired, though he is not challenged. We have found that most counselors and rehab people "talk a good game" and actually do very little.

I was in denial for years after Donald's diagnosis. I kept thinking that any day he would "get better." I have been emotionally distraught from the day he was born, with very little let-up. I would like to be free from the responsibility and guilt. I wish I could let him be totally independent without hearing from his case manager about all his negatives.

Donald's father is in a lot of denial, very saddened, and took his frustrations out by being a "workaholic." I was affected the most because I have had to do most of the "dealing" with counselors, teachers. I have had to do most of the caregiving, too. Our two older girls used to babysit for him, change his diapers, helped him to learn to walk, etc. None have ever expressed any anger to us as care providers. They didn't have to do it that much, and were extremely supportive in times of crisis.

We mainly talk in terms of the worry we have over all his problems and how we have "matured" because of his situation.

Donald does not think of himself as disabled and has great compassion for those who are. I think he would have been a great asset to the world with his warm personality. I would have been more of a "free" and happy person. I have screamed many times at God that Donald's situation is "just not fair."

I blamed myself for years, because I smoked during my pregnancy with him. Parents always tend to blame themselves. I tried for years to pretend that Donald was normal and could learn like all the other kids.

I wish I knew about the future. Hopefully, he can be a functioning, contributing member of the community. I'm afraid that he will not get to realize the dreams he has for himself. I've learned that every little difficulty they overcome is so beautiful.

HIS EDUCATIONAL EXPERIENCES HAVE BEEN ROUGH, TOUGH, SAD, FRUSTRATING, HUMILIATING, TIRESOME, DISCOURAGING, DEMANDING, STRESSFUL

Twenty-four years ago this man, now 59, became a father to a son with mental retardation:

Our son has Dandy Walker Syndrome. A shunt was not put in until age 17 months, resulting in brain damage and mental retardation. It is basically a birth defect due to lack of proper diagnosis by the attending physician.

My earliest memory is of a sad, sad, sick feeling.

My wife is an RN, and I left it up to her to deal with the doctors. I was with her for most of the sessions but I rarely participated in the discussions.

Watching my son suffer was the worst. His life was most at risk between ages nine and 11 months, when he had intensive seizures and convulsions resulting from pressure on the brain. He quit breathing at age 17 months for approximately five minutes resulting in further brain damage.

It's tough to have a mentally-retarded child.

His educational experiences have been rough, tough, sad, frustrating, humiliating, tiresome, discouraging, demanding, stressful.

His employment has been mainly janitorial and menial labor. Very demeaning.

Organizations that helped? Absolutely none! We've really received no help at all.

I have always had some degree of depression the entire 24 years of his life. I can never completely shake it. I wish I didn't have to be in the relationship with a disabled son. I wish I would have pushed the doctor harder for a correct and timely diagnosis.

We were and are all devastated. We're all very weak. I've had the most trouble coping. His mother did most of the care. His older brother and sisters usually resented having to take care of him and were by and large ashamed of him. The impact on them has been devastating.

I've got to blame someone, so I guess the attending doctor for lack of correct and timely diagnosis.

I wouldn't consider suicide. I have a lot of other things to live for.

I would just want other families to know that you're all alone in it.

What happens when he no longer has a mother or father around?

I WAS ON A BEACH THAT WAS DESERTED, WITH A MAN. IT WAS HOT AND SUNNY AND I WAS WEARING A VIRGINAL WHITE DRESS

Sexuality is a key issue in the life of this young woman who was diagnosed with cerebral palsy as a baby:

Adolescence for me was terrible because I suffered from untreated depression because of the disability. The first ten years of my life were very happy and care-free because I never thought I had a disability. Doctors have treated me very well, they have given me respect, caring, and dignity, and they give me time to talk about problems. When I was younger this was especially true. I never was my orthopedist's "meal ticket" as far as surgeries, and I have him to thank for not surgically touching me.

Even though my cerebral palsy is minor compared to other people I have known, I suffer a lot emotionally because of my condition. It is crippling to me in the way I see myself and how I am perceived by my family. My family thinks I am selfish and ungrateful because I only think of myself. The way I deal with my disability isn't the way my family would like me to deal with it. I think they want me to talk about what's bothering me and I won't.

I should have had psychological counseling but my mother didn't think it would be important. Don't get me wrong. I'm not indicting my mother for what she didn't do. I think she thought I would tell her everything; but instead I told her nothing, maybe because her attitude is "I don't care." I have to live with my parents because I have no money and am unable to find a job. I long to be able to drive so I won't be so dependent.

There are times I totally forget that I have a disability because only my legs are affected. I think, too, that I am seen as being fragile, which I'm not, and I don't think I'm seen as a sexual being by my family. As for how I see myself, I don't see myself as a woman. In my dreams I am not disabled. In my favorite dream which also turned out to be a sexual fantasy dream, I was on a beach that was deserted, with a man. It was hot and sunny and I was wearing a virginal white dress.

I have a disabled friend who I met when I was 14 who has the same condition as mine. She also is married, which gives me hope that I can have what she's got, which is a husband and two kids. My disability has affected my sexuality in I think a very bad way, and I blame society for it. No, I have not had any important sexual relationships at all in my life and I really wonder if I deserve, am capable of, or have the same rights as disabled males and normal healthy people to have one sexual relationship that leads to marriage.

I believe with all my heart the things just mentioned, and no one has changed my opinion otherwise. The reason I have such a negative opinion on this is because I have been taught or brainwashed that I shouldn't even attempt a sexual relationship. Even though I personally don't believe this, I have been taught that I am crazy to want a man to love and marry. I blame this negativity on society because nobody teaches people that disabled women, especially, are sexual beings just like everybody else.

I feel it is more acceptable for a disabled man to get caring and nurturing from a woman than vice versa. And for me that is bad news because I need a lot of TLC to feel that I am a woman, that I'm a worthwhile person. Please, please don't preach to me about finding love and nurturing in another area of my life. It doesn't work. I need to prove myself in this area more than any other part of my life. I just don't know how to go about doing it.

I CAN DRAW FROM A "WELL OF PATIENCE" THAT TOOK YEARS TO DRILL, AND IT SEEMS TO BE DEEP AND FULL

Twenty-two years ago this 43-year-old mother gave birth to a beautiful baby boy who was subsequently diagnosed with Down's Syndrome. She writes of her struggles on behalf of her son, and of her love for him:

My earliest memories are of having a happy baby, a good baby, without knowing he was Down's Syndrome. My doctor didn't tell me until Rick was almost a year old. No one noticed, not even my mother or mother-in-law, until nine months old when he was slower than other babies. A specialist finally told us. It was very hard on me.

I used to believe doctors are so wonderful and know it all. I had such trust in them. I believe that the doctor who delivered Rick knew he was Down's Syndrome and could not tell us. When I would take him in, he seemed so uneasy. I finally took him to a big clinic about 45 minutes away. They were better. Rick is scared of doctors. "No shots," he always says. And dentists: one dentist wanted to strap him down, including hands and feet. We never let him touch him. It takes understanding, time and patience to work with a mentally-handicapped person.

Once when Rick was young—three or four—and he was acting up in the doctor's office, the doctor told me I had a monster and would have a lot of problems. I was so upset. I did not need to hear that. Most kids show off and won't listen at one time or another. I also remember a specialist who was doctoring Rick for an ear problem. He acted as if he despised him. Rick was so upset, he picked up on those feelings. He cried when the doctor worked on his ears and we were told to find a different doctor. Even now we see "family practice" doctors, a different one each time. Rarely does one take time to listen to Rick or understand his fear of them. He had one good doctor, a baby doctor.

Living on a farm, we have had several very tragic close calls with Rick. I get upset thinking of them. I watched him close, but a child is quick. He has put the tractor in gear and the truck. Fortunately, both had been in park and not running. One experience with an auger I do not want to think about. He does not understand danger. He is much better now that he is older, but we still have close calls. Once he tried to shave with Dad's electric razor, he almost put it in the water. I caught him just in time. It was plugged in and I'm sure it would have killed him. There have been times he does not understand the danger cattle pose. He could get kicked or knocked down. He is doing better now.

I have had those days when I want a normal child. I ache for one. But it is not his fault. The pressures of life, dairy cows, get me on the down side. I love Rick so much. He is the center of my life.

[Educational issues?] This is a big department for me with small space to answer. When Rick was in school he spent the entire 12 years in one elementary school. He did not receive art, music, phys ed at all until a group of us mothers fought the school board and won. I have learned through his school years to fight for his rights. The school system is not a good subject for me, I have a lot of heartache from the way he was treated.

I can't stand it when people stare as if we were from an alien place. Strangers have come up to me and told me they are sorry for me and glad it was not them. Many mistake Rick for someone else. Down's look so similar. Once I told a lady she was mistaken and Rick showed her his ID. She told me she didn't believe me. And they talk to him and do not introduce themselves. He loves everyone. I get uneasy not knowing anything about the stranger talking to him. He does not understand and I answer for him.

The things I would do different are many. I would not be so quiet and passive over the way he has been treated by "professionals": doctors, school authorities. He has every right to programs and to be himself without the putdowns. I would start working with him sooner, rather than wait a year.

I regret that I cannot be a grandmother. My friends are, and I see and share their joy, but I must accept the fact that I never will be. And Rick even tells me he will get married and have a baby like me and Bill.

Life itself has so many ups and downs. He is almost always on a straight and even course. I don't get upset or mad very often at all. I can draw from a "well of patience" that took years to drill, and it seems to be deep and full.

Do I ever get mad at God? I just do not think that way. If anything, I do get the blues at times, but everybody does. God has helped and guided me through such joys and deep heart-breaking sorrows. I try to take each experience and learn, then go on with life.

I have thought of suicide, years ago. I feel most people do at one time or another, but it wasn't because of Rick but all the other problems life throws at me.

I sometimes fear that if I would die and not have plans made that he would not be in a safe, happy, loving place. I understand him and not many others do.

SHE WAS CINDERELLA WHEN SHE DANCED WITH HER FATHER

Twenty-two years ago this woman, now 52 years old, gave birth to a daughter who was later diagnosed as having mental retardation. The daughter died in her late teens:

My earliest memories are of her crying, day and night. She didn't want to be held, kissed, or hugged. She would not sleep in her crib. My husband or I slept in the rocking chair holding her all night, till she was at least two years.

The first doctor we had ordered the test which confirmed our suspicions that Sandy was mentally retarded. The doctor said, "Find another doctor. I don't treat these kinds of people." She was seven months old. We didn't even know what retarded meant, let alone how to deal with anger, rejection, and fear. We had three normal children at home. Tests were done at the Mayo Clinic. Same answer, retarded. "Take her home and put her in a home. There's no hope for her." As parents this would be the best we could do for her and not ruin the lives of our other three children.

We went to the state home two different times. These were the only times I saw my husband cry, besides at his two daughters' funerals. A home was not the answer for us. Another doctor sent us to another clinic, same test results. They gave us no hope.

The most difficult thing is feeling "hopeless" but yet we hoped, and then the pain of hearing more test results. We had no other parents at that time to talk to. Times have changed. We got pity from parents and friends, never a helping hand.

No one ever told us that she could die from the seizures until after she died. We always feared she'd injure herself falling, hitting her head or limbs on something during the seizures. She knew no fear, in the early years. Would walk into a swimming pool, go out into traffic. She did learn dangers after she was older. Probably because she was told so often.

We had hoped that someday she could have worked in a nursery or greenhouse surroundings. She was very knowledgeable about plants.

We would have liked for better conditions in the sheltered workshop. She was distracted a lot by other clients and what was going on around her. I worried about her safety, and of her being hurt by one of the other clients.

We all worked together. All would say, "Okay, yes, I've seen her do this, and this is what I do to make her stop, or try to accomplish the task." We would make a plan, and all use it. If it didn't work then we'd try a new plan. She was always #1. No one ever lost sight of that fact. How lucky she was to have so many people to love her and help her to her full learning ability. No one lost hope.

The last two years of her life she knew she was different mentally. She said she hated the seizures. It tears a parent's heart out and you can't change it.

[If you had life to live over, would you do anything differently?] My husband and I did the best we could for Sandy. We had five months together after she died and we talked about this very question. The only thing my husband regretted was that he had not had the opportunity to physically hurt the house father who beat her with a belt and the buckle. She was a beautiful person. She could sing so beautiful. She was Cinderella when she danced with her father. She had more love to give to her family in the short time we had her than most people ever receive. Her sister became a special ed teacher. Her two sisters could laugh and cry all in one minute. Such feelings as a family! How lucky we all were, and aware of our feelings for other people. We hope that her happy life was the result of a family working together to achieve the best we could.

We felt helpless sometimes. We all had brains that functioned, why couldn't she learn? We all gave our weekend time or whenever she was home, just to her. Both kids gave up activities, dates, work time to spend with her. My husband and I worked different hours so one of us would always be home with her. We had few baby sitters, and felt we couldn't trust anyone to deal with her seizures.

Our daughter Chris was the oldest child. We expected her to help with the care of the other three children. She taught Sandy to use silverware, then how to dress herself correctly. Her speech was slow, she just made noises. This wasn't really acceptable. We wanted her to learn words. Chris had patience, a trait her mother was short of. She is a teacher.

Karl, Jr. was her "warden." Caretaker. She liked to be outside and had to be physically restrained at times so she would come back out of the street or whatever danger. He helped her to learn to walk, play ball, pat the dog or cat, hold it and not hurt it. She loved riding on his motorcycle. She'd ask him to play banjo or guitar and they'd sing together. I think all of us showed anger at some time. We all cried in frustration when the houseparents beat her. We were afraid the first time we left her at a hostel house with houseparents and drove away. We had doubts. Was this the right thing to do?

A family member was always with her. When Chris was in college, she'd come home every weekend to help out with Sandy's care. She took her to visit her friends, shopping, out to eat. After she married and moved, she asked to have her come visit by herself. We put Sandy on airplanes many times and sent her. We went as a family once a year to visit, also. She could hardly wait for these visits. When Karl, Jr. moved out of the family home and got married, he didn't spend much time with her after that. We just felt he couldn't change things for her betterment, so out of sight out of mind.

All of the people, family and friends, accepted Sandy and her disability. There were over 300 people at her funeral. She touched a lot of people with her lovely smile and happy thoughts.

Did I ever get mad at God? Yes, I was very angry. I'm still angry. We had two daughters die. Why did he take the perfect child first? Sandy had so many difficult times in her life. Pain, frustration, so much sadness. I felt she died just when she was seeing the sunshine. For the first time in her life she said, "Momma, I had a good day."

Who do I blame? The doctor who delivered her. I was in labor three nights and four days. He would not do a C-section. I'd had three other children normal. My husband and I always felt this was when the oxygen supply was cut off. Her head was very deformed when she was born.

TEN YEARS

Stories told by individuals and family members who have been challenged by a disability for one to two decades.

I WISH MOST OF ALL THAT I COULD DANCE, ESPECIALLY WITH MY CHILDREN

For 20 years this mother of two children has been challenged by paraplegia resulting from a car accident when she was 20. Today she demonstrates wisdom gained from a difficult experience:

I was in a one-car roll-over when I was 20. I was the passenger in a car that went off the road on a sharp curve and rolled down a hill. I was thrown around inside the car, then fell out of the car and it rolled on top of me, crushing my upper torso. It crushed my spine, collapsed both lungs and broke 12 ribs. I also had a broken collar bone, and a huge cut under my right arm. I also hit my head, causing nerve damage in my right ear.

I am an L1 paraplegic. My right leg is completely paralyzed, and I have very little muscle use in my left leg. I can stand briefly with crutches. I have spotted feeling from the waist down, and can feel very little in my feet and nothing in the back of my legs.

I first remember lying in a hospital, completely hooked up to machines. I couldn't talk because of the respirator tubes. I was really scared.

My medical experiences are so numerous it's hard to know where to begin. I guess the ones that stand out are the bad ones. The doctor that laughed when I thought I could feel some in my foot; the nurse that seemed to enjoy seeing me in pain when they turned the circle bed. There are so many stories like that. I have often wondered if the medical profession has been given any sensitivity training.

There have been good experiences, too. They are the ones that talked to me, explaining things, answering questions. The people that would treat me, the person, rather than the disability.

Being a young adult was the hardest time in life, mostly because of the big change from being "normal" to being disabled. I had to make a lot of new friends and a lot of big adjustments.

I think the most difficult thing has been the majority of the medical profession not giving me credit for knowing anything about my own body. They can be very patronizing. The best thing people can do is treat me like they would anyone else. I don't want their pity or anything special.

I hate it when people assume I can't do anything just because I use a wheelchair. I also hate it when I get the "you poor dear" smile, usually from older people. A support group might have been nice in the earlier stages. I still sometimes think it would be nice to talk to someone that faces the same things I do.

To be disabled you always have to fight for your rights. You always have to prove you're normal and not a freak or something. You have to be able to let a lot roll off your back, because there are a lot of people that are very insensitive and just plain stupid.

I wish most of all that I could dance, especially with my children. I've always loved music, and dance is such a great way to express yourself.

My dad blamed himself. He should've kept me home that day or something. Somehow he thinks he should've done something to prevent it. My mom was the caretaker. She was always there to be there for me. My older brother and sister were married and moved away and have never talked about it or have given much support. My next sister was very supportive—she had had major heart surgery when she was younger—so I feel she kind of knows what it's like to deal with a disability. My younger sister really rebelled. She was very jealous of the attention I was getting and all the time Mom and Dad spent at the hospital. She partied and tried to ignore me. My youngest brother was ten at the time. It was very difficult for him, not only because his sister was now a paraplegic but he grew up in a hurry. He had to go to neighbors' houses after school. Mom and Dad weren't there for him because they spent so much time in the hospital.

Sometimes my dad would get really angry with me. I know now that the anger wasn't really me, but his feeling powerless over the whole situation. As a parent myself, I know how difficult it is to see your child suffer or struggle. I think it's hard for my parents to see me deal with the daily things life puts in my way.

We have definitely been affected financially. My children and I are living on social security disability, and it's very difficult to get by. I can't afford to go to work and lose my medical assistance and Medicare. My long-term plans are to continue my education and, hopefully, get a job somewhere that has good medical benefits.

I try not to let it [the disability] affect my relationships. It did right after the accident because many of my friends found it too difficult to deal with. So they distanced themselves, rather than deal with it. Now, I've had many people tell me they forget I'm disabled. It's just not an issue with me. When I first meet some people they are afraid of the chair, but when they get to know me, it's no big deal.

I don't think my disability really affected my sexuality. Up until a couple years ago, I was never comfortable with my sexuality, but I think it was more my upbringing rather than my disability. I didn't have much self-esteem which naturally affected my sexuality. Now through Al-Anon I have a good feeling about myself which in turn makes me more comfortable about sex.

My sexual relationships have been few. I was married for almost eight years. The beginning of the marriage, the sexual part was okay. It was never anything great. The marriage was never great, either. As the marriage began to deteriorate, so did the sex. The man was a taker—never a giver—in all aspects of life. I have been in one relationship since my marriage that was wonderful. There was great communication and respect, which is needed, I think, for a good sexual relationship.

At the time of the accident I was drinking and partying more and more, and really had no direction in my life. I believe that God has a plan for us even though we may not know what that is. I may not always like the way things are going or events that happen and sometimes I get mad at God—especially like when I see someone I love hurting.

Just before my divorce I seriously throught about killing myself and my children because I didn't see any other way out of my situation.

I have had severe bouts with diarrhea and pain on my right side that the doctors haven't been able to diagnose. It makes me frustrated with doctors that don't always seem to care very much.

An 11-year-old son:

I don't really think about it [the disability]. [I know] you were in a car going around a curve, the car slipped in the sand and rolled over. You got hurt because you didn't have a seat belt on. I don't feel sad—well, kind of sad.

And her 12-year-old daughter:

I don't mind [about the disability]. It doesn't bother me, but sometimes people make fun of me because of it. [I know you're disabled] because you crushed your back. I'm not afraid of the future.

PARENTS OF A DISABLED CHILD MUST BE "RETARDED"

For 19 years this 49-year-old woman's daughter has dealt with some type of seizure disorder. The mother's encounters with the professional world have been very difficult for her:

Some doctors say Erica has Lennox-Gastaux Syndrome. She started out with petit mal seizures as a baby, and had grand mal seizures by age four. She may have an undiagnosed degenerative disease. She is on large doses of anticonvulsants and the seizures are uncontrolled. She can walk with assistance, but uses a wheelchair to avoid injuries. She wears a helmet and has had many stitches in her face and head from falls.

She doesn't talk much anymore, has no bladder control, and wears diapers. She is mentally about two years old. No one has been able to determine what caused her retardation or seizures. She had a normal birth and was not diagnosed with a problem until she was four. We felt she had a problem because she was slow in learning to talk and wasn't trained until four, but we could not get her doctor convinced there were any problems.

We have had Erica to many doctors and have had both good and bad experiences. Her first two neurologists were very poor. The first one was very very BAD. We went to him for years and he kept telling us that she had seizures to get attention and her EEGs showed seizures every ten seconds so we knew he was crazy. He finally let us go to the U of M for testing. They were very understanding and good. They did extensive tests (two-to-three weeks at a time) and changed meds, etc. We came back home to be followed up by another doctor who took away her meds and changed them....

We contacted the U of M and continued to doctor there. A few years later we tried to go back to the old doctor and he put her in the hospital and forbid us to see her.

He took away the Tegretol which nearly killed her. The nurses called for us to come when she was in ICU. We finally quit seeing him altogether and have excellent medical care now. The doctors and nurses get more upset than we do during her static seizure times because we have seen them so many times and know how to deal with it.

We had one teacher who was physically abusive to her and that was unbearable. We finally made the decision to put her in a group home at that time and she went to special education. She cannot even dress herself and has to be fed part of the time. She has so many seizures and her brain doesn't allow for any thoughts to materialize far enough to do a task.

Psychologists and counselors were the worst experiences we had. When we first sought help, a counselor told me Erica was fine but I needed help because I thought she had a problem. How upsetting!

School officials could be more understanding. Their attitude is that parents of a disabled child must be "retarded". You learn to be defensive. I used to teach school myself and I knew what to expect and would not let myself be put down as an idiot. I cried a lot when we first put Erica in a group home (160 miles away) to go to school and still do some, especially when I discuss it with someone. It is always hard to leave her when we take her back after being home, especially after Christmas.

Our family is really close because of Erica's problem. Her two sisters learned to help care for her and were very adult for their age, even as very young girls. They are excellent students and one is a teacher. They are very high achievers. We all work well together to help with Erica. The girls kept Erica while I helped in the field, etc. She loves her sisters and loves to hear them on the phone now and really enjoys when they come home. We always have her home when they come home, too.

Our lives have been centered around caring for her and we still make all of our plans around when we're going to get her, when she'll be home, and never know when we'll get a call to go to the hospital.

The girls learned at an early age how to deal with a hyper, upset sister and learned to take responsibility at an early age. They were deprived of social activities, etc., because we couldn't take them because we were tied down with Erica.

We have had people suggest that we take her to a "healer" but we don't believe in that.

She will be in an adjustment training center or nursing home after age 21 and come home every two-to-three weeks to visit us as long as we can manage it. Or she will go into static seizures and the doctors won't be able to bring her out of it. We feel sorry for her and what she has to go through.

YOU LIVE IN A NEVER WORLD. IT IS LIKE A DEATH THAT LIVES ON

Nineteen years ago this 46-year-old mother gave birth to a son who was later diagnosed with mental retardation:

The doctor miscalculated the child's due date. Due to medication given during the time of the pregnancy. It was a cover up by all the medical people involved. He was meconium stained, and put on a respirator after birth. I had a fever and infection at the time of the birth. He was born by C-section.

My earliest memory is probably when he was a day-and-a-half old. I was very ill and medicated. The doctor's first words to me were, "We really had a hard time getting him going." I sensed something at this time because I felt so bad, such a bad experience could not be normal.

The most difficult thing of all was never getting an answer that could place him in any area for aid of any kind. We were just pushed on to the next doctor with little information of why this had happened.

At age 18 months he had a very high fever and went into grand mal seizures. I was so afraid, I would not even go to the child for a long time in the hospital because I was so afraid he was dead. I have never been the same. He was in my arms rocking him when this took place.

When he was about age five or six he could not breathe due to swelling of his body from hives. He had been given high amounts of medicine, and this would not help. The doctor said we have done all we can. It is in someone else's hands now.

It makes me feel many times that I am unable to function. It is like I am paralyzed myself.

Each age just has a different heartache. None ever get solved, they remain with more adding to it. The older the child gets it is more noticeable. The gap gets larger.

He is still in school and will remain there until age 21. He is isolated a lot of the time from the "normal" school setting, and it's difficult to work with teachers that have the book learning but not the real-life learning it takes to handle the person or the family.

[What things do people say that aren't helpful?] God only gives you what you can handle...You are a person with lots of patience...I don't know how you do it, I couldn't...These are special people. You were chosen because you are special...I have never seen this before. You are the first I have seen...You are lucky, he could be a lot worse...Don't be impatient, time will take care of it...If you can't deal with it, put him somewhere.

No compassion.

I am drained of all future thoughts. I feel like I just exist, that I don't really live. Always waiting for something that is not there.

As a mother you never get any dreams that come true. It is like it is over before it begins. You live in a never world. It is like a death that lives on.

[What do you wish you could do?] Walk away from it. Hope that it never would have happened. Accept the disability for what it is. Forgive the doctor.

We have no finances. We barely live from day to day. Medical expenses from day one were very high. We now have no insurance. We have no financial plans for the disabled person. He now receives SSI only after age 18. No financial assistance has ever been received. No one would diagnose his disability to help. We carried the entire load.

Suicide is a quitter's way out. There is always hope to win. Even though you know you have lost the battle.

Our moods and feelings change a lot. It is like you are always waiting for the next thing to happen. What life will hit you with next. It is like we are always in a mixer.

SOMETIMES I GET A SICK FEELING, EMPTINESS, A HOLLOW FEEL-ING, FEELING LIKE I'M MISSING A LOT OF THINGS IN LIFE

A 48-year-old father talks about his 19-year-old son's disability:

The diagnosis was mental retardation, caused by malpractice due to the doctor's miscalculations in dates and times, also prescribing the wrong medications during pregnancy. During the pregnancy, the doctor lied about a lot of things. The worst was the unknown: "What will happen next?" In the early years of his life he had so many hospital stays. And we had so much lack of knowledge.

I dreamt once about him being normal, and that if he smoked marijuana, he would be normal.

The preschool years were the easiest because he was more accepted at that age. Adolescence was the most difficult because you could see other kids doing things that he won't be able to do. He attended special education in the public schools, went through many programs and different schools. He never had a chance to make a long-standing friendship. He lives for the Special Olympics.

No one will hire them, also if they are collecting SSI, they're limited to what they can earn. People avoid them when the disabled person is talking and they don't pay attention to what is being said and maybe walk away in the middle of the conversation. We get no help from anyone because they won't talk about it. You are shunned in your group. Parents need more support in the beginning. Tell the parents what is to be expected.

Sometimes I get a sick feeling, emptiness, a hollow feeling, feeling like I'm missing a lot of things in life. Sometimes being with my son is exciting, sometimes real sad. I wish they would find a cure so that they might enjoy something in life, like drive a car.

I get my strength from the Lord. One thing, He is not a quitter.

Our family has been affected by many emotions, some jealousy, some bitterness, feeling cheated, missing part of things in life, never being able to teach him how to drive a car, those things you miss.

Some mutual funds programs are set up. Financially we have no money. It took it all we've got [to pay for this] and we're not able to restore it. I have no job, just temporary positions. In the beginning, we had to pay all the hospital and doctor bills without insurance or anything else.

We talk about how it is to deal with. What hurts is when people with kids the same age never talk about yours. No support from your old friends and family.

We talk about the disability and the services you get but have to fight for. At first you are full of energy but you just get burned out.

I believe the Lord is the Supreme One and if you have faith everything will be okay. Why does this have to happen? Is it punishment for something we did?

Suicide? No, a dumb thing to do. What would the disabled person do then if he or she lost their best friends—their parents?

What is hard is to never to be able to see him do the little things in life. The acceptance of it is a hard pill to swallow.

Please let the parents know immediately what is happening and don't lie about it.

In the future, hopefully maybe he'll live on his own, I mean in a supervised area where they won't take advantage or hopefully, a sibling will jump in and take over.

And from their 13-year-old son:

I think it's real bad [the disability]. I'm sad because he can't do a lot of things, he's unable to do things normal kids can do. [His] birth was two months late and this caused the problem. Sometimes I'm afraid when I think of the future. People will take advantage of him. Comfort me [when I'm sad].

CHRONIC GRIEF

This middle-aged mother describes the early, very difficult years she had in coping with the brain damage her daughter experienced at birth. The daughter is now 18 years old:

It was like a nightmare that you didn't wake up from. My doctor induced labor, but I was allergic to a drug and my labor contractions became abnormally strong and close together for an extended time. I had no dilation after two days of hospitalization. A C-section was finally done. Julie did not breathe on her own for 70 minutes and she started having seizures the first day.

I felt instant love for her. She had seizures in my arms almost daily. I was constantly afraid she was going to die. She, at times, had several seizures in a row. I was always fearful she would die. Her blood sugar would frequently drop and she wouldn't wake up. There was constant crying day and night. I slept very little.

Julie was in and out of various hospitals during the first six years due to seizure problems, digestive problems and severely-agitated behavior. It was extremely stressful. It seemed there was little they could do to control the screaming and agitation. Different medications were tried to control the seizures. She seemed traumatized by the testing and constant lab work to monitor the blood level of the anticonvulsants. I felt very frightened, protective and alone. Looking back, I know that I lost my perspective and all I could think of was keeping her alive.

I did not have an adequate support system for such a stressful situation. My husband at the time was uninvolved and detached. I felt trapped. It is like the grief of losing someone you love by death, only it is not confined to a few months. Watching someone live a frustrating uncomfortable life and fearing they will die, causes chronic grief.

I've always felt responsible to fix her and make her life more comfortable and I feel guilty that I can't do enough. I have always provided most of her care. My ex-husband became very irritable if I did ask him to help. We are divorced now because my former spouse was oblivious to the effects my child's disability was having on me. He changed the subject if I tried to discuss the situation at all.

The disability was definitely a variable involved but probably not the sole cause of the divorce. We needed counseling after she was born and from there on out. Or, we needed to be involved in a group with other parents of the disabled. I wish that her grandparents, sister, father and stepmother were willing to take her with them more often, so that she could enjoy more experiences rather than be excluded.

Now whenever she gets a common illness, such as the flu, I worry that it's something from the long years of meds and I think she is going to die. Over the years she has grown healthier and the seizures have been well-controlled for almost eight years. I've tried to learn to relax more, but I'm occasionally reminded it might be a false sense of security. People tend to want to do things for her that she can do herself, and they become impatient because it takes her longer or they think they must help her. It is helpful if people look at her and talk to her as if they respect her like any other person. It is helpful when they take time to understand her language and show interest in what she has to say.

It is hard for those of us without disabilities to truly know how the disabled person really experiences life. We need to always try hard to be patient and accepting of their feelings. I believe all of us are our brother's keepers.

"THIS MUST HAVE COME FROM <u>YOUR</u> SIDE OF THE FAMILY BECAUSE WE DON'T HAVE ANYONE WITH PROBLEMS ON <u>MY</u> SIDE"

It took a long time, but this 38-year-old mother finally found a partner who could love and accept her son:

Sean is learning disabled with integrated sensory dysfunction. He is 5'8" and weighs 120 pounds, and from all outward appearances looks the same as any other 16-year-old boy. His actions, thought processes, vocabulary, and pastimes reflect those of an eight to ten year old. I have no clue what caused his disability other than the fact that I had toxemia for four to five months of the pregnancy and was treated with medication. Other than that the pregnancy and delivery were uneventful.

Since Sean was my first born and since there had been no other small children in our family, I did not think much was wrong until after the first month of his life. My girlfriend had a child born at the same time, so I was watching the milestones of the other child and realizing that Sean was nowhere close to those.

Early medical experience was that when Sean was born and they had him in the nursery he was what they called "highly nervous." He had these ticks that came and went. He vomited every feeding. The ticks went away, but the vomiting lasted three to four months. I had him at the doctor's office or hospital regularly, because I was concerned that he didn't seem to keep the formula down. They changed the formulas, etc. Eventually it stopped. Then the concern over the constant drooling that went on and on. Again, I was told he was teething, but my friends' children did not have this excessive drooling.

Sean also enjoyed rocking himself in his crib, in his high chair, anywhere. He would sit and rock himself back and forth. I asked the doctors, but they didn't think it was much to be alarmed about. He then had delays with things like crawling, walking, etc. Eventually, I convinced the doctor that something was not right. He agreed hesitantly to have an evaluation done. There were no significant findings.

It was not until he went to kindergarten that the teacher called me and said there seemed to be a problem with fine motor and gross motor skills. She noticed he drew numbers and letters backwards. Eventually the parochial school he was attending told me he needed to go to public school where he could get special education. I then had him evaluated again and he was placed in a resource room. He also began to receive occupational therapy treatment twice per week for about a year. This seemed to help with his motor skills.

To make a long story short, Sean is now a sophomore in high school, age 16, operating at about a ten-year-old level. He still has great difficulty reading, and math is not something he can grasp. He is still in resource room full-time.

So far as medical people went, I feel I was the one telling them what was wrong, and they were telling me that I was imagining it and that "boys eventually grow out of it." That was their famous line. No one has ever given me any direction on what to do for Sean. I have done it myself, and I have made all the calls to everyone trying to get him help in any way I can.

This part also is very difficult and painful for me to discuss, but Sean's biological father and I had been married for about four years when he was born and once the problems started happening, this man could not deal with the idea of a child that was not perfect. He was very verbally abusive to Sean, saying things over the dinner table like "get with the program" if he spilled his milk (which he did almost every day). My ex-husband would ask me questions like, "Is he ever going to be able to do anything in life?" When I look back on those times, I cannot believe how any father could not love and accept his own son unconditionally. As a result, I was overprotective of Sean and would not allow anyone to hurt him in any way. His father and I divorced, although it was about eight years later. He never played with Sean like a father does. He never took him fishing, or played ball with him. He just couldn't accept the fact that his son was disabled. His famous line was, "This must have come from YOUR side of the family because we don't have anyone with problems on MY side." I laugh about that now because he was actually the one with the biggest problem.

Sean is 16 now, I have remarried to a wonderful man who is more of a father than I could ever have asked for. He has rebuilt Sean's confidence, given him back some self-esteem, and encourages him in every way. Sean sees his father, who has now remarried and had two daughters. But they are not close, they are more like acquaintances. My ex on occasion still calls me and asks me if he is ever going to be able to do anything in life....

Adolescence is hard. Sean is interested in a social life and wants to get a driver's license. I'm afraid he's too easily distractible to be able to concentrate on driving.

The people I find most helpful are parents who are in the same situation. They point you in the right direction and they are compassionate about their and your child's difficulties. Sometimes it is helpful to me when people notice just how far Sean has come along over the years. Also it is helpful when other parents invite your child to a party or to come over to play at their house. Presently, a teacher that Sean has in school gave me lots of encouragement about the possibilities for his future. He told me of others who had been in the same category who turned out just fine, who got jobs and licenses, etc. He made me feel that there really could be a good future for Sean.

In some ways it has hurt me to watch him suffer through without friends or a social life. It is difficult to watch him interested in girls and not knowing what to do about it. I worry for him that he will be dependent on me for life and worry what will happen to him if I ever died. After my divorce some years ago when I was out on the dating scene myself, I wanted to meet someone to get on with my life again, but felt a real pressure to meet the right person—one who would be able to be a father to Sean. I was very fortunate, but the criteria I had set up for the person I needed in my life was driving me to find a close match for Sean. I realized the stress that a disability places on my family.

I feel like the protector, the coach, the support, everything. I feel that I have to be. Sometimes I am a mother, sometimes I am his best friend, sometimes I am his fishing partner. I'm happy we are close, but I want him to be happy and fulfilled in his life.

My husband, my father, and my daughter are a tight family that is caring, kind and compassionate. We stick together and try to do family activities. We support Sean and each other. We are Sean's support group and provide him with an opportunity and environment where he can be himself and be happy. My daughter who is 14 also shares with Sean an interest in music and clothes. She is a bit like a mother hen to him, getting on his case when he needs to take a shower or wash his hair, etc. She jokes with him to get the point across. I pray each night for the strength to help Sean get situated in life and that he will be happy.

I work full-time making $32,000 per year. My husband has been laid off for two years with his recall rights running out. I am supporting the entire family, including my 79-year-old father that lives with me. The pressure on me the past year or so has been difficult, but I keep trying to look at the bright side. There are always people who are worse off. We have a nice house, and so far I have been able to keep paying the mortgage and I am hopeful that my husband will be able to find suitable work soon. I have some savings for a rainy day, which I hope doesn't come.

I worry about what the future holds for us.

Knowing that there is a possibility that this child will be dependent on you for life. Most kids grow up and leave. He may grow up and stay. And that's all right with me.

This is probably stupid, but I do believe that these special children are given to people who have the capability to love them and nurture them and care for them.

It takes a lot of strength to handle all of this and this is where I believe the strength comes from, a power greater than myself. No, I don't get mad at God, because I feel that I was selected. If I had the money and the means I would even adopt more children who have this disability, because I feel that I have something special.

I handle the stress by realizing that nothing on earth is worth killing yourself for.

The hardest thing to accept is that there is nothing I can do to make it go away. I can't make him smart, or able to drive a car, or to be able to tell time, or to fall in love, etc. I can only hope that things will fall into place sometime or other, if it is meant to be.

One time I had had the last straw with kids making fun of him. Some kids put a "post-it" sticky note on his back that said "kick me," and all the way home on the bus kids were kicking him and laughing at him. And when he came home, he told me what they were doing. Then I saw the sticky note. I took it off his back and I went out in our shed in the back yard where we keep the lawnmower and where I knew I wouldn't be found and I sat in the corner and cried my heart out. Then when I was done I decided to transfer him out of that school so he could start over again someplace else. In the shed that day I cried so much that I thought I was going crazy. I prayed for an answer and that is what I got.

I DON'T FEEL GOD PERSONALLY SENT IT,
BUT I OFTEN FEEL IT ISN'T FAIR

Sixteen years ago this mother, now 49, gave birth to a son who was subsequently diagnosed as autistic:

My son has autism. He withdraws socially and has little desire to communicate. From birth on, he always seemed to be aloof and in his own world. Our family doctors had no experience with autism and didn't detect the disability. They hinted that I was the problem. The most difficult was having professionals who obviously knew less about my child and very little about autism.

When he was younger, his behavior was very abrasive. There was always tension, embarrassment, and anger in our family relations. Now that he is in adolescence he has become more dependable and able to reason with. The high school activities suit him better than grade school ones.

Preschool and elementary years were the most difficult. He was very difficult to teach, very stubborn, would scream or run away easily, and seemed to have little inner reflection. Though his behavior improved, he was usually the "misfit."

His disability has made me much more sensitive and open to other families and children with disabilities.

I wish our family would not lose our temper so easily. I had to deal with guilt, what did I do/not do to cause the disability. His father has been embarrassed by the behavior that goes with the disability. His sister is somewhat embarrassed by his behavior as both are in their teens.

Although he has difficulty relating socially, he much prefers to be around well-controlled, emotionally stable, kind and mature people.

Most disabilities stem from very complex factors and are not directly willed by God because he wills good for us. We can work to make something beautiful out of even a disability. I don't feel God personally sent it, but I often feel it isn't fair.

The hardest thing to accept is that perhaps I could have done something to prevent it, i.e., more rest, better food during pregnancy, that it took me a long time to "bond" with him and to accept him as he was. Yes, I've shouted at him, spanked him.

[The future?] Hopefully, college or some training and a job he likes.

WE SHOULD MAKE THE WORLD BETTER,
FOR IT BELONGS TO EVERYONE

Though this 15-year-old boy endures life with a communication disorder and suffers from depression, he also enjoys many aspects of his life and has hope for the future:

My disability is not communicating with others, and getting upset, and jumping up and down.

I don't want to be disabled. My disability makes my parents feel bad. I can't make friends.

I would have been happier if I were not disabled.

I get mad at God for not protecting me from fate. I enjoy my life. I wouldn't commit suicide. My biggest fear is being in bad moods forever.

We should make the world better because the world belongs to everyone.

I HAVE SAT IN A FETAL POSITION IN A CLOSET WEEPING AND BANGING THE WALLS WITH RAGE FOR 15-TO-30 MINUTES

Fourteen years ago this mother gave birth to a mentally-retarded child. Today at age 45 she struggles to live with the present and visualize the future:

Sally is mildly mentally retarded, undiagnosed, with pronounced speech and language delays. In spite of delays, she functions semi-independently and one may not notice her disabilities until after five-to-ten minutes of interaction. Also, she has cyclic vomiting syndrome: unexplained, unpredictable episodes of vomiting and sleeping lasting one-to-five days.

I remember the immediate and overwhelming bonding at birth. I remember the view of her head in the mirror crowning, the blue skin quickly turning pink, the heavenly cry of filling her lungs. I breast-fed her for about 45 minutes surrounded by Dad and two siblings.

At home I am the primary caregiver during episodes: IV care, nurturing, decision-making about when and how to intervene, innumerable washloads and wipe-ups of vomit. In the hospital—12-to-15 times per year—for hydration, surgery, evaluations, I have been the sole decision-maker with minimal support (my choice) from stepdad, who is a lawyer. In all of this, the decision-making and coordinating of care has been the theme. I speak for Sally, always letting her speak first if possible. I have much emotional turmoil in striking a balance of assertive, aggressive, passive behavior to get what I think we need.

This disability has been so unresolved, unpredictable, and unexplained that sleep is often the only escape from the constant involvement and exhaustion from thinking of the future.

Let me cry, hug me, listen to me without judgment and advice, elicit the bottom line problem from me, and help me to delineate a step-by-step coping or action plan.

I wish I would have done a literature search to find descriptions of vomiting syndrome; also, more foresight into public-school programs available.

My personality has changed: the frustration/rage at unresolved difficulties; constant repetition; being "on guard" to control my daughter; the intense ambivalence of loving and not liking so much of the time has drained me emotionally. I feel numb, protecting myself from the rage and regret. I feel deeply bonded to her and love her intensely, but ambivalence is nearly a constant—resentment and frustration looms—yet I find much good.

I wish I could look forward to a time when Sally would be leaving home, for education, or marriage and to have children, living without my assistance. I don't like knowing I'll have to stay so involved.

Her stepdad is deeply affected by having Sally in his life, repulsed by her, impatient, some verbal abuse, resentment of her needs and the time she takes. Her two full sibs worry about the genetic tendency to have a mentally-retarded child of their own, fear their responsibility for Sally in the future. My husband usually feels my pent-up emotions and prods me to talk; I emote with frustration the unresolved issues, how my personality has changed, how the family is affected.

Stepdad expresses much grief about the effect of Sally on me (his wife). He expresses repulsion: "She is the worst thing that has ever happened to me." In spite of these expressions, we feel a deep level of committment and we'll get through this.

Sally is intensely affected by other people: peers and adults stare, avoid her, are uncomfortable with her, and yet some are deeply caring, loving and do much to include her. The theme is that Sally wants constant activity and company, and she is rarely the one sought after. She almost always initiates contact.

Without the disability, I'd have much more emotional energy. I'd be less numb about life's ups and downs, I'd have more energy for my marriage and the other children. I can predict that I wouldn't be doing this IV and vomit cleanup!

Being agnostic, I have no clear belief of what things happen in the universe. There is not enough information available, so I don't attribute "bad things" to anything other than the random flow of the universe.

The hardest thing is the long-term nature of Sally's needs, which will impinge on my life and on her stepfather's life.

I have felt numb on the outside, to avoid "feeling" the pain. I have sat in a fetal position in a closet weeping and banging the walls for 15-to-30 minites with rage, frustration, it's all so unresolvable.

How did it happen? What level of independence will she achieve? What is the emotional impact on her personality?

As an adult we think Sally may live in a semi-supervised setting, apartment or house. She could use public transport to get to and from some type of job. Maybe a mainstream job. Possible ongoing health problems which may limit her life-style, probably some feelings of isolation and loneliness as well as feelings of accomplishment and independence.

Sally's two able-bodied siblings also talked about her.

A seven-year-old brother:

I feel sad about Sally having brain damage. [I also] feel sad when she feels sad about being teased. [Why was she disabled?] She was born that way. I'm afraid that something [Sally's friends] might come out and chase or hurt me. It helps when you take care of Sally, [but] don't let her come to my birthday party.

And from an 18-year-old sister:

I think this disability has been a learning experience for me and the rest of the family. I can't think of very many good things that have happened because of it, but it has made our lives interesting. I am sad for Sally having to live with it, but especially for my mom because of all the grief she has had to go through dealing with the disability. She is my sister and I feel happy that I have her—disability or not. I am very afraid about her future. No, actually I am more curious about what her life will be like in the next few years.

WHY ARE HIS EARS SO BIG?

Fourteen years ago this mother, now age 40, and her husband adopted Craig who was eight years old. She does not blame God, but she does blame Craig's mother for drinking while pregnant:

Craig has Fetal Alcohol Syndrome. He also has emotional problems from his first home being so rough. He has chest deformities, small stature, large ears, and has weak arms and little strength. He has reading disabilities, has a hard time understanding directions, and frustrates easily. He throws temper tantrums and will tear things apart or cuss out of control. He won't think about what he does, he just does it. We adopted him at age eight.

Education…Horrible! You have groups of people putting you on the spot to make decisions. No matter how it works the parents always get blamed. Craig went in and out of counseling, resource people, and teachers who just didn't have time to deal with his problems. I had to be a strong advocate, often causing trouble at home and school. He has problems following directions and keeping his mind on what he is doing. He doesn't know what is good behavior and what is bad, sometimes.

What helps? Just come and give me a break. Ask him to stay over night to give me some time. It also helps when someone comments, "Craig is acting so good lately."

What doesn't help are comments like, "Why do you keep him?"

"What ever made you adopt him? You should send him back. He is such a mouthy kid."

"Why is he so small? Are you feeding him? Is he sick, he's so skinny?"

"Why are his ears so big?"

Never a break. He is always doing something that I have to answer for. I get upset. I can't sleep, I cry. My husband and I fight over ways to handle the situation. We usually give up or overreact. I am very tense at school, wondering, "What did he do now?" I am always the one to get the phone call and have to apologize or work it out. Never a mental break. Always worried "where he's at, what's he doing…."

Craig does things that kids laugh at. He looks different and has a problem talking in complete sentences. Kids that are popular tease him. He has a good sense of humor, so he has a lot of friends, but he has trouble fitting in.

I'm not mad at God. He gave us Craig to help him have a good life. Something is very important about him for God to change his life as he did.

I blame his real mom for drinking while she was carrying him. It makes me angry she hurt her baby like this.

I can't change the world but I can make him fit better by my teaching him how to overcome.

This mother's two children also talked about Craig. Her 14-year-old son:

[I feel] sad. He acts strange, won't play. He doesn't eat. I get his dessert then. It's his problem. Our real mom drank and took drugs while he was inside her. [It makes me] afraid because I can't ever drink because I might be an alcoholic already. Craig will be sad forever. He may never be happy. [But I] don't worry. He always gets better in a few days. [I like it when you] make him stay in his room and read books.

And the 12-year-old son Craig with the disability adds:

I know my real mom drank and caused the FAS. It isn't my fault. [I hate] my ears, cuz they're so big. Sometimes I'm afraid, will I ever get a job? Help me with my schoolwork [when I'm frustrated].

MY FEAR IS THAT HE'LL ACT OUT SEXUALLY
OR RAPE OR SEXUALLY ABUSE SOMEONE ELSE

This 43-year-old mother describes graphically the stress of caring for an angry, unhappy 13-year-old son:

Our son has attention deficit disorder. At first it was with hyperactivity, but he's pretty much outgrown that. Also oppositional defiant disorder. From birth he was always slow at things, crawling at a year, walking at 18 months. Talking at about two. We had trouble also when he started eating. He would gag and throw up. He didn't want to play by the rules. A lot of tantrums. He couldn't entertain himself. Always wanting lots of attention. The older he got, the worse he got: lying, sneaky, just hard to trust. He has no friends and he can't get along with anyone.

At first, our family doctor said he was just a boy and would outgrow it. The older he got the worse he got, so we told the doctor we needed help. The specialist said there definitely was a problem. They admitted him, ran a series of tests and evaluated him. Then they diagnosed him with ADD and put him on ritalin. Then things were better, but we were having lots of problems with him in school and his teacher didn't help.

She ridiculed him, wouldn't help him, hollered, and picked on him all the time. Finally the Educational Service Unit tested him and found him behaviorally impaired. He was put in a another school and did better, but life at home was continually getting worse. We had his medication changed a couple of times. We finally had him made a state ward and he was put in a special program. He came home after five months with no follow-up by social services. We finally got him admitted to the state home when we found out that he had sexually abused our daughter.

I worry about his future and what's going to happen to him when we're gone. Also, now that he's 13 and acting out sexually, who's he going to hurt? Or when he gets mad, who's he going to hurt?

His body and hormones know he's 13 but his mind is only nine or ten. He's feeling things he doesn't understand. He's acting out sexually and doesn't know how to control himself. He's very angry because there's something wrong and he can't fix it.

Most people don't understand disabilities and shy away from disabled people. The only people who REALLY understand are those who've lived it. The others try to make recommendations. Some people, especially kids, would make fun of him, tease him, and wouldn't want him around. He has no friends.

When social services took our son, we all were in a very explosive situation. When he acted out sexually to my daughter the last time before he left, I was so angry I took a belt to him. I whipped him. (Not beat.) We had a therapist coming to the house at the time. He asked my permission to put the whipping in his report. This finally got us the help we needed.

All we want for him is to be able to live in society and be happy. We want for him what we want for our normal daughter. No matter what happens though we will always love him and never abandon him.

Our son has controlled our household for years. We had given up hope. We just got to where we couldn't handle him anymore. My husband and I would fight, we'd take our anger out on the kids, and they'd fight and cry. Allan's been at the state home for three months and it's been like heaven. We couldn't take him anywhere because of the way he acted. So we were more or less shut-ins other than work or school.

We have been provided with some respite care, funded by the state. Right now we're paying child support to the state and it's pretty hard to come by. It's caused a lot of stress and fighting, and we've been embarrassed to take our son out of the house much because of the way he acts. We've had a pretty miserable existence until now and hopefully we'll learn from this.

I think God wants us to suffer to make ourselves stronger in our beliefs. It's very hard though, because you get mad and blame God because you don't know who else to blame. I prayed and prayed for help and guidance and it's taken seven years to get it. In the meantime our son has emotionally hurt and sexually abused, and it's put an awful lot of strain on my marriage. I've beat my son when the stress got too much, I'd lose control.

My fear is that he'll act out sexually or rape or sexually abuse someone else.

And from their 10-year-old daughter:

I feel sorry for him. I'm sad. [He has problems] because of his brain. I'm afraid, maybe. I don't know [what will help me].

I EVEN DREAMED OF HOW I COULD GET UP, STRANGLE HER WITH MY ROBE SASH, AND GO BACK TO SLEEP FOR SIX HOURS OF UNINTERRUPTED SLEEP

This 45-year-old mother of a 12-year-old daughter with mental retarda-
tion, epilepsy, and mild cerebral palsy tells of her struggles over the years to
create a safe and kind world in which her daughter may live. The mother has
succeeded:

Alyssa is mentally retarded due to anoxia at birth. She was three weeks over-due, a C-section was performed after five hours of induced labor. Brain damage was evident immediately, she was not breathing at birth, stayed in the neonatal ICU 11 days.

Before birth she seemed a normal pregnancy. A week before the birth I knew she wasn't moving much but the doctor wouldn't do anything yet. On the day of birth I could tell there would be problems from the way the baby's heartbeat responded in labor on the monitor. After the C-section I saw her when she was about four hours old—asleep in an isolet, naked, and ready to be taken in the ambulance.

I have been at every medical and therapy session Alyssa has had except school therapies. When Alyssa went to the other hospital at birth I could not visit for a week because of the C-section and the fact that she was 125 miles away and my husband, who is blind, can't drive. So when I got out of the hospital, a friend took us to see her. It was quite an emotional meeting. No one had asked for her name and we each thought the other had told the hospital staff!

She responded well to me but sluggishly to hospital personnel. She came home after 11 days. Thereafter I had about monthly visits with the neonatolist who cared for Alyssa. He had spoken to me on the phone many times after Alyssa was born but apparently thought I didn't care about her because I could not come to see her for seven days. When he met me in the office, finally, he said, "You sure aren't the person I thought you were." He answered any questions I had but didn't volunteer too much. After I realized Alyssa would be mentally retarded and asked him the prognosis he said, "You'll just have to wait and see."

I could not accept such a bland statement when she was already perhaps six months old, so I stopped him from leaving the room and demanded to know what to expect. He then told me she would probably be moderately to severely retarded and not progress beyond the mentality of an eight-year-old. He never admitted that she had cerebral palsy, however. He only seemed interested in mea-suring her progress, not helping me to get therapy. He said, "Good," when I told him I had found out about a local Infant Stimulation Program but he was never too interested in telling me directly what should be done for her, so I stopped going to see him and just saw a pediatrician in town thereafter. (Why go 125 miles to hear nothing much?) The pediatrician was at Alyssa's birth and had been clued in to my previous first pregnancy (stillbirth—three weeks late) and successful second pregnancy, but he was somewhat airy and unconcerned about her lack of development, I thought.

Then when she was 14 months she had a terrible seizure at home—we had never seen anything like it. She was seen by a neurologist who prescribed Phenobarb. "Oh, it's nothing, just a seizure and it's all over." He never mentioned that a severe seizure could cause brain damage or death. Never really told us what to do.

Alyssa had more severe seizures and developed a terrible problem of not being able to sleep at night for more than two hours and would just wake up screaming. It got so bad that I would wake up just a minute before she did. I took her to the pediatrician and the neurologist, each several times over the next two-to-three years. But they had no good suggestions except, "Give her Dimetapp (sinus med) since that usually makes people sleepy" (said the pediatrician), and "We might change her meds, though Phenobarb is the safest for children...." (said the neurologist).

I was going nuts never getting any sleep. I became abusive with her, having tried everything else—milk, water, food, rock her, walk her, keep her in an upside-down playpen, so she couldn't stand up and scream, put her far away in the other end of the house so we couldn't hear her so well when she screamed. Finally I started smacking her. That, of course, didn't work either.

Then I took her to a United Cerebral Palsy clinic for another full eval. When the neurologist walked into the office, Alyssa (now four) was zooming, and as usual, opening all the doors and drawers. I was too exhausted to interfere much. The new neurologist said, "I guess she's a little hyperactive." He asked what meds she was on and when I told him, he said half the kids on Phenobarb are allergic to it. They get hyper! They can't sleep. He put her on Tegretol and she was a new child in one week.

Alyssa loves school, regular hours, lots to do, lots of people, rides the bus, eats in the cafeteria. School is good in that teachers and aides are very good and try hard to integrate her and make sure she does activities that stimulate her. They treat her like the fun-loving kid she is.

The hardest thing is when she's made fun of, or when people do too much for her, or expect too little. And then when they say to us, "Maybe she'll grow out of it," or "She's your gift from God." I love friends who have disabled children, or adults with disabilities—and most of all BOOKS!

I have been very strong-willed and opinionated, perhaps too bossy. Since I've had Alyssa I'm probably a lot more empathetic to all sorts of human problems now. (But then, I'm older, too.) I'm more intense and tense when I have something to accomplish. Less tolerant of people who whine about minor problems. Very fierce and protective of my three children. But I'd like to be just a "regular" mom rather than feel I have to always be involved with everything having to do with disabilities.

I'm lucky in that I can stay home rather than work fulltime, so that allows me to be more tolerant of her than I would be (probably) if I had to rush home each day and deal with her as well as supper and maybe bills and maybe an unreliable husband. I don't worry too much about the undisabled children in our family, so we have more "worry" time about Alyssa and to deal with her foibles.

Yes, we won a lawsuit which gives us support now and for her entire lifetime. What I would do different is I'd go to a different doctor and demand to have a C-section when my baby was a week pre-due date as I did with my last child who turned out great.

As the parents of a child disabled at birth we were traumatized by the situation, embittered toward doctors in general, shocked into realizing what retardation really means. The whole situation has made us more cynical than we already were and much more critical of people who are careless of life and especially of their children's lives and well-being.

My husband and I get along very well and usually agree about what to do concerning the children. I'm the most overloaded with concern and responsibility. Their father has a very big worry for the future, as well as the present. Her oldest sister was jealous of how much attention Alyssa took away from her. Our youngest tolerates her, makes fun of her sometimes, though. He's somewhat self-conscious that his sister is at his school.

I don't believe in God. If there were a God in my thoughts, you bet I'd be mad about all this!

Suicide? Why, and miss the rest of the story?

Several times I have gotten too rough with Alyssa over really minor things, but no harm really came of it. But when I was going through her screaming period I did bang her around too much, and even dreamed of how I could get up, strangle her with my robe sash, and go back to sleep for six hours of uninterrupted sleep. (Fortunately, I got help in time.)

I envision her going through school in a good number of work and integration experiences, then living at home with us until we no longer can care for her and ourselves. During all the years we will strive to see that she has companions and caregivers that she likes, so that she will get used to living with other people and being as independent as possible. I'd like to see her have a stable relationship with a good, clean, quiet man who also is mentally retarded, who would love her, but not just use her for her money and sex.

Disability doesn't have to ruin everything. There are still lots of things to do and enjoy. It just makes life more challenging and interesting, in a way.

This mother has two other children who shared their thoughts. The seven-year-old brother:

It's bad [the disability]. I'm dad because Alyssa can't do the same things I can do. I don't know why [she is disabled] and I'm afraid that we might have another accident.

And from the 15-year-old sister:

[I] don't know what you want to know. I'm used to it [the disability]. I have no idea what Alyssa would be like if "normal." At least she's alive. She was born too late—not enough air. She's got a "cushy" life because she's got money for the future. Don't feel sad [for me].

HE PASSED AWAY LAST WEEK. I'M JUST SO AT PEACE
AND HAPPY FOR JOSH NOW THAT HE'S OKAY

Eleven years ago Josh was born, and this mother, now 33, and the rest of the family began a long, extraordinary journey together:

Josh contracted spinal meningitis when he was two weeks old, and suffered brain swelling, resulting in brain damage. Due to brain damage he was very spastic. The brain shunt at 18 months helped, but the tightness affected his hips. He had to have ITOs and abductor releases on both sides. Most noticeable, due to the spasticity his tongue could not handle food or liquids, so feeding was a major problem until the gastro-tube was inserted at 18 months. I remember nursing him in the hospital when he was a day old.

Hospitals are the WORST. I left this question for almost last, because I hate to think of some of the experiences. Especially with interns who try and be big shots and only show their ignorance. Also at hospitals they would never take instructions as to how to position Josh so he wouldn't be on his back. It was like talking to a wall.

Josh's pediatrician, neurologist, neuro-surgeon and pediatric surgeon—they ALL were wonderful and did outstanding jobs.

But then there was the orthopedic center—unorganized, different doctors each time, interns who had no concern or compasssion, did "cut-downs" on Josh to find a vein, sent him home without a cast after a hip surgery and said, "don't move him or it could ruin the surgery." Oh, yeah! If I knew then what I know now I'd have never brought him home without a cast on. It was removed because of swelling, and they just didn't put another one on. That was probably the experience I'm most bitter about. That he was in pain unnecessarily. I had to really pray for forgiveness to get over being angry about that and I still don't like to think about it.

He's always had a lot of upper-respiratory problems which have caused a lot of choking and gagging and the possibility for aspiration. So every time he was fed with a gastro tube we were constantly monitoring his breathing. The closest he came to death, besides the initial spinal meningitis, was when he was 18 months old and was severely dehydrated with the flu and I took him to the doctor every day and finally when he was admitted to the hospital it took a long time to get IVs in him and a week to get his sodium level normal. There were also times I'd be driving and Josh in the backseat in his wheelchair and he'd start projectile vomiting and aspirating. Talk about intense, trying to pull over, get to him, etc. Over the years the kids learned to put his head forward when I couldn't get to him. The school had an aide park at our house to ride on the bus with him in case he gagged in transport.

Although there were some really rough times of feeling helpless when new problems arose, I always found strength in knowing God is in control no matter what happens.

It helps when people acknowledge Josh and just being comfortable around him. Or even saying, "I don't know what to do or say" and asking for direction on what Josh would like. It doesn't help when people try to come up with a reason "why." I had a person once say, after I'd poured my heart out in frustration when Josh was two years old, "You people, how long are you intending to keep him at home?" I was devastated. After that I was very careful who I shared my negative feelings with.

I wish more people would have called me, letting me know they were thinking about me when Josh was in a body cast and I couldn't go out for weeks.

I have different emotions at different times. Helplessness when he was in pain for no reason. Burnout, having to feed him every four hours for years and years and years.... Total frustration when Josh needed to be tube fed, one of the others needed to be nursed, the phone rings and I haven't had time to eat all day.

I love Josh more than ever, there's always been a special closeness between us. We've been through so much together. I basically grew up after having Josh. I was 22 years old and just out of college when I had him.

The biggest frustration was not being able to hop in the car and go places. And by the time Josh was eight years old it was almost impossible to get a sitter. Everyone was afraid of his breathing. So we placed him in a care facility 35 miles from our home. THAT was by far the hardest, most devastating decision we EVER made. He was there for almost three years when he passed away last week (July 19, 1992). The three years he was at the care center were easier in terms of care. I remember after he was admitted it was such a big deal, we just hopped in the car with the other three kids and went and got a Christmas tree. My husband and I just looked at each other: "So this is what it is like to be normal?"

But emotionally it was HARD, especially after six weeks there he got a fractured leg and it was left untreated. I took him out and had it x-rayed myself and was told it had already healed crooked. I was so angry and hated to take him back, but after three days they called and said if I didn't bring him back, I'd have to pay hundreds of dollars for a deposit. That was really hard. I was just ready to bring him home, but I called everywhere around here but no one was qualified because of his needing suctioning, etc. We really had only been signed up to just have Josh go to the care center for the summer because it was just too difficult to do anything when he wasn't in school.

But when they said they had an opening they said if we didn't use it, there's a two-to-three-year waiting list. Oh boy, what a choice. That always puzzled me. Why would the state pay $3,000 per month to care for him in a care facility, but yet not provide any kind of respite care so I could keep him at home and save them $36,000 per year? It just doesn't make sense.

Anyway, after the leg episode, they changed doctors and called immediately anytime Josh had a problem or change in meds, etc. Over the next three years he had several more leg fractures due to brittle bones caused by so many years on seizure meds and muscle spasms. I'm convinced now they really took excellent care of Josh.

I got your reminder card to fill out these questions a few days after Josh passed away. So, how did that affect us? (Glad you asked?) Seriously, surprisingly enough we are doing GREAT. I'm just so at peace and happy for Josh now that he's okay. His brothers never stopped praying for God to heal Josh. Every time we sat down to eat they'd always pray for Josh along with the food. I was concerned how they'd take it. But Steve, age eight, said, "Mom, God answered our prayers. Now Josh can walk and talk in heaven." John, age five and a half, still comes to me and says, "Mom, I wish God could have healed Josh so he could play with us and go to church." That's hard. I just try and explain that God doesn't always answer our prayers how we want and it's okay to miss Josh. David, almost four, it's over his head. He says Josh is sleeping.

We put all our faith and trust in God and have a very supportive church family. My husband and I fortunately burn out at different times, so one of us is able to encourage the other. I could have never kept Josh home for eight years if my husband hadn't been so much help with his care for Josh and emotional support for me. We both centered our life around Josh. I didn't realize how much until he went to the care center. I then realized how much stress there was even putting Josh to bed at night and then listening for an hour to see if he was going to cough or go to sleep.

It's a lot more relaxing now when we can just put the kids to bed and go to bed ourselves and relax and enjoy each other. It's not too romantic jumping up and flying into Josh's room to change his position so he doesn't choke. Since he was so stiff, if he coughed instead of leaning forward, he'd throw his head back and was always at risk for aspirating into his lungs. So he spent many a night on his tummy over a bean bag chair.

All in all, I'd say it's been a positive experience for the boys in the fact that they are very comfortable around disabled people and they have an understanding and compassion thay never could have had otherwise.

My husband and I always did everything. I did most of the meds, laundry baths, etc., because he went to work. But anytime Tom was home he always helped feed, hold, move, and position. There were even times he would INSIST I go spend the weekend with my mom or a friend because he thought I needed a break from Josh. Steve helped open doors, pushed Josh's chair, read him books, etc.

Tom always could handle any situation with Josh which is why I only could get a break if he was caring for him. If we went somewhere together it was always hard for me to relax because I'd worry, "Oh, what if his tube comes out? What if he vomits?" etc. We've never been angry about caring for Josh but I do remember getting really burned-out having to feed him every four hours. The last feeding, whoever was the least exhausted, would do it. We had a joke: "Time to feed the Josh." (Remember the doughnut commercial about the guy who said, "Time to make the doughnuts," and he was worn out?) But it always wasn't funny. We were getting weary and had to pray about our attitudes by the time we let him go to the care center.

The nurses at the care center were very concerned and caring. They were very close to Josh. They all came to his funeral and the doctor said a grief counselor might have to come in. The chaplain said that Josh seemed to be the most of the nurses' favorites. I guess he just had a really sweet spirit.

Actually we've always been in just the right categories to qualify for SSI, a medical card, etc. Unlike some of our friends who have split up over the money problems of disabled kids. Anyway, either our insurance or Josh's med card always covered all his surgeries, meds, equipment, etc. We've been very fortunate there. We've never been ones to use credit cards. I'm sure that's helped. We don't have real lavish vacations to the Caribbean, but we've never had a late bill and I get my monthly fix at the Mall. I love to buy clothes! And we're still able to give 10-15 percent to the church for missions, etc. So we feel God blessed our finances.

We're very close and talk about everything. As far as Josh, we just always tried to keep each other encouraged. The only tension I remember is when I insisted on having Josh go somewhere (to a care facility) when I was pregnant with our third child. The waiting list was too long so he didn't get in anyway. When I was pregnant with the fourth Josh did go to a care facility for three months and it worked out fine. We were able to do more my ninth month of pregnancy with Josh gone than we did for months before.

We've learned to accept what comes. I'm especially appreciative of the three normal kids. When I give them a bath I notice how straight their backs are or what excellent range of motion they have, etc. There have been times people see me in the store and say, "Oh, you look busy" with the three younger boys. And I just think to myself, "Hey, you don't know what I've been through, this is like being on vacation compared to what I'm used to." Not all of the negative effects have we learned about yet.

The kids at church have grown up with Josh and are real comfortable around him. His cousin who used to babysit him is an occupational therapist, now just due to Josh's influence on her.

Without Josh my life would have been more stable, of course, but I wouldn't be as content with just "normal" life as I am now. When I first had Josh I thought, "Oh boy, I finished college, got married, and had a baby, What's left? To change diapers and diet for the rest of my life?" But two weeks later with Josh in ICU my life priorities totally changed. I had a whole different attitude and perspective. We've always felt that God had a purpose for Josh's life. In fact when I was six months pregnant with Josh an evangelist came and professed I would have a boy and that he would be born normal and not to worry. So we felt like God was preparing us for what was ahead.

Suicide? Never, ever, ever been a thought. I don't want to die until it's time for me to go.

The hardest thing to accept about the disability is that Josh has a cousin two weeks younger than him, and it was a little hard when she started walking and started to school and started band. Now she's old enough to babysit and sometimes I feel a little cheated. But now that he's deceased that doesn't seem to bother me as much. It's like the story is finally over and I can go on with my life and three kids.

Twice I've thought I was going crazy. Once when he was seven weeks old and had been home several weeks from a hospital meningitis episode and he cried for six weeks without stopping. Mom kept saying, "He's allergic to milk, try meat-base formula," and the doctors said "no, no, no". They gave him chloroform so I could get some sleep but I didn't give it to him. Finally Mom just bought some meat-base formula, I tried it, and he was fine within 48 hours. It pays to listen to your Mom sometimes.

Anyway, during this time I remember rocking him one night really rummy from lack of sleep thinking, "Oh, I wish I could put him in the refrigerator to get away from this crying for a few minutes." Of course, as soon as I thought that, I kind of jolted and thought, "This must be getting to me, but I love Josh more than anything and will hold him forever if I have to."

The only other time I remember thinking, "I never want to come this close to a nervous breakdown again," is when my second son was born a month early and nursed every two hours, plus Josh had bronchitis and was up a lot, plus we were managing apartments so the phone and door had to be constantly answered. I did not sleep more than two hours at a time for over a month. I was so rummy, I remember the pastor came to see me and all I could do was cry. That's why I insisted on getting help for the next two births and those experiences were much better.

His condition was deteriorating and I was feeling really helpless and it was scary. Maybe that's one reason his death hasn't been as traumatic because I feel better thinking about him now not having any problems.

What I am looking forward to is seeing him in heaven. There wasn't much for him to look forward to before in life unless God had healed him.

JASON NEEDS NO PHYSICAL CARE NOW. HE DIED LAST WEEK.

Ten years ago this man, now 33, became father to a baby son with cerebral palsy. During the time when the family was participating in this research project, Jason died:

Jason has severe brain damage, leaving him with very limited voluntary muscle control. He is classified as having cerebral palsy with seizures controlled by medication. His bones have deteriorated to the point of being very brittle. He can't talk or eat anything orally. He is totally dependent on others for any stimulation including movement. He constantly fights a battle with respiratory problems.

Jason contracted H-flu meningitis at ten days old. His spinal fluid had 300,000 white cells per cc of fluid. The normal amount is three. He was hospitalized for three-and-a-half weeks, during which time his brain swelled up due to inflammation of the spinal fluid.

He was perfect for ten days. Then he wouldn't eat, so we had him examined and they immediately hospitalized him. They had to shave his head to place IVs. He was so innocent, it didn't seem fair.

From the onset, we were totally involved. During his initial stay I worked daily and would travel 30 miles each evening to see him. Meeting with new doctors daily as his problems increased. During the first stay the doctor told me that he nearly asked me to "let him go." Scarey!

When he was released, we had to take him to numerous doctors. Because of his orthopedic history, he was given therapy for use of limbs. He would cry as they moved him. But they insisted that they were helping him. Despite therapy, his hips began to dislocate so he had hip surgery. It was a nightmare. The doctor was very cold. Jason was in real pain. When he came home, we had to care for the op sites. Then he dehydrated, so another surgery to place a gastro tube. One week later he was having headaches—he would just cry and we could do nothing. So a shunt was placed in his brain. This doctor was super. No more crying. Two more hip surgeries to go.

I didn't always know that I was doing the right thing. What if he didn't really need that procedure and I caused him pain for nothing?

When he was first sick his brain swelled and he was on total life support. Then the doctor talked about "letting him go." Then when he was dehydrated, they couldn't find any veins for IVs so they could get some fluids in him. During one surgery we were told that it would take an hour and a half, but we waited five hours for him. Nobody informed us that he was out or anything. They wanted him to cry before bringing him back to his room. But he only cries if he is in pain. At night when he would vomit, I would wonder what would happen if he choked to death. After his shunt surgery the surgeon told us that he should have no infection in his body at all, or it could ride the tubing up to his brain and kill him. Scarey!

He has had such a miserable life, there have been times when I've wished God would take him home.

We placed him in a full-care facility at age eight years. The everyday pressure was removed at that point.

His preschool years were his worst years and therefore our worst also. As he aged, either he got easier or we got better at it.

It doesn't help when people say "they know how you feel." Every instance is different and has unique circumstances.

At times I would just cry and wonder, "Why?" But all in all, it has made me face situations that build character. My faith in God steadied my emotional self. I believe that we did the best that we possibly could. Always trying to make the decision that was in the best interest of the entire family.

I wish we could travel with ease. Jason was a poor traveler, making trips and vacations less than optimal.

He is a child of God, therefore God is in control of his life. He is part of our family so no matter what the situation, God gave him to us and we will prevail. I would like for my children to develop even more compassion for the less fortunate and never become callous and uncaring.

Actual care was either through us or a professional. Jason was so involved that others were a little frightened of him. So most care was through my wife and myself. Anger was not a problem.

Jason needs no physical care now. He died last week.

We are comfortable financially. "Godliness with contentment is great gain."

Trying to manage and cope under the medical pressure wears you down. If you are not careful, you can allow circumstances to destroy you. Your faith has to be in God.

At times the other kids had to take a "back seat" to him. His needs were uppermost at the time. Although they never showed resentment, I'm sure it was sometimes difficult for them.

Without the disability, life would have been totally different. He could have had a normal childhood. Because of the severity of his handicap, Jason never experienced but a few of the so-called joys of life.

"All things work together for good to them that love the Lord and are the called according to his purpose." We don't always understand, but God is in control. Getting mad at God would not solve the problem. I don't believe that God made him sick. He allowed it to happen—that is all. He had a disease. Placing blame is a waste of time and energy.

Being unable to do anything to remedy the problem gave me such a total feeling of helplessness.

[I have] No fears anymore. I used to fear a slow agonizing death, but that was not the case. I'm looking forward to joining him in heaven where he is a "regular boy."

An eight-year-old brother describes his feelings:

[I didn't like it] at the nursing home: sick people, coughing, gagging, broken bones. He was in pain and we didn't get to see him that often. Nothing would really make me laugh [about the disability], but I did feel happy since he was my brother. He had brain damage. I always picture him falling off a rocking chair and hitting his head. Now he's in heaven and he's not sick anymore. I don't think anything bad of it. I won't be sad that often now that I know he's better.

And a four-year-old brother:

[The disability made me afraid] because it was just like that he was sick and I was afraid that he had to go to the hospital.

A five-year-old brother says:

[I'm sad] because I didn't want him to be sick anymore and it's sad to have a brother that's sick. It was a little funny because he had two buck teeth and he had to drink through pipes. [Why the disability?] because he was standing up on the rocking chair and bumped his head. What scared me was when his temperature got up to 60 something because I thought he was going to die. [He became teary-eyed at this point.] It helps when you read me a story out of the *Bible*.

FIVE YEARS

Stories told by individuals and family members who have been challenged by a disability for five to ten years.

BRANDON'S DAD SEEMED AFRAID, BUT HE NEVER COULD TALK ABOUT IT

Nine years ago this young mother gave birth to a special, beautiful little boy who was later diagnosed with cerebral palsy:

Brandon was three pounds, 12 ounces at birth and 19 inches long. I remember my first thought was how he resembled a skinned squirrel. I bonded with him when he was three days old and felt like it was my calling to care for him and do it better than anyone else could, regardless of the outcome.

Brandon was born two months premature in an inadequate hospital facility. After birth he was transported to a hospital with a neonatal unit. He suffered a cerebral brain hemorrhage and three strokes before he was 12 hours old. Brandon's doctor was not present until only two minutes before his delivery, and I feel he suffered trauma because that could have been avoided if I had had proper medical attention.

The most difficult is to have to see him suffer through the pain and be in casts. I don't know how much Brandon comprehends about all the treatments and I hate the scared looks.

Being so premature and with all the complications at birth, the doctor said he may not live past the first 48 hours. Every day past that was a positive sign. Brandon prospered after the fourth day, steadily gained weight and had few complications after the birthing complications. We were fortunate to be able to hold him the third day and immediately I knew he was going to be special and I desparately wanted him to be at home.

He is very social and has many people that visit with him. He now makes me feel special to have such a special, beautiful little boy. Brandon was in an infant stimulation program for three years. After turning four, he attended a daily school for six hours at a developmental center. He now attends the State School for the Handicapped.

Often people are judgmental. It has been suggested that Brandon is too much of a burden. Often it is said that I won't always be able to care for him. Maybe not, but right now I can, so why worry about tomorrow when we've made it ten years?

He has such limited speech but is always available with a hug. He knows when I'm feeling blue. My sister has been there to always offer encouragement and helps by reading up on new treatments and passes along the information. Sometimes my girlfriend just telling me how bratty her two boys are helps. She doesn't know that sometimes she makes me feel lucky.

It has been a challenge. I was divorced after 14 years of marriage when Brandon was five. It's been easier on my own. I can make my own schedule and budget for his needs. When I just found out that he would be disabled I cried a whole night away. I got up the next morning and have gone forward since then.

If my marriage would have remained secure, Brandon would have benefited from a brother or sister. I felt cheated not to have had the chance to raise a "normal" child and he missed out on the sibling interaction.

Brandon's dad wanted perfection. He couldn't cope and actually seemed angry at me for being able to. He chose to ignore Brandon rather than interact. He seemed afraid, maybe, but never could talk about it.

No one in the family has ever offered to provide care. My mother (Brandon's grandmother) felt she couldn't handle him, so has never tried. His dad walked out.

Brandon is on no medication. His only expense is $14 weekly for diapers. Brandon is no more expensive than any other child, but people don't see that he does have expensive equipment needs. So far this has been covered through Crippled Children's.

I have a strong, personal relationship with God. I am an extremely independent type of personality, but am overcoming this. If people ask if they can help, I'll let them now. I don't believe God caused his disability but I do know he could have prevented it or could heal him. I do know he has given me the strength and attitude to deal with it. God knows what my life holds for me. I don't. I trust his decisions.

RIGHT NOW THE WORLD IS HER GUMDROP, SHE BELIEVES EVERYONE LOVES HER

Nine years ago this mother, now 42, gave birth to a daughter who was subsequently diagnosed with cerebral palsy. Thoughts of the future cause her pain and fear:

I grieve over the loss of my dreams of having a normal child. I fear for her future. When participating in a school program, I feel as if I'm hit with a "hard slap" because suddenly I am aware of just how disabled and different she is from other children. My eyes tear and my calm face suddenly falls apart. I'm very intense now. I don't laugh as much. I'm too serious. My marriage has suffered. Lots of stress. However, on the other hand, I am a lot stronger because of her. I am more involved in helping others, more compassionate, less selfish, more understanding of others, more patient and forgiving.

We all need to help my daughter be more independent. To see her as a ten-year-old, not a five-year-old. We tend to do too much for her and it scares me that it could hurt her more than help her to be independent.

The effects on us? Mother: extreme depression, denial, stress, overeating, high blood pressure, anxiety. Father: excessive drinking, treatment for drinking, no self esteem, fear, anxiety.

Our relationship is secondary. I'm more withdrawn, obsessed about my child's needs, don't listen well. But, I'm working on it. A lot!

I am Catholic, although just confirmed to be an Episcopalian. I was raised in "fear of the Lord." If you do wrong you are punished. My husband and I lived together three years before we were married. A very unacceptable Catholic thing to do. My mother disowned me. You can believe my first questions were, "What did I do to deserve this? Was this a punishment? Was I really that bad?"

Was I mad at God? In the early years, definitely! Why should any child have to suffer if you are a loving and forgiving God? And I don't believe I was chosen, either. My child's disability is just fate, not punishment. So I can't be mad at God. Now I turn to him for strength, guidance, to handle every day one day at a time. And once in awhile to just pray: "Make it all go away. Help me get through this!"

For three years I blamed me. I was overweight. On blood pressure medication. I remember using shellac on the walls of our house and wondering if fumes caused her CP. I was innocent and naive about childbirth. I lost some water early and never thought to call the doctor. My husband drank heavily and alcohol is related to her problems. When she was four, after many doctors' opinions, one finally said to me: "You are not to blame for this. Many things can cause CP." Finally, I was ready to let go of the guilt, accepting his word and accepting her.

It will never go away. My child will never walk. She will never talk to me about what's truly in her mind.

I fear her lack of independence, having someone other than family care for her. I fear that she'll be taken advantage of sexually and can't defend herself. Right now the world is her gumdrop, she believes everyone loves her. I fear the hurt that adulthood brings.

What about the future? Loving friends, husband…This question is emotional for me. I don't plan a future beyond today. I'm afraid to look forward. I tear up….

IT KILLED MY DREAM. I PRODUCED A BURDEN TO THE WORLD

Though she dreamed of having a child who would play an active part in life and help solve some of the world's problems, this 35-year-old mother feels she failed when her son was born with cerebral palsy nine years ago:

Most difficult was the initial diagnosis, learning to come to terms with the death of my "dream child," to the reality of this brand new life at an end before it could begin.

Darren is a cerebral palsy victim. His primary disability is aphasia, the lack of talk, although he can intonate sounds consistently, and says many words. His secondary condition is mild retardation. His gross motor skills are poor, but he is functional.

When we can't see our regular doctor, it's frustrating to have to explain who and what Darren is for a newcomer.

It killed my dream—my life goal was to raise my children to play an active part, and to help in the world to come. Instead, I produced a burden to the world. I see the burden of housing the child for life, not having a relationship as I age with my spouse alone. I feel a failure. I feel embarrassed.

If I knew this child would be handicapped, I would not have had this child—whether through choice of childless marriage or abortion.

The strength of my family is me, my determination to be a family, to make Darren's life as "normal" as possible, to make society realize that he is a valuable part of society. My husband works hard so I can be home to do this.

The disability makes it hard to be a friend, so he can't participate as well with other people. It turns some people away, so he has no chance to try friendship.

I was very angry at God after the diagnosis for how he could do this to a beautiful child. How unfair to pick a child, his creation.

It was meant to be.

IT DOESN'T MATTER NOW, WHAT'S DONE IS DONE
AND WE'LL DEAL WITH IT

Eight years ago this mother, now 34, gave birth to a baby with develop-
mental disabilities:

My son was born with spina bifida and hydrocephalus. Spina bifida means
that the spinal column didn't form properly, at about 28 days gestation, and
paralysis resulted at the level of the lesion and below. He has no movement in his
lower limbs because his lesion is at L1 in the lumbar region. Also, as a result, he
does not have control of his bowel and bladder. Hydrocephalus, or water on the
brain, also resulted from the spina bifida. This has been controlled by a shunt,
which drains the fluid from his brain. When he was six days old, his bowel perfo-
rated and the infection spread into his abdomen. He was given an antibiotic to
clear up the infection, and as a result he became deaf. The bowel problem was not
connected to the birth defect directly. He also has visual-perception problems
because of the hydrocephalus.

I am his primary caretaker. As a result, I have the responsibility of taking him
to his appointments. Also, because I can sign fluently, I have always stayed with
David in the hospital following surgery. I have had good and bad experiences
with doctors. Some doctors have been very negative with the prognosis they gave.
Others have been very positive. When he was six days old and had to have emergency surgery to remove his large colon we had one resident tell us that David
probably would not come through the surgery alive and if he did, he would not
live long afterwards. The doctor who performed the surgery assured us that other
children in worse shape than our son came through the surgery okay and recovered from it.

I had one doctor, a physiatrist, tell us that he would never walk. The orthopedic doctor said there was no reason why he wouldn't. The physiatrist had also not
wanted him to stay in a manual wheelchair but to get a battery-operated chair.
The physical therapist treating David at that time worked under this physiatrist
and was not working on strengthening his upper body in preparation for walking.
I got another therapist who worked independently and who felt David's potential
for walking was good and was being wasted. We worked together toward that
goal. Each of his therapists since have also worked toward that goal and although
David will never walk long distances, he is able to walk around at home and
school.

We had his hearing checked at four months. We were told at that time that
there was a delay between the time the sound entered the ear and the time it

reached the brain. The doctor who interpreted the test said this was the result of the malformation and that he would outgrow it. When David was 17 months we had him tested by a different doctor and a different kind of test. He fell asleep during the test. That doctor told us that she tested him down to conversation level and that he could hear at that level. When David was three we had him tested at a different location by a different doctor than the previous two and found that he was profoundly hearing impaired.

Upon further investigation we learned that deafness is a side-effect of the anti-biotic he received following his bowel surgery, but we were not informed of that at that time. We also learned that the first hearing test done on our son had showed a severe loss, but the doctor had made a wrong call. The second doctor was just plain wrong. Most of our experiences have been very positive. We've learned that if we have a bad experience with a doctor or a therapist, we usually have the option of finding a new one.

I love David just as he is. Although there are difficult times (surgeries, etc.). I wouldn't change him. He is such a blessing to our family. I believe in a God who makes no mistakes and I'm thankful that God gave us this special child.

I guess I would like most to be able to go anywhere for whatever length of time without having to be concerned about if I had everything I'd need to cath him and whether or not he'd have a bladder accident.

I do most of his care and always have. My husband helps whenever I need his help and is more than willing to do so. David's care in the past involved cathing every three hours, bathing daily, feeding, dressing, and physical therapy exercises done at home. Also, when he got into preschool, I transported him to and from school and have always been responsible for making appointments with the doctors and taking him there as well. Now that he is older he is learning to do many of those things himself, and I just have to supervise and be sure they're done properly. We are not angry about having to care for him. There are times I start to feel burdened by all the therapy, so I give David and myself a day off and that takes care of it.

I am a born-again believer in the Lord Jesus Christ. I was saved when I was nine years old. I believe in a sovereign God who controls everything that happens in my life. Although I may not always understand His reasons for doing things, I believe He knows what is best for me and I accept that. I sometimes think it was to draw my husband and me back together because we had started drifting apart. When David was born we prayed together and drew strength from each other like never before and it drew us close together again.

To some extent I think I blame myself. If it's true that spina bifida is caused by a lack of folic acid in the mother, I blame myself because I was somewhat anorexic when I got pregnant and did not eat properly the first month of my pregnancy. However, it doesn't matter now, what's done is done and we'll deal with it.

I think my biggest fear is that something will go wrong during surgery and that his life here on earth will be ended. Although I know he would go to heaven and that I'd see him again, it would hurt a great deal. Another fear is probably that no one would hire him and he would have to do something like sell trash bags and light bulbs to earn a living. I want better than that for him.

We can't control much of what happens in life, but our attitude about what happens to us is something we can control. Having a negative attitude will do nothing to help ourselves or anyone else. We all need to strive to reach our highest potential and challenge others to reach theirs.

And a four-year-old sibling says:

I don't know why [he's disabled]. It's okay that he is in a wheelchair. It doesn't make me sad. I don't know why.

IF I WERE TO DO IT OVER, I WOULD TRY
TO UNDERSTAND THE PARENTS MORE

A 75-year-old grandmother writes about her autistic granddaughter and how the family faces the challenge:

My granddaughter is autistic and hyperactive. No one knows what causes this problem. One psychiatrist said it was due to a "refrigerator mother," but that has long been discredited and was a cruel thing to say. It is probably a brain disorder. About two years ago I realized that something was amiss, due to her lack of eye contact. For awhile she walked on her toes which I read was an early symptom. For a very short period she had to wear a helmet to protect her from terrible headbanging. One doctor questioned the mother about the possibility of grand-mother abuse.

She has been in pre-school and now elementary school, always with a one-on-one relationship.

It keeps one in a mild state of depression much of the time, worrying for her future and her happiness. Her parents keep me informed of any life-style changes. My spouse understands her strange behavior.

There was nothing to do, just wait for acceptance.

It has been devastating and, for awhile, divided the family. Her parents thought we should help more but we have all finally improved the relationship. If I were to do it over, I would try to understand the parents more.

Physical disability would be easier. As long as you have your mind, there is hope and understanding.

I feel helpless because I have no control and feel my advice is not always welcome so I "mute" it.

The relatives are considerate, but no one really "feels it" except the parents and grandparents. The loss of not being able to care for her at home is devastating and hard on their self-esteem.

The future seems so murky. I fear abuse by uncaring attendants.

WE HAVE LEARNED WHAT IS MOST IMPORTANT: FAMILY, LOVE, HEALTH, AND HAPPINESS

Seven years ago Jesse was born into this mother's life. At age 37 she reflects on the struggles and blessings:

Jesse was born premature—merconium stained with apgar of 2-7 at 1-5 minutes. Developmental delay with poor proprioception, fine/gross motor development was present from birth. Diagnosed EMH, IQ of 67. We have experienced multiple problems with my pregnancies. One 13-year-old son, six known miscarriages, and two full-term stillbirths. The neonatologist felt I had some type of autoimmune disorder where my body rejected the fetus, because of evidence of chronic placental insufficiency.

As a registered nurse who has a master's degree and specializes in pediatrics, I can tell you it's shameful how little is known about developmental delay. Every specialist, and believe me there have been many during these seven years, seemed to have a contradictory explanation of why he had problems and plans of treatment. A wise, white-haired physician warned me early on to be "conservative" in diagnosing Jesse's problem, as a child could quickly become a "Guinea pig." Ninety percent of the professionals gave me little hope that he would function as a normal child. If his family had given up on his potential, I'm sure he would end up very dependent on others all his life. As it turns out, I believe he will function independently as we continue to fight for his rights. The pessimistic attitude of the professionals is the worst part of all of it.

Jesse spent five days in neonatal ICU and I, having lost a baby stillborn four years earlier, did not want to see him as I didn't want the hurt of losing another baby. The evening of his birth my husband insisted we go see him. He was bigger than most babies in that unit. I stayed home with him for six months until I felt his health was not fragile. I prayed that he would not die. All the testing would not give conclusive diagnoses, although it was evident that he was motor developmentally delayed. When he began to crawl at 12 months, walked at two years, spoke and potty-trained at three years, even though no diagnosis was ever revealed, I knew that he was a survivor, a fighter, much more than most everyone gave him potential for.

It's not easy fighting every inch of ground for what your child needs. I would rather be physically than emotionally exhausted, but it is not an easy task. The elementary years were easier to handle, and I have become more confident in my abilities to nurture him. During preschool there was so much unknown, so much pain, fighting school systems, listening, evaluating, researching, trying to determine what were Jesse's needs to achieve optimal development.

I wish there was more money and emphasis nationally on child health and education needs.

Jesse brings joy to every day. He is sweet, positive, loving. He is full of energy, enthusiasm and smiles. At times I get frustrated, but most of the time I count my blessings as he has brought much love and faith to our family.

I wish I would have trusted my own intuitions sooner, and not put him through so many evaluations, but hindsight is great, isn't it?

He needs no real physical care, just the constant supervision to prevent injury as Jesse has no fear, and although independent has to be observed more than other "normal" kids. Sometimes it is frustrating to answer constant questions, but it sure beats the alternatives.

My husband stays home to be there with and for Jesse. During school he transports him to motor developmental lab several times per week. We are happy to provide this wholesome environment for both our boys. As an RN myself, we have not qualified for any financial assistance. We are not able to have savings for the future. We have good life insurance, which I hope will take care of the boys if we were unable to provide for them.

People either love to be around Jesse with his happy, inquisitive, non-stop activity, or they become very uncomfortable. There seems to be no middle ground here. I thank God he did not die in utero as so many of our other babies did.

We don't blame anyone. We had the finest medical care. I don't even blame myself, although it has taken time to come to this understanding.

Stress is part of dealing with people when one is so emotionally involved with the situation. Thank goodness my husband and I can keep each other in balance when one of us feels overwhelmed. My husband was very crushed by the pain and hurt we've been through. Together we are overcoming these sad feelings. We have learned what is most important: family, love, health, and happiness.

I HAVE LEARNED TO WEAVE THE THREAD OF PAIN
AROUND EVERYTHING ELSE, AND NOT LET IT TAKE CENTER STAGE

This 40-year-old mother gives a riveting picture of the stress she faces in her efforts to raise a son with severe disabilities:

My son has cerebral palsy, multiple disabilities including epilepsy and mental retardation, spastic all over.

It was caused by a CMV infection (cytomegalic viral infection) infection in the first trimester of pregnancy. I suspect now that the hepatitis I had during the first trimester was CMV-related. I think now I got the hepatitis from my now ex-husband, who might have had a homosexual experience with a hepatitis carrier.

I remember a baby with a tiny head, who was very healthy and happy but had weird episodes. I didn't know until he was a year old that he had been experiencing seizures.

I am intensely involved in medical experiences. He has had two surgeries. I will NEVER permit surgery again, as it is too upsetting and I have a jaundiced attitude toward professionals who, although well-meaning and experts in their field, seem to have no long-term view of the disabled person or no sensitivity to the family. I have fought numerous education battles to get PT, OT, and ST into his education plan. He is now seven and this is the first year I feel he almost has gotten everything he needs. Up to now it was a hodge-podge of school, private and hospital-based services. Too often professionals tell me what to do. I just want them to do their job. I've got plenty to do.

The impersonality of hospitals is crippling to families.

I monitor his life closely, as he cannot go about alone or speak for himself. He is healthy, hardly ever sick. My co-worker's kids are at the doctors all the time, but not my child. His only contact with the medical system is on account of his disability; immunizations and eligibility forms to be filled out by doctors so he can get services, e.g. a form for a handicapped parking permit, etc. I resent the fact that the medical profession exercises such control over his life. These visits cost money and time when you get forms filled out. There is something wrong with our society when his access to the mainstream is influenced so heavily by medical people. I offer no alternative, however.

I have learned to weave the thread of pain around everything else, and not let it take center stage. I see no let up in the stress level. As soon as one problem is resolved, another emerges.

In seven years he has been to four different "programs." Only two were easy to get into. He has been discriminated against already many times, i.e., they don't want him "too" disabled. We have spent close to $6,000 in legal and professional fees to get the right placement for him.

This is wrong.

There is no one in my family who has positively supported me except my brother, occasionally. Family is no different than society in general, in terms of reaction. Your [the researchers'] assumption is invalid...that families help emotional adjustment. It has forced me to go deeper, be more serious, and generally more responsible, and not at all carefree. I am very strong as a result of this, more stoic, more accepting and tolerant of others.

He and I have a special quality that I love and hate simultaneously. His dependency can be overwhelming. I can't go for a drink after work with co-workers as I have to get home to relieve the personal care attendants.

I would like to have a more extended family; possibly a live-in person who cares for him. I'd like less turnover of people in his life. I'm the only constant.

His father: emotionally crippled, became unpleasant, failed in the marriage to cope with the demands, ran off with another woman

Stepsister: became a better person. Has developed an understanding of disability and motherhood that the average 19-year-old does not have.

Parents-in-laws: pretend a lot that they care and help but really do nothing. None have gone out of their way to assist me or him. They denied a lot. They don't want to hear about problems, just successes.

His father and I "took turns" taking care of him when married. However, as part of his denial of the situation, he worked more and more hours and took on other interests so, in reality, I got "stuck" with his "share." Therefore, the marriage collapsed. Similarly, the lack of system support contributed. Until divorce, I got no respite. Now it's mandated via the child visitation arrangement. I have more "time to myself" since divorce than in marriage.

The disability has impacted every financial aspect of the family, including what job I hold (it has to have good benefits), to greater use of utilities (more mess, so more laundry), to no vacations as there is no discretionary money. We have never been eligible for anything because I work full-time. As long as child support is paid by my ex I can pay for a personal care attendant after school, so I can keep my full-time job. If that falters, big problems.

I have faith. I'm not sure if I'd be different without a disabled child. I resent being called "saintly" or a "special parent" or statements like "God picks those who can handle it." I do remember saying "Why me?" at first, but this child with a disability is so part of my life I cannot separate "Why?" in general from "Why this?" any more.

A few times I have wished my disabled son were dead, so I wouldn't have to deal with everything. I worry about the future and what happens if I get old/disabled or lose my job. I screamed and hit him once or twice. I can tell him I'm losing patience and lock him in his room till I'm able to control myself (about 10-20 minutes).

A child's questions are easier to answer. Stupid questions from adults like, "When will he walk?" enrage me. My ex-mother-in-law aggravates me by asking, "Can he walk yet?" I asked her once to not ask this and asked my ex-husband to speak with her, but he "failed" to do this for me. These are typical examples of lack of family support.

I hope he dies before I do if he doesn't get to lead a normal life. The thought of institutionalization is unspeakable.

There is always someone worse off. Keeping a sense of humor and seeing the absurdity of it all is very important. Friends are important!

Another member of this family, a 19-year-old daughter talks about the disability:

The disability limits to some point what he can do physically, but he can overcome it with technology and benefits from society. The whole country should do more, cater to, the kind of disability my brother has. He has a better/greater personality than other kids his age. He knows he's special in some way. The disability was caused by hepititis while his mother was pregnant. Everything will be fine. He'll learn. I'm not worried a lot. I keep updated on his progress and what he does, as I don't live at home now.

SHE DOESN'T UNDERSTAND LOVE AND HUGS AND KISSES. I FEEL AS THOUGH SHE'S EMPTY INSIDE

A 32-year-old mother talks about her seven-year-old daughter's challenges:
She has always been described as developmentally delayed, but has been diagnosed within the past few months as having pervasive developmental disorder. Also, she has a seizure disorder which I had noticed from about eight months, but was not diagnosed until she was five. When you first meet her, your impression is that she looks and talks normally. However, it becomes clear soon after that most times she has no idea what she's talking about. She uses words she hears, but not in the right context. She is about two to three years delayed.

There was lack of oxygen at birth. She had the cord wrapped around her neck five times and I had an emergency C-section. She had stopped moving at 36 weeks, however, was not taken for another week. I always knew she was delayed but I never thought it would become so severe.

Since her birth I have been to many hospitals and doctors. I feel I have not had the best understanding and listening from doctors, especially her own pediatrician, whom I have since changed. I've felt very rushed in office visits and not given the amount of attention to my daughter's needs and what I'm telling them. However, I have made a total change in all doctors involved with her and am much happier. I still believe that it's too hard to reach doctors when you need them and sometimes feel put off.

Very often when I'm dwelling on her problems, I want to go to sleep so I stop thinking about them. She's only six, but so far the easiest time was when she was an infant. Every year has gotten more difficult. I have not had any support until recently. She has some wonderful doctors now. I'm also hooked up with respite care.

Since my daughter's handicap is not something you know about unless you really get to know her, only close family knows. My family does not really talk about it. The worst I've heard has been from my own family saying that "things could be worse." I don't think they should minimize her problems. You always know someone has things worse.

The disability has changed my whole life. Some days I can't think straight and I feel like a basket case. Other days I'm a fighter for her. I guess I have my ups and downs. I still don't know a lot about her diagnosis, so I'm still looking for information.

Because of her handicap, she does not have normal emotions which makes me sad because she doesn't understand love and hugs and kisses. I feel as though she's empty inside and that's very hard.

I think that we are an average family and the best thing is that my other children treat her the same as anyone else. We go and do the same things as everyone. We stick together, and even through the hard times, we talk a lot. My children are small, so I don't think it has had a big impact on them yet. My husband has and still does have a hard time accepting it. I think being a mother I have mostly been affected by the fact that she is not a loving child and it hurts to know that she doesn't have the proper feelings for anyone. Also, her behavior has put a big strain on me. This has been emotionally draining.

I guess it has made us discuss things more. My attention is geared to her sometimes too much and I feel I neglect others in the family.

My children are all very close and don't really understand that she has problems. Her behavior has had some effect on them because at times she tends to be very mean and aggressive.

Without the disability, my life would be different. I wouldn't be beating myself up every day trying to get someone to listen to me. I also get mad at God because I wonder what I did to deserve all her problems. I really believe she should have been delivered before she was. I blame the doctors.

I have a hard time because I think that something worse will happen, because for six years, every year it has gotten worse. I'm afraid she'll be teased in school and may not be able to function on her own when she grows up.

I have learned how important family is.

LIFE GOES ON

Seven years ago this 33-year-old father found out his daughter had a seizure disorder from birth:

Our daughter has a developmental seizure disorder. It has been the most difficult trying to find out the correct diagnosis for her disability, [and getting] some answers. I can see how it affects her and I know there is nothing I can do to help her get better.

All of her years have been equally hard because everything is very hard for her to learn and comprehend. She started in an early intervention program at eight months and has been in a school environment ever since. She is always behind in something, the older she gets, the more delayed.

I wish she had a disability that could be seen so it would be easier for people to see that she is disabled.

My wife is very aggressive in finding answers about our daughter from the doctors. Our other daughter helps care for her, also.

We are finally getting answers from doctors; these answers are helping a lot with our daughter. I think our strengths are very good as a family, but there is always the need for continuous improvement. As far as her siblings go, they are not old enough to understand the problems. My wife was affected the most by the disability because none of the doctors would answer any questions about our daughter. It took five years to get answers.

Without the disability, there would have been less stress on the family. I blame the doctors who were caring for my wife before the birth. My advice would be to keep pressing the doctors so you can get all the answers.

It's very hard to accept that my daughter will always be delayed. Hopefully, she will have a normal life. My fear is that she will always have to be taken care of. The disability has taught me that life goes on.

I FEEL WE HAVE MADE MOST OF THE RIGHT CHOICES
AND SO FAR DON'T LOOK BACK WITH MANY REGRETS

Seven years ago this 42-year-old mother gave birth to a son who was diagnosed with Down's Syndrome:

I was frightened when I saw him as a newborn because he was the reddest baby I had ever seen. I was afraid for his health and that he would die, but yet I wondered if that might not be best. He seemed so fragile, his muscles were very weak, he would not nurse well; I worried about his appearance to others and our acceptance in general as a family.

At birth the doctor told us immediately of his handicap. We were glad of that—to be told then and not later on. He encouraged us to love and care for him and treat him as much like our other children as we could.

One of the most difficult things was accepting that things would not get "better," and that developmentally Don did not "fit into" the guidelines of normal children.

It helps when they [teachers] give examples of ways and instances where they have seen improvement: he's talking better at school, he's independently got on and off the bus.

It has drained me at times, physically and emotionally. It has affected my patience with my children. It has caused an emotional strain on my marriage at times. Accepting Down's Syndrome as a disability was very hard the first three years. I had a hard time emotionally because I was afraid of things people would say about him and how I would react in public.

I feel we have made most of the right choices and so far don't look back with many regrets.

I wish I could make learning easier for Don so that he could feel more positive and his limitations mentally could be less, so his level of frustration could be lower.

I think I possibly spent less time with our other two sons the first few years after Don was born because I was so dedicated to trying to speed up his development. At times the boys have been embarrassed by some of his actions, but in a positive aspect they have accepted him for what is also, and for the most part they don't avoid having friends to our house because of Don.

I believe God gives us all kinds of situations to deal with in our lives. We are not "special" because we are given a "special needs" child, but because of this child we may become better people.

Many nights when he was sick and we couldn't get him to stop crying, he would kick and wiggle and didn't want us to hold him. This might continue all night and he couldn't show or tell what was wrong. It was very draining and made me feel like I was "losing it" at times.

My main fears are if something happened to one of us as parents, who would be able to care for him and understand his needs?

And from a 15-year-old sister:

I'm not sad about his disability. It's something you can't do anything about and I like him the way he is. Sometimes he's silly and I laugh. He's disabled because he has an extra chromosome. No, I don't think about the future.

And a nine-year-old brother:

Sometimes I'm sad, sometimes not. It's hard to explain. Because he doesn't act like he has a disability. I'm sort of afraid of his future. When I'm feeling sad, I want you to answer more questions for me. Explain more about it.

OUR FAMILY TALKS THROUGH OUR FEARS
AND FEELINGS TOGETHER

Six years ago this 42-year-old father found out his newborn daughter was mentally retarded:

She was first diagnosed as developmentally delayed, but it was later changed to mildly mentally retarded. The cause is unknown. In May of 1986 it started with hand tremors, and the tremors moved throughout the body. She lost all balance by July. In early July we took her to the Mayo Clinic. All tests came out clean. No diagnosis. She started walking again in September.

The rate of her deterioration was such that we didn't know if she would be around or not. We feared for her life during the time she was at the Mayo Clinic for tests.

I feel like she is improving all the time. She has been in special education since she was three. She has improved all the time so far. It's important to encourage the disabled person, not feel sorry for them. Our family talks through our fears and feelings together. Just to know what happened to her would have helped.

There isn't too much we can't do, but we always have to keep an eye on her. We are a Christian family. We all work together trying to keep our family normal. The disability has helped me to realize that there is more to life than all work.

I love her very much, she is improving all the time. She tries us all. She has a mind of her own and we love her.

Our older children went from being very protective of her to being embarrassed by her actions. She has changed my outlook on family and work.

God always has a reason. We may not know it at the time but sometime we will understand why. My hopes are that she can have a somewhat normal life. She keeps improving so there is still hope.

I'M AFRAID SOMETIMES THAT THINGS WILL BECOME
WAY TOO FAST-PACED FOR THE DISABLED,
AND THAT SOCIETY WILL FEEL THAT THE DISABLED
HAVE NO CONTRIBUTION TO MAKE

Six years ago this 31-year-old mother began her journey with her severely-disabled baby daughter:

My child was born with myelomeningocele, an open spine, and fluid on the brain. She also has numerous respiratory complications. She is paralyzed from the nipples down. She has a super sharp mind and great use of hands and arms, but severe bladder and bowel problems. We do not know for sure what caused her disability. This birth defect occurs in the first trimester of pregnancy. I did not do drugs, alcohol or smoke. My husband works at a lead foundry and it is possible that this contributed to the birth defect.

This disability has always been fresh in my mind. My earliest memory is of her lying flat on her stomach because she could not lie on her back. She had an extremely abnormal-sized head. It was very large and did not have very much bone structure. We had to hold her on a pillow to feed her.

As her mother, I am her primary caregiver. I tend to all of her needs. When she is in the hospital, the involvement on my part varies. Most of the time I am allowed to fully take care of her. The doctors in the hospital are seen very few times. You see a lot of medical students. Most of them leave a lot to be desired. There have been numerous mistakes made in the emergency room, on the doctor's part. For example, on one occurrence they gave her a spinal tap and she had a reaction. The doctor got scared and left the room and never came back to see about her. Later on, after being seen by someone else she wound up in ICU. Needless to say, my involvement is much greater now and I stand for no nonsense where my child is concerned. I keep pushing until they get a real doctor to see her and take appropriate action.

There have been many times when she has been close to death. She had a seizure that lasted approximately 30 to 45 minutes and she was then in a coma. She was really very sick and they expected her to die. Another time she had back surgery on a Tuesday; on Thursday she filled up with fluid and her heart rate dropped, and breathing was very shallow. They called us back to ICU and told us they had done all they could.

There have been several times when she has stopped breathing and come close to dying. Once her lung collapsed and she couldn't get her breath and they were never sure she'd make it. However, through all of these experiences she has come through because people have prayed for her and because my Lord saw fit to let her live another day. She is here with us now.

There have been times when emotionally I have been down. Sometimes I feel like I should be able to do more. You feel as a mother you have let your child down. There are the feelings of guilt. Why me? How do I change things? I think as a family we should work on letting go a little more, and also saying it's okay to be angry about her disability sometimes.

Her dad is angry, confused, hurt, and feels guilty. Her brother feels sorry for her, confused as to why this has happened. Her sister is embarrassed by her, and very much afraid of her dying. Me, her mom: I'm confused, hurt, questioning lots of things. Her father used to be pretty mellow, easy-going. Since she was born, he became very stressed, wired up and ready to explode at the drop of a hat and resented our financial situation because of her disability. He is involved in all aspects of her care. He does a wonderful job, and as time has gone on he has become less angry and resentful and has truly learned to love her in a special way.

Sometimes her siblings are afraid to be angry because they are afraid that something might happen to her. The embarrassment they sometimes feel makes them uncomfortable. And their lives are disrupted whenever she is in the hospital.

I don't get mad at God because I trust God to do what's best for me. He knows what I need so that I can be what He wants me to be. And, without having a child with a disability I would never have got to this point in life. He knows what tomorrow is going to bring.

What is going to happen to her if her dad and I are not around to take care of her?

People automatically think that birth defects are caused by something you have done, and this is not always true. This is hard to answer when people ask.

I'm afraid that sometimes things will become way too fast-paced for the disabled, and that society will feel that the disabled have no contribution to make.

A 13-year-old brother writes:

I'm sad because she doesn't get to do as much as I do. She's different than most kids and she gets to do lots of things other kids don't. She is funny. She was born that way. Because God wanted her that way [disabled]. I'm afraid because she may die. Listen to what I have to say. That helps.

And their ten-year-old sister:

It's kind of good and bad [the disability]. I'm sad sometimes because she can't run and play when we do. I'm happy because we get to learn about prople with disabilities and and how different her life is sometimes than mine. [Why disabled?] Because God wanted her to be like that. I'm afraid because she might die or get really, really sick. Listen to me when I need to talk about it [what helps].

IT'S WONDERFUL TO BE AROUND HER.
IT MAKES LIFE WORTH LIVING AND SHE LOVES ME

Six years ago this 64-year-old woman became the grandmother to a baby girl with an open spine and other severe physical problems:

Her breathing is bad and she doesn't walk. Speech, digestion, her kidneys and bowels do not work properly. She is very bright and intelligent. The day she was born, the memory stuck in my mind was when she had to have oxygen and when realizing she had stomach trouble. The day she was born she had such a large head that you could not see her eyes because of the fluid.

When I babysit, I suction her as needed, hook her up to her monitor, and take care of feedings. I have stayed with her in the hospital on several occasions. I can suction her, but the rest is done by her mother or the nurses. When I first started babysitting, sometimes I was afraid of her stopping breathing and having to take her to the hospital.

Her life has been at risk several times. The worst I think was when she had a seizure. It lasted almost a half hour and she almost died. While the seizure was going on she shook real bad, bit her tongue, and was very dysfunctional. Dealing with the nurses was very frustrating.

At first, I really didn't want to deal with it and I thought it would be easier to go to sleep and not wake up.

I hate it when people stare. People should ask and not just stare. They pity the handicapped. They should not always want to do for the disabled person, let them do for themselves.

It was a shock when we first learned she had a disability. There was some discouragement, some anger, questioning as to why, and sometimes sadness because I wanted to be able to change things for her but realized I couldn't. It's wonderful to be around her. It makes life worth living and she loves me.

I wish I would have learned better how to take care of her and how to do more for her. I should have had more training than I did.

Without God and my faith, I could not cope. He makes everything seem better.

The disability gave me a broader outlook on life. My son didn't deal with it; he blocked it out. My daughter was sad, and did lots of questioning. Natalie's family was made stronger; it drew them closer together, caused their faith to be stronger, made the siblings love in a different way. They are closer to each other and have learned a little more love and understanding. They have not been able to have and do things that they normally could. When she is in the hospital, it has an impact on them.

I know God has a reason for whatever He does and He makes no mistakes. When she was first born I was so upset over the effect it had on her dad that I was angry at God. The hardest thing to accept is her inability to walk and her speech impairment. With God all things are possible and maybe someday she will be able to get rid of the trach and oxygen.

My fear for the future is that someone will mistreat her. I have learned not to take life for granted.

ONLY YESTERDAY

Stories told by individuals and family members who have been challenged by a disability for just a few weeks up to five years. It seems like "only yesterday" when their journey began....

NO ONE CAN SEEM TO PUT ANY NAME TO WHAT IS WRONG WITH HIM

This 33-year-old mother cannot seem to find the help she needs:

My son is five. He is not potty trained and he does not speak in sentences. He seems to just now be starting to try to talk. He does not test easily, so trying to get an idea of what he knows is not easy. No one can seem to put any name to what is wrong with him.

Frustration abounds. I have been through six pediatricians who would only say, "Wait six months or a year and he'll grow out of it," or want to check his hearing. This child has had his hearing checked more times than I can count. When I finally find a doctor that is willing to test him, my insurance company says no. This could be a pre-existing condition. Meanwhile, a little boy waits. My big problem in trying to get help for him is that no one seems to be able to return my phone calls. Right now I've been trying for two months to get my son to see a psychologist that my insurance company says I have to go to.

People are real good at saying, "If he were mine I would…" Sometimes they act like he's lazy or defiant, when neither are true. I just don't say anything anymore.

I can accept the disability. What I have a hard time dealing with is the "professionals." I hate the constant apathy.

I am a Catholic. I believe if you have a problem you face it head on. I don't sit around and wait for God's will. Nor, is my god a mean god. I don't feel blaming God or anyone is helpful.

THEY SAY, "GOD ONLY GIVES YOU WHAT YOU CAN HANDLE." SOME DAYS I CAN'T

Five years ago this 36-year-old mother gave birth to a baby with cerebral palsy. It has been a constant challenge for her and a stress on her marriage:

Ted has spastic quadriplegic cerebral palsy due to prenatal distress. As an infant he was very fussy and sensitive to noise and also to touch. Looking back at baby pictures his legs were always bent at the knees. He was very stiff and hard to diaper also. He underwent a rhizotomy August of 1990. Since then the leg spasticity has greatly improved, although his arms are still very involved. Putting on winter coats is a hard task and also buttondown shirts. His arms bend at the elbows and come up towards his chest. Finding a walker has been very difficult with his arm involvement. He has good control of the right hand but not much grasp with the left.

The disability is due to prenatal distress. There was meconium-stained fluid and no beat-to-beat variability of heart rate with contractions. The doctors noted after birth some type of utero placental insufficiency, causing his placenta and cord to show signs of starvation. Ted was also born in the middle of a blizzard which added to the problems. They were unable to transport him 30 miles until ten hours later. A blood sugar problem was handled as best they could until IV therapy could be started.

Most difficult is sitting in therapy sessions. It becomes such a power struggle. Also in clinics they hurry the kids through without much discussion. It's hard, just the constant reminder of his disability; they dwell on what needs to be, instead of what has been gained.

Ted was at risk after birth because he would not eat. It was a battle to get an ounce of formula into his little stomach. He also had colic and colitis to add to the problem. His weight gain has always been slow but we continue to see slight increases. After that point everything went pretty well until the rhizotomy. He lost a pint of blood during surgery and this also was a very stressful time. Also, morphine was given and we understand it is a fine line to adjust the dosage. Anyway, they over medicated and everything shut down. It was very frightening when he stopped breathing. We were lucky everything went all right and other serious problems were avoided. Five days post-op therapy was started. It was terribly difficult to justify therapy with a five-to-six inch incision on his back. I thought he would open up. But they were right. Those kids bounce right back and must be re-trained quickly.

It gets so stressful. I feel the majority of the work is on me. I have no time for myself. My life has been put on hold for five years. It all becomes so overwhelming. My occupational therapist said it best, "It's too bad you can't be just a parent. You have to be everything, legs, hands, therapist, etc."

I have always found it difficult when people ask if Ted can walk, right in front of him. He is a very bright little boy. But it's possible that it hurts us more than him. The majority of people have no idea how much time and patience it takes to care for a physically-challenged child or adult. I also have a difficult time with him as a "special" child, and you are "special" parents. Yes, Ted is special but I don't feel that way about myself. Some days I'm not very proud of my feelings. When I stop and think about it, I guess another thing that people say that bothers me is "God only gives you what you can handle." Some days I can't.

When people just listen and understand how frustrating it can be, it helps. The people that work with physically-challenged children do seem to be the most understanding. They have some idea of the time and energy it requires.

I should have listened and found caregivers for him at an earlier age. But in a small town that is a problem. It is like a roller coaster ride. There are highs and lows. In our small town you are sheltered from disabilities. There are only two other kids in our school system. But the majority are "normal." You are faced with what should have been. Then off to Des Moines to the doctor and a stay at the Rainbow House, and you find you are very, very lucky. That was a turning point for me and my husband. Sitting in doctors' offices, clinic, etc., you see many more problems. Then you step back and are grateful.

I think I wish I could be working outside the home. I had always worked up until Ted's birth, and it has been a hard adjustment. We could use the income, and the extra self-worth to me would be a help. Also just getting out.

Our family does lack communication. I also get so wrapped up in Ted, I forget there are other things in life. My husband and I lack time to talk about other subjects. We need to start going to church. That might be a way to strengthen our family.

From my standpoint, my husband has been the most affected. He still has not accepted Ted's cerebral palsy. I feel I have, but my life has by far changed the most. I have given up the most. All grandparents have accepted, but Grandpa just wishes Ted could walk. We all wish that, of course. My sister does a great deal of worrying. Being eight years older than myself, she cared for me as a child and doesn't like everything to be so difficult. Also, she has a son one year older, and I have always felt that it makes it hard when we are together. The closeness of their ages and what could be. She can't stand to see him go through all of this.

I made a mistake of not making my husband care for Ted as a baby. He didn't want to or claimed to not know how. I feel he was angry when he did finally have to. I was told he wouldn't keep him again. This is better now, but I would tell other mothers to make fathers get involved early.

I wish I could say it has brought us closer together, but I can't. I hope our marriage can weather the storm. I've always been glad we were married 12 years before Ted was born or I don't know if we'd still be together. We have lost our social lives. Finding babysitters is awful difficult and as a baby we didn't ever leave him, and now it is even harder. I devote my life to Ted and don't really know who I am except for his mother, therapist, legs and arms.

He relates really well with adults. I think being an only child and having teachers and therapists since an early age has contributed. I worry about his relationships with peers. He is a very vocal child and kids don't always follow him. He is a child that grabs your heart and holds on tight.

I guess I sometimes need someone to blame and lash out at. I think to myself, "Why him?" And, "Why us?" It took us five years to get pregnant and then, "Why us?" I used to blame myself. The guilt got to be too much for me to handle and I finally decided I didn't cause this.

Yes, there are times I just can't continue. Trying to get everything scheduled for him and keep a household running. Yelling at a five-year-old when I get frustrated. How must he feel?

Don't take anything for granted. Like picking up a Cheerio. Such a small thing can be a major accomplishment for a physically-challenged child or adult.

I THINK THE FUTURE LOOKS BRIGHT...HE CAN CONQUER THE HARDEST CHALLENGE AND REACH THE FARTHEST STAR

A 38-year-old father talks about his son who was born five years ago:

He has cerebral palsy. The cause is unknown. Possibly attributed to complications around birth. There was partial deterioration of the umbilical cord. Low blood sugar count. He was born in a snowstorm, delaying a C-section until the surgeon could get to the hospital. There is tightness in both arms and both legs. An inability to perform fine motor skills.

I think my memories are similar to any first-time father, gazing at a newborn son in a hospital nursery.

Handing our son to a surgical nurse was always the most difficult.

He spent a half year in school with other physically-challenged children. Then two years in pre-school with both disabled and nondisabled children. The biggest change we've seen is in development of social skills.

Every parent has guilt trips at one time or another, but emotional pain is something you learn to live with.

Please stop and visit instead of stop and stare. Give the disabled person a chance to show that he is a real person with real dreams and expectations of his own.

A disability puts an emotional strain on the marriage, on accepting it and learning to live with it. Adjusting is hard for everyone concerned.

It makes you become more aware of the way you look at other disabled persons and how their everyday lives differ from able-bodied persons.

[If you could pick another disability, what would it be and why?] If I could change or pick, I would pick no disability.

As every day passes, you see things that you would have done different the day before. Part of living with the disability is learning what should be done and what should not be.

The family helps by giving each of us a chance to get away occasionally for a little time for ourself. I would like for my wife to have more time to do things she enjoys and a chance to get away more often.

My wife was forced to retire from her job to devote her time to caring for our child. She has lost contact with many things and friends because of full devotion to doing all she could for the child. I had to learn to accept a different lifestyle than was planned. I'm trying to understand how my wife felt about leaving the workforce, losing her financial contribution to the family. Our social life has become nearly nonexistent.

[Do you ever get mad at God because of the disability?] "I don't feel angry" are the correct words for describing what she felt. I believe not knowing what caused the cerebral palsy, learning to accept it, deal with it, and to do everything we can to help improve his condition has brought more frustration than anger.

Any family that has a medical problem is affected financially. We are fortunate to have good insurance with my employer. We have also used Medicaid and some services offered through social services. We have set up a trust fund in his name and have enlisted the skills of a financial planner to manage its monetary value.

We have talked about parts of our lives that have been most affected: our marriage, social life, personal lives, what we have missed by being committed to his care. We make decisions together, expressing our love for each other and to our son. It's hard not to be able to identify with "normal" developments and milestones that other parents enjoy.

Until he was about three years old, he would not accept anyone else to have him but his parents. Fortunately, this has greatly improved the last two years.

I do not believe that God would intentionally inflict a disability upon any person. I don't get mad at God because I don't feel that I am being punished by God just because I have a son who is not as able-bodied as we would have hoped he would be. If I were one to place blame on someone it would probably be the weather conditions at the time of birth.

My biggest regret is that my son may not be able to enjoy every aspect of life that other boys enjoy as they are growing up.

I think the future looks bright. With the computer age being introduced to children as young as two or three, the opportunity to enjoy life to their fullest abilities will be a goal they can achieve with the help and encouragement that we can provide. He can conquer the hardest challenge and reach the farthest star.

My fear is that we have failed to do our part of the process of giving him every chance at living a fulfilling life. We are hoping that he will be able to be a self-supporting adult able to live his own life.

LIFE IS PRECIOUS, I DON'T TAKE IT FOR GRANTED

Five years ago this 35-year-old mother's son was diagnosed with hydro-
nephrosis. For five years she has lived her life one day at a time:
"Mom, why did this happen to me? Will I always be like this?" That is the
most difficult question for a mother to hear. Sometimes I don't always understand why this is happening, and why not me, instead of him, but I've never lost
faith. It has opened our eyes to how precious life really is. We don't take it for
granted. God is a very big part in our life.

Our son has hydronephrosis, a chronic illness which started when he was ten
months old. His urethral valves were blocked when I was pregnant with him
which therefore caused all the urine to back up which resulted in kidney damage.
Tyler has had two surgeries and kidney infections since then and is on five different types of medication. He is incontinent due to the surgeries.

Due to Tyler's young age he has never been alone during any testing, treatment, hospitalization, or office visit. Even though we have two other children we
always have thought that it was critical that he would never be alone—even when
we had to travel 120 miles for his surgeries and weeks of hospitalization. Family
members and friends really pitched in and helped so that we were able to do this.
We have watched many IVs, blood tests, catheters, ultra-sounds, etc., being done
on our child—however, now that he is getting older and used to the procedures,
it is easier than when he was a baby. I was always glad that I was there sleeping in
a chair in his hospital room at night—especially when they were understaffed
with nurses, such as the night his IV came out in the middle of the night and he
woke in a pool of blood. Yes, it was worth every minute.

The first surgery was done when he was diagnosed at ten months. His blood
levels were still high and his blood pressure was very high. They were at this time
considering another type of surgery but Tyler was not strong enough or in very
good health to have another surgery. We just hoped and prayed. He pulled
through. Our lives changed—we had blood tests done every day and also his
blood pressure checked. A year later he had another blockage. Two years later he
got a kidney infection. Each episode was a setback. But he pulled through.

I handle all the crises really well in the hospital when I have to be strong, but
when I get home and reality sets in, that's when I fall apart. Dad was saddened,
and felt helpless. The two brothers worried, and missed us being together. The
grandparents helped with watching the other two kids and I know it puts a strain
on them even though they have never complained. I felt torn as to where I should
be.

I feel some organizations have good intentions, but the people there really just go there to have someone to talk to about their own experience—in some instances I've left worse or more down than when I came. Being that treatment was done out of the area, when we came back home to our town, I felt I lost a lot of support because I couldn't find another parent who had gone through a similar situation. The support groups were too general. But then we have been very fortunate to have family and friends. Being together as a family is more important than anything money could buy. They don't have to say anything—just a hug. I'm a very sensitive and loving individual. Sometimes I feel I love my kids too deeply. Life is precious, I don't take it for granted. I really do live day-to-day.

Even though we have insurance, being on a single income is hard. We have not used any assistance programs because Tyler is not classified as disabled. I worry about long-term care because of the pre-existing condition clause in so many insurance companies. I stay at home because I want to be the one to administer his medications and be there for him, like helping out at school in the classroom. I wish I could be there to always protect him from the teasing (wearing diapers), and to explain his condition to other people. I'm his mother. I love him no matter what.

Not knowing the outcome is hard. Will he need a kidney transplant and be incontinent for the rest of his life? Are we getting the best medical care we can? Why do I have to see my child suffer?

And the three children speak. The 10-year-old brother:

I hope he outgrows it. Sometimes when he's sick, I feel sad. I laugh sometimes when he wets the bed, even though I know I shouldn't. I'm afraid that he might die before me. That he will be in the hospital for a long time.

An an eight-year-old sister:

I don't think about it that much. I feel sad because he is the only one in the class who has it and I don't want him to feel left out. I don't know why, some people are just different. I'm afraid that they'll have to take his kidneys out and put new ones in. Talk about it, hold me.

And the five-year-old son with the disability:

I'm sad because I want to be like the other kids, but it's not so bad.

CHILDREN ARE HERE TO SHOW YOU HOW TO BE GOOD PARENTS BECAUSE YOU'VE NEVER BEEN PARENTS BEFORE

This 32-year-old mother of four children talks about her five-year-old daughter, who has multiple disabilities including a heart murmur and mental retardation:

The most difficult aspect was not getting any answers. Having never experienced this before, I didn't know what to ask. Therefore, I didn't get any answers. In the medical profession, a lot is expected that anyone should just know.

Our biggest fear with Tami is her lack of fear. She has no inhibitions and acts as though everyone is here just to love her and protect her. She will walk up to anyone, go anywhere, fall into anything simply because she doesn't have the mental capacity to understand all the implications. Because of her sensitive gag reflex, she has been very prone to vomiting. When this occurs, she will turn blue and not be able to breathe for a time. She always pulls through, but occasionally it has been scary.

It would be nice to be able to talk with someone that follows the whole history of our child and have discussions when the need arises, and can answer some questions and help direct us to know what steps to take.

She helps all of us keep a better perspective about what really matters in life. Our children are always reminded that they are learning things that others may never learn.

This is an ongoing process. We are daily affected by the disability. But as normal children grow and develop and go through their own stages it's hard to pinpoint exact details. It seems everyone has different needs at different times. That's what makes it all so challenging at times.

The physical care she needs is close supervision. Each member of the family knows this. They know they have to take the responsibility of caring for their own things and putting things away or Tami gets them and she doesn't understand. This does develop into anger oftentimes, but the blame is not hers. We try to remember and express that perhaps we don't like what happened, but we still love that person.

Sometimes the responsibility is too much so someone else helps carry the load or they vent their feelings and we have lots of talks. Sometimes she is just in their way, and Mom or Dad have to help give that child some space of their own.

Tami looks normal and the older she gets the more is expected from her. Sometimes we just don't feel like explaining about her everywhere we go, so sometimes it seems like we answer for her a lot. At five or six years, her peers are developing major play skills. Her inability to communicate makes it so she doesn't have children come to play with her.

We are LDS (Mormons) and feel that she was sent here to get a body. She doesn't need to prove anything to anybody. She doesn't need to become "normal." She will return to our Heavenly Father, but as long as she's here we may as well learn as much as we can from her because we can only become better from this experience. We feel like she was sent here for us and not the other way around. So we are blessed. I know she was a perfect spirit in the pre-existence, and I will have the chance to raise her as a normal child later, if the need be. I know she knows more than me, because the veil is thin for her. But as for me, my eyes have been closed to the pre-existance for now.

Why suicide? What would that solve? It would make matters worse for those remaining.

Have I felt like I was going crazy? Perhaps, but not in the real sense. Being a parent isn't an easy task and sometimes we do things we regret doing that makes us wonder why we did such a stupid thing. But like our oldest son said just yesterday, "Children are here to show you how to be good parents because you've never been parents before."

Everyone has disabilities. Some are just more visible than others. It's most important to learn how to live life to it's fullest in spite of those disabilities.

We don't know what the future will bring. That is the topic of many conversations as we plan our life together as a married couple. We put ourselves in different scenarios. "What if?" Because no one knows. We plan on keeping her home with us as long as possible, knowing also that we may not be able to.

Three children in the family share their experiences. A nine-year-old sister:

[I'm] sad, because she can't do as much as we can and because she's my sister and I don't like people to call her names. Sometimes she makes me laugh. She has a disability because the Heavenly Father wants her surely to come back to him. In the future I think people will laugh at her and make fun of her. [What helps?] Tell me that she will go up to the Heavenly Father and that she won't do the wrong things. Hugs help!

And an 11-year-old brother:

[The disability] doesn't really bother me. I have gotten used to it. I'm not sad because it doesn't bother me any more. I have kind of grown used to it. [Joking] If someone makes comments, they aren't alive very long. I laugh if she does funny things. Maybe born too early? I'm not afraid of the future. I know I will protect her or I will get someone to protect her.

A seven-year-old brother:

[I'm] sad, because she can't do all the things I do. I'm happy when we laugh and she laughs. I'm afraid she might get hurt. She needs me to protect her, love her, and hug her.

I FEEL TRAPPED, NOT APPRECIATED, AND SELFISH
BECAUSE I DEMAND TIME FOR MYSELF

Four years ago this 48-year-old mother found out her son had muscular dystrophy:

At every visit we must repeat the same information up to four times. It just drills into us the seriousness of the situation and time. We have to be absolutely sure each new person gets the information because most doctors in this area have never dealt with M.D. before. In a hospital it is aggravating to be made to repeat it so many times. It hurts emotionally. Having to face the brutal reality that he has M.D. and that despite our very best efforts, it continues to get worse. Away from the medical world, we can create a "fantasy" life and have many enjoyable times.

It's not helpful when people start talking about someone else that has a severe physical problem. I know there are others who are in worse shape, but this isn't easy either! It's not a normal life and we struggle to make it a good life. I don't want to hear about someone worse because what most people don't understand is that this is HARD enough and in our case, it's going to get a lot harder. M.D. doesn't get better, it gets worse. I don't want pity but I would like acknowledgement that I'm working with a difficult situation that saps my energy.

Don't tell me about someone else who really is worse off in an effort to make me feel that I don't have it so rough. I play that game with myself all the time and am grateful not to be in the other person's shoes. But having another person tell me that is like making light of our problems, especially when they aren't dealing with any disability in their own home. They have no idea what the daily struggle is like.

Don't tell him he CAN'T do something. He likes to try and thinks he does it, even if it is terrible. In his mind he DID IT.

I no longer feel carefree and joyful. I often fight depression. I have to work at finding happiness. I resent demands from others. I feel trapped, not appreciated, and selfish because I demand time for myself.

When this happened to us, each family member became depressed for awhile. Our daughter had to face the possibility that she might be a carrier of M.D. We in a sense "gave up" the child we thought we had. My husband worries about extra expenses, and I must learn to be a caretaker and a nurse. We had to sell our home because he needed a wheelchair, and it became necessary to make modifications in our new home. We are struggling to find money for a special van. Travel is now limited.

We encourage many activities and conversations. As a result many people go out of their way to speak to him or open a door. But as he becomes more physically limited, his friends come over to play less often. He seldom is invited to parties, because of the difficulty of getting him inside or his inability to play the same games.

At this age, he would not have received as much special attention (radio, newspapers, special treatment at amusement parks). He would be gaining independence rather than dependency.

Once in a while I blame myself. I always wanted a "special" child that was extra intelligent or achieved a highly-respected job, and I was given a very difficult "special" child. It doesn't make sense but that's the way it is.

I HAVE NO EMOTIONAL PAIN!

This 31-year-old mother of three children gave birth to a baby girl with Down's Syndrome four years ago:

Children with Down's are about 15 times more likely to develop leukemia and that possibility concerns me, although I don't dwell on it.

I have no emotional pain! It hasn't really affected me emotionally. I guess I am personally much more accepting of people's limitations, but I don't have any sadness or anything. I am simply the busy mother of three young children, one of whom happens to have Down's Syndrome.

If I knew now what I did when my daughter was born, I would not have been upset at all when I initially learned she had Down's Syndrome. She's a joy and a regular kid. It's not an issue in our lives.

[It has affected the family] The same. We all accepted it and went on with life.

Really, we only discuss it in passing. Down's Syndrome has not affected us much.

HE IS VERY HAPPY, LOVING AND SPECIAL

Four years ago this 30-year-old mother gave birth to a baby boy with Down's Syndrome. Her second child, a girl, two years later, was born without any disabilities:

Our son has Down's Syndrome. He is developmentally delayed in all areas (speech, motor, fine motor). He also has physical characteristics, some which require medical attention and monitoring. He is also mentally impaired.

I was 25 and he was my first baby. My first memory of him was when he was delivered. I fell in love with him immediately and felt that all was as it should be. I didn't know until several hours after his birth that he had Down's Syndrome.

Some doctors have been very arrogant and ignorant. We really try hard to find doctors who will work with us. My biggest frustration are those who only know the stereotypes of Down's Syndrome. I wish there was a specialist who could provide more answers and guidance.

There will always be some degree of emotional pain. I guess I try to use that pain to learn from and to grow from. Of course, there are some days that are very difficult but we muddle through.

I questioned if something was wrong with me that I would produce a child who wasn't "normal." I felt angry at friends who couldn't understand what we were going through. I felt I was being punished. But in the long run it has made me stronger and more confident in my beliefs and more sensitive to those with disabilities. I still feel overwhelmed by the responsibility and when things are especially stressful, I get very sad, angry and irritable. Because of the extra demands, it has been difficult remaining close friends to some we had before his birth. We felt they didn't really understand what we were going through on a daily basis. It was sad, but we drifted apart.

He is very happy, loving and special. He tries so hard at all he does. We enjoy just sitting close to him and taking him to parks, zoos, etc. The expression on his face and his hugs make us feel very lucky and happy.

I wish I didn't have to worry so much about his education. I wish I didn't have all the extra meetings and "battles" that sometimes go with it.

He was our first child. My husband and I were affected emotionally and dealt with sadness for a long time. We felt isolated from friends who just didn't understand. We've had to find information about what raising a child with special needs entails. We are currently moving for a second time in his four years so that he can be in a program suited to his special needs, so, of course, there has been a financial change. Our daughter, age two, is growing up very flexible and loving toward her brother. We know that our family doesn't center around him alone, but while she is so young, we feel these moves won't hurt her emotionally. We both had to change our plans and our ideas about raising this child. When major changes take place, people are affected.

We have not qualified for any financial assistance programs. Until last year my insurance was paying for private speech therapy. It no longer does. We paid for it awhile but it became too expensive. While we work full-time, our sitter takes him to school, and used to to therapies, so we had to pay extra for these services. There are more doctors for him to see, and sometimes our insurance doesn't cover the whole fee. We have to make sure he has certain shoes, so that's an extra cost. Financially, a disabled family member is more costly. At present we have no long-term financial plans for our son.

Kids will often comment on either how he speaks or how little he speaks. I think he is aware there are differences. He's very shy when meeting new kids and doesn't always play with kids he knows. He just appears to have an awareness that things are more difficult for him.

Sometimes life gets crazy and overwhelming and I wonder if I'm being punished for something. Then I feel angrier because I can't think of anything so awful that I've done. However, it's not just the disability that makes me at times feel angry and cheated, but it certainly contributes.

The feeling of being different and the misconceptions people have is hard, but also very hard is keeping up with a good medical schedule and finding doctors who are knowledgeable yet don't take advantage of your situation.

At times I find it a full-time job, etc., exhausting and overwhelming. At those times I am easily set off and lose my cool. When that happens, I feel I am going crazy because I can't control my tears and say some bad things.

Things do seem to get better, although there is a long road ahead where stereotypes are concerned. I hope our son will be able to reside in a group home and to hold a job in a setting that isn't necessarily an organization that has a majority of disabled workers.

I'm afraid of his vulnerability and I wonder if he'll be accepted.

WE'VE LEARNED, HURT, AND GROWN

Four years ago this 27-year-old mother gave birth to a baby girl diagnosed with Cornelia deLange Syndrome:

[My earliest memory of her is] The moment they showed her to me in the delivery room. She was so small and had so much hair. They said she had a cleft palate and missing digits, and I didn't know what they meant!

I have been involved since she was born. I spend almost every day at the hospital with her while she is there. She spends less days in the hospital each year, last year only 158 days. Our regular hospital is family. We are treated by nurses, the doctor, administration to housekeeping with respect and friendliness as you would from your own family.

At times when things are very touch and go, and her death seems near, it is at this hospital with these people that I want to be. There my child with a disability is treated as their own and loved. We've had experiences at larger hospitals where they have treated me like I was in the way and why give my child respect: she doesn't know anything anyway, she's disabled.

It has been difficult to learn how to patiently wait during surgery and how to willingly hand my child to the OR nurse and turn and walk away.

She has at two separate times had a malfunction in her central nervous system controlling her thermostat. This left her temperature out of control; it could go up five degrees in a matter of 30 minutes, and at one time, it dropped 12 degrees in an hour and a half. That is the closest she has been to death. Since the cause is not known, there is no way to prevent it from happening again.

With sudden temperature changes, she has seizures where she stops breathing. She has coded once officially and once without the code called. We have since listed her as a no-code: no medications, ventilators, CPR; only hand-bagged ventilation till we as parents can arrive if we're not already there, and till the doctor can arrive. She has cerebral atrophy, it is not known if it causes these problems or if it is the result. She has had pneumonia countless times and because of this she has severely scarred lungs. We never know when they will cause other systems to shut down.

She has been taught homebound since six months of age. She has a wonderful homebound teacher and wonderful physical therapist. Her OT and speech pathologist have been changed several times and have not been constant. We have problems because she is hospitalized so much and it makes it difficult to receive services.

The social worker at the hospital after the birth: she was the greatest!

There are some people that treat you as an outcast and as people that would be better off if they would die.

Other families at the hospital with "chronic" kids have been great. One mother, when our daughter was first born, reminded me that she was a baby first, a disabled child second.

How has it affected me emotionally? My daughter was not the child I imagined, so of course I mourn for the child I lost when she was born. People didn't realize that I lost a baby when my baby was born. The thought of dealing with and making decisions about what's best for someone else the rest of my life scares me sometimes. The effects of this daughter on her sibling and what she has and will go through worries me.

I wouldn't want any other disability. I don't want this one. All disabilities are bad. They all have something better or worse than the one before.

I can live with the disability, except there are children with this disability that don't have the serious health problems my child has. It would be nice to have a healthy disabled child.

My life has changed to almost the opposite of what it was, and I still mourn for my lost child. We've learned, hurt, and grown.

[I worry about] The uncertainty of the future and the fear of her death. Not because of her dying, which is only a matter of time. But how it will affect everyone that loves her.

And a five-year-old sister shares:

I think that she doesn't like it. If I was her, I wouldn't like it [the disability]. I'm sad because I think she might die some day. That she might not be able to talk ever. That she'll never get to do what I do. Sometimes I feel happy because she can do some things that other kids with disabilities can't do. I worry about the things she might not be able to do and that she might not be here [death]. [When I'm sad] tell me she might keep well, tell me stuff that she might be able to do because it makes me feel good to know what she can do.

SHE SOMEHOW DOESN'T COUNT AS MUCH AS A NORMAL CHILD

This 35-year-old mother tells of her daughter, who was diagnosed with microcephalus at 13 months of age, and has a severe expressive language delay:

I fear every time my baby gets sick that it will make her too weak to fight any more. She is already very frail. I get this sick feeling that the doctors will let her die because of their prediction about her life. I get the feeling that doctors feel that she somehow doesn't count as much as a normal child, that somehow her pain is less and her life not worth as much as the normal child.

Cara does not speak at all. Her eyes began to cross inward at ten-to-12 months. No known cause. By accident, I discovered a few notes in my baby's medical records that several other doctors had noticed something and suggested to my baby's doctor that she be taken to children's hospital for further testing. The doctor had made notes as early as two months that he noticed her head was not growing, but this was never mentioned to me. I was later told that the skull closed too early and therefore the brain was unable to grow.

I was very upset and demanded that every test be run that they could think of. Everything came back "normal." I was told, "She is just a little small and slow for her age. She'll be fine. Take her home and love her, Mommy." So, life went on.

I had to put up a big fight to even get an appointment to even see any doctor. I did not care if the insurance didn't cover it, I would pay the visit myself. The most frightening time was when we were asking questions about her, but not getting answers. Why was she doing this and that? Where should we go for help? We could not get the insurance company to approve visits to doctors. Everyone seemed to be afraid of her. I felt we wasted a lot of time just watching and waiting, while the doctors kept saying she was fine, just a little small and slow. By the time they had changed their minds, it was too late.

My husband and I have drifted apart. He works and pays for everything I want to do for Cara. Sometimes I believe God gave me Cara so I would never be alone. One time I charged $7,000 on four credit cards to buy her clothes, shoes, hair bows, anything to make her the cutest dressed-up kid around, hoping no one would realize anything was wrong with her.

An 11-year-old sister talks about the disability:

I am sad because I feel like she will be teased her whole life. It makes me happy that she is learning and she won't be as slow as she is now. She was born too early. I am afraid she might not learn enough and she will never be able to feed or dress herself and will have to have someone help her. You can't do anything. I have to live with that.

And a 13-year-old sister:

I am sad because she doesn't know right from wrong and she can't understand the things I know. I am sad because she can't talk, "why can't she talk, I don't know". I am afraid because we never know what is going to happen to us and people will make fun of her if we aren't there to take care of her. Teach me something Cara knows when I'm feeling sad.

SOMETIMES I THINK IF I ATTEMPTED SUICIDE, MY HUSBAND WOULD THEN KNOW WHAT I GO THROUGH AND HE WOULD HELP MORE

Two years ago this 33-year-old mother gave birth to Leigh. Their lives have been very difficult:

My daughter was born with her disabilities, but all the doctors still have no idea why. Leigh is severely developmentally delayed. She has very low muscle tone. She will be two this month and still cannot sit up. She also has seizures. She is fed fluids through a G-tube. I will always remember her being taken to the ICU at birth because she was premature.

I am very involved with my daughter's medical care. I stayed with her when she has been hospitalized, because once her apnea monitor went off and no one came to check on her. Another time they forgot to get her her seizure medication. I work with both her physical and occupational therapists so that I can learn how to do different exercises with her. I think doctors' offices need to be a little more sympathetic to how much time we spend in many different doctors' offices. I have had to wait 45 minutes past our appointment time before being seen, which sometimes means we are running late for our next appointment, or there is no time left to even eat or go to the bathroom.

The most difficult aspect was when I knew there was something wrong with my baby and my pediatrician kept putting me off.

Just before she was a year old she had gone to bed fine, but when I woke her the next morning she was burning with fever. I was afraid she would convulse because of the seizures so I called an ambulance. By the time we got to the hospital her temp was 106. She had pneumococcal pneumonia. I didn't realize how close I had come to losing her till a week later when a nurse explained how some people can die within 24 hours if they don't receive treatment. It turns out that she did not swallow properly and the fluids were going down into her lungs. I had been telling my pediatrician that I thought her reflux was getting worse and that I would like her to see a gastroenterologist, but he kept telling me to wait. It turns out that the specialist I went to told me her lung damage was irreversible and that she needed a G-tube for fluids.

I usually just want to go to sleep and hope that I'll wake up and it will all have been a bad dream. I see other babies and cry because they are so much younger than my daughter, but they are able to do so much more. She is totally dependent on me. Sometimes I think I could just run away and rest. If I had known what would happen, I would not have planned this pregnancy.

I wish we could do things with the other children like we used to, but it's very hard to find a babysitter for Leigh.

My oldest daughter had to have counseling. She couldn't understand why our baby was handicapped when I did everything "by the book" during my pregnancy. My husband tried to deny her disabilities for the first year. He kept telling me she would be all right. My life has had to change the most. I still have all the other responsibilities I used to have plus now I have to make sure she gets the best care available.

My parents had to learn CPR along with us before she could come home from the hospital. They were glad they could receive the training.

Her medical bills have been extremely high. If it weren't for the Medicaid program we would have lost everything.

Her siblings want to be able to do things with her and they can't. They get very upset when she is in the hospital because they can't see her.

Usually everyone falls in love with Leigh. She is very beautiful and they tell me she steals their heart away.

Sometime I think why me? But then I think why not? God knows I'll do a good job and I'll still love her in spite of the burden she has caused.

Sometimes I think if I attempted suicide, my husband would then know what I go through and he would help more. But my children need me too much! It's so hard that her future is so limited.

I hate it when people ask us what is wrong with her. I feel so stupid and helpless saying, "We don't know."

A 10-year-old sister speaks:

I don't see her as being different. I love her for being just herself. It makes me sad because she didn't do anything wrong. Why should she have to go through this? She was born this way. I don't know why. Will anyone want to date me [because of her]? Will they accept her or make fun of her? When I feel sad, talk with me and comfort me. Yes, I want a big hug!

Another six-year-old sister:

[I'm] sad, I want her to be like the rest of us. I don't like her being handicapped. I'm afraid something very dangerous will happen to her. Cheer me up by hugging me and telling me everything will be okay.

THE HEALTH CARE SYSTEM IS THE BIGGEST FRUSTRATION

Two years ago this 31-year-old mother's second daughter was diagnosed with cerebral palsy:

I remember asking myself, "What did you do to her? Why was she born so early?" My memories are of holding her, loving her. But seeing her right before the doctor took her to ICU. Calling out her name and her opening up her eyes. It was great! To me she is beautiful anyway!

Our five-year-old daughter had a little hard time with it. She wishes that her sister could play with her. She is still adjusting. We are grateful to be her parents. She has taught our family so much. We want people to be kind to her, smile, and understand. Treat her as if you were the one with the disability. What is hard are the questions and comments, "Aren't you glad you don't have to run after her? I'd sure like to be in a chair and pushed around. I wish I had a stroller like that one. She can't be in this area, she's blocking an aisle."

She does get frustrated and because her mind is fine, she is aware of what she should be doing. But her body won't let her do it.

Medical bills are the hardest. And people are not always willing to work with you. We are in collections with at least four medical bills. The hospital where our daughter was born received over $71,000 from our insurance, but put us in collections for $1,500. Plus they've arranged that they will take our income tax return for the next eight years or until paid. We make monthly payments also.

This is all I know. We take it one day at a time.

And a five-year-old sibling talks:

I think that it's not very good to have a disability. I am sad because I can't play with her with my friends. [I'm mad] Yup, cause my sister has cerebral palsy. I'm afraid because I don't know [what will happen to her].

SHE LOOKS SO NORMAL AND I FIND MYSELF YELLING, "WHAT DO YOU MEAN YOU CAN'T TIE YOUR SHOES?"

Just ten months ago this 40-year-old mother's life was changed dramatically by the closed head injury her 13-year-old daughter experienced on the playground at school:

She was playing field hockey at school and was struck by a stick between her eyes. She then fell back on the pavement. While she was in this huddle, several other blows struck her. The kids were trying to hit the ball and in their excitement didn't realize she was hurt. The teacher was around the corner, and when the children told her that Janet was injured, the teacher told the kids to take her to the office. The kids shook her until she "woke" up and took her to the nurse. The teacher never came over to check on her. The shaking caused a neck injury, since her head was flopping around.

When we picked her up from school she could not walk unassisted. She complained of being dizzy. Even lying down she felt she was falling. At the hospital she was asked to write and draw, and the results were quite infantile. She couldn't answer orientation questions. She managed to fall out of bed in the hospital and when she tried to get up, because of the right side weakness, her right leg turned in and she tore ligaments in her knee and ankle.

I thought she had just had a concussion, and it really "rang her bell." My earliest memory is a social worker patting my hand and asking if I had support. I thought this to be rather melodramatic at the time. Next a neuro-rehab nurse came in with stacks of booklets on head injury. The big clue was when the ER doctor told me they were calling a neurosurgeon. Strangely enough, my thought at the time was I didn't want them to cut her hair. Bizarre concern, wasn't it?

I felt the nurses were overworked. Once, I went to tell a nurse that CNS fluid was coming out of her nose. The nurse ran around trying to find a bottle to collect a sample, and never did get one. Janet had little memory at the time and couldn't tell nurses if she'd urinated or not. At shift change one morning, the head nurse noticed that she hadn't urinated in 30 hours. It was quite obvious, because she couldn't get out of bed and needed a bedpan. Yet no one noticed. This meant she had additional problems and we needed a urologist to boot. I wanted to be present for MRIs, but you couldn't narrow time down with them.

If I went to the hospital at 5 a.m. the neurosurgeon had come in at 4:30 a.m. If I went at 5 p.m. he came in at 11. I felt that my whole life centered on the ten minutes a day that rounds occurred. When she had a photo-evoked EEG, the tech asked me if I was staying in the room. I said yes. Janet started twitching and jerking on the table, and here I am trying to find a nurse or somebody to come and check on her. I felt the most empathetic and efficient medical personnel were in the trauma room.

Before we were done, we were involved with 18 doctors. Everything from a neurosurgeon, pediatric neurologist, pediatric opthamalogist, orthopods, physiatrist, urologists, etc. After discharge and before rehab hospital each one wanted a follow-up visit. I averaged three therapy sessions a day: PT, OT, CT, and 1, 2, or 3 visits to a doctor each day for the month after the hospital and before inpatient rehab in another state. I will say that everyone was very patient with waiting for the three insurance companies to pay. The bills are well over $200,000, and her day therapy is $3,000 per week right now and the psychologist is $250 each week. Fortunately, we are only dealing with a physiatrist right now. What doctors seem to know best about head injury is that they just don't know. The only consultants left out were faith healers and psychics!

Was I going crazy? Oh, call it hysteria. When Janet was discharged from the hospital, I thought I could handle her wheelchair, dressing and feeding her, and her catheter. But the second night home she had a *grand mal* seizure. We were talking and all of a sudden she screamed a sound I've never heard before. She went stiff and then shook violently and then wet her pants and crumbled in a very still lump.

I was home alone, we live in a small town about 20 minutes from a hospital. I thought it faster to drive myself than wait for an ambulance. She was so still. I couldn't lift her to her wheelchair, so I rolled her on to a comforter and dragged her through the house and down the stairs and shoved her in the car.

I went to the edge of Reno to the first casino you come to and started blowing my horn. Security came over and took her to the hospital in a shuttle. They paged my husband at work who came and got me. I sat in the car with my foot shaking so bad I could barely stay on the gas pedal. My body lost control and I started retching and wet myself. I was sure she was dying, she just didn't respond.

She had a small bleed that is common days or weeks after a head injury and things worked out. The ER doctor talked to me like I was real smart. I could rattle off history and tests like a pro. He made me feel like I was very knowledgeable and responsible.

It is like the child you knew has died, and there is this stranger you're to take care of. You don't have time to grieve because from the first minute you've got to be the caregiver. I am so sad for her loss and the loss of some of my dreams for her. I am afraid for her future. Sometimes I'm so angry at her, and it's easy to forget she has problems. She looks so normal and I find myself yelling, "What do you mean you can't tie your shoes?"

I am like a mother bear protecting and advocating for her. I feel burdened and resentful. I feel tired and stressed. I am thrilled at each progress: the day she took halting steps without a walker; when she remembered all the steps to brushing her teeth. I have a lot of guilt over my negative feelings.

Dad held things together initially. Very good with doctors and hospitals. When things got to him, I was then ready to start reading up on head injury and soliciting info on rehab. I called and talked to everyone from medical schools to rehab facilities to call-in talk shows to library and computer services.

Dad hurt worst in the beginning. I was, and still am to a degree in denial.

I provided most of the care. In the beginning it involved lifting her to the wheelchair, helping her to the toilet, brushing her teeth, helping her shower and dress. I had to watch her eat because she wolfed food or choked. She would wander away when she learned to walk. I put bells on all the doors. I would hold her and rock her when the headaches were bad and the medicine never cut the daily pain. Later on, I made lists for her to do things, step-by-step, for washing hair, brushing teeth, changing her sanitary napkin, getting dressed. Her short-term memory was awful. Now I have a big chart that she checks off what she needs to do at night after therapy.

I've been angry a lot. Sometimes I yell at her when she says she can't do something simple. She looks so normal it's easy to forget, and I think you want to forget. I hated that damn heavy wheelchair, and hauling it in and out. I realized, though, that I could really harm her by my anger, so I started seeing a psychologist. I don't think the rehab people realize the load they put on you. The PT wanted her to do balance exercises every night, OT wanted three household chores done by her, CT wanted her to work on a computer, the homebound teacher had homework to supervise. The nightly shower/hair, etc., takes twice as long now. She comes home tired after seven hours of rehab, and it's a fight to get anything done.

When the psychologist wanted her to take a couple of classes at the YWCA for interaction, and to play with a child each day, this was the final straw. I had six hours of stuff to do with her each night after 4:30. All of it important. Finally, we all had to rework the plan. I'm down to a manageable three hours.

At first there were lots of calls and visits from her friends. As the months went on, her friends basically abandoned her, all but one. She didn't remember people and couldn't do their activities. I think the kids were scared. The teacher said the kids were afraid to play on the playground after she got hurt. Although she could have attended birthday parties, she wasn't invited. I think the moms didn't know what to expect of a child with a wheelchair, etc. and didn't know what to say to me, either.

She tells me, "I'm just me, I'm not stupid, I just got injured." She explains herself and her limitations fairly well.

Do I get mad at God?…Why me? Why not me?

I got "crazy" with a doctor. He told me I was being silly to be so worried. He treated Janet with a bored comtempt and I really let him have it.

I fear that when she goes back to school next month in special ed that the cruelty of young adolescents may destroy her. What if she's miserable, what if she gives up?

AUSTIN SHOULDN'T HAVE BEEN PLAYING AROUND WITH THE BAT

A year before becoming involved in our research, this 12-year-old boy had experienced a head injury:

I cant remember have to go to therapy all the time i get lost or cant remeber fhon numbers i cant ride a bike cant run can't jup

at schol was playing hokey got hit with the stik cant remember getin hit

one time i got hit in the head after my head injury at got rely sick and had a cesur went to hospital

I wish they believed me whn i told them i was hurt and was dizzy

you don't get to do stuff you know you did befor

I wish I wouldn't have to go to therapy every day in the summer

Austin shouldn't have been playing around with the bat

TODAY AND TOMORROW

By John S. Campbell, M.D., and John DeFrain, Ph.D.

THE AILING HEALTH CARE SYSTEM

We believe that the preceding narratives illustrate not only how people with disparate health problems and disabilities have common problems complicating their lives, as well as the lives of their families and friends, but that they have very significant variations in their abilities to cope with these challenges. People with similar difficulties may have better or worse outcomes. We are convinced that better health care, psychological care, rehabilitation care, and social support likely would have improved the chances for a better life experience for all these individuals.

We feel the narratives presented in *We Cry Out* of some of the most severely functionally impaired citizens of the United States have wider implications for our health care system. We have documented in Susan Dahl and John DeFrain's research, and cited many references which support the assertion that many suffering chronic illnesses and disabilities are receiving less than optimal care. At the very least, they are experiencing less empathetic and sensitive assistance than they deserve. This is an on-going problem with deep historical roots.

Our health care system is simply not organized adequately to meet the needs of the chronically ill with multiple interacting problems. Professionals are not effectively coordinating their efforts with each other. They are often failing to understand the need to individualize their management plans, not adequately taking into account their clients' perceptions of their own needs. This is most obviously true in their failure to understand and respectfully assist with the emotional, psychological, and social facets of client problems.

Our aging population has an increasing number of citizens with one or more chronic illness, condition, or disability. No one ages without something eventually going awry. Our national success with high technology in medical care has contributed to this scenario by keeping many people alive who would in the past have died. Because of the chaotic health care delivery, finance, and insurance systems, many U.S. citizens are unable to afford or have inadequate health insurance coverage. More and more people, often the elderly, are having to choose between buying food or paying their rent and seeing their physicians or taking their increasingly expensive medicines. Dr. LeBow's book, *Health Care Meltdown*: *Confronting the Myths and Fixing Our Failing System*, comprehensively explores all these issues and offers his well-considered solutions, based on years of frontline medical practice as well as extensive research and consultation all over the world on health-care delivery systems. [21] Other books also document these critical problems in our healthcare system but suggest different solutions to these problems.

NO SIGNIFICANT IMPROVEMENT HAS OCCURRED

It is discouraging that no dramatic improvements have occurred in the healthcare system to better care for multiply and severely handicapped individuals and their families, as far as we can see. This conclusion is based on a review of research literature over the past 30 years, and our three decades of clinical experience.

This failure to improve health care is also apparent in the stories presented in this book by looking closely at the number of years the respondents have lived with their health problems. There seems to be little difference in approach to management between those having lived with their disabilities for 50 years and those whose health problems were diagnosed within the five years prior to telling their stories to Susan and John. Many people throughout all those years had less than positive experiences in interactions with the health care system and its professionals.

The threads making up this book weave a fabric portraying a society and a medical system failing to adequately help individuals with the most complex health problems—among the most vulnerable members of our community. The most important elements necessary for more adequate care include: accurate information, especially from clients and their families; as accurate diagnoses as possible; and attempts to evaluate prognosis without taking away all hope, since any prognosis is really an educated guess—by no means an absolute truth.

Active listening to the ill person and their loved ones is a key requirement for competent professional help. Many professionals give advice and plan management of care for patients without asking enough questions, or the right kind of questions. Really understanding the facts of these people's lives is essential, as illustrated in *We Cry Out* and the other books and sources listed in our References and Resources sections. The emotional travails of chronically ill and disabled people are especially not well understood by many professionals. Chronically ill people are often cranky, fearful, and self-absorbed, which must be taken into account in knowing how to best approach them in a helpful way.

An understanding of the grieving process and its relationship with healing, especially when cure is not possible, is also essential to being truly helpful. Suffering is unavoidable in any life crisis; that fact should be overtly and empathetically recognized by health-care professionals. Suffering should be respectfully acknowledged, remembering the dignity of the victims of disabilities and illness. Patronizing people is not helpful.

Although there is no best way to help in the grieving process because it is a unique experience for each individual, empathetic advice and support are always appropriate—dignified, warm, recognizing human emotions. The emotions of the professionals involved in care must not only be recognized, but can assist in understanding therapeutic approaches likely to prove beneficial. A multi-professional team approach often is helpful in planning health-care management because the complexity in the lives of these clients is beyond the expertise of any one profession. In all situations, listening to, and respecting, the affected individuals' and families' perception of their needs should be given first priority in planning.

It is not surprising that professionals and non-professionals are intimidated and discouraged by multi-need clients. However, there are always means to respectfully, competently offer effective assistance. Although suffering cannot be banished, it can be eased by human interaction including respect, caring and love. Professionals should freely admit what they do not know, as well as what cannot be known because statistics are unable to predict individual prognoses. The power of the desire of people to heal, the natural tendency to *heal* should never be underestimated.

Quality of life can improve even in the face of overwhelming odds, including expected death. Lives can be *reinvented* even after a catastrophic occurrence, assisted by hopeful encouragement. Professionals who deny the existence of hope cause as much harm as those who offer unrealistic hope. When cure is unlikely, amelioration of symptoms is possible in any health condition. Ill and disabled clients are truly the experts about the facts of their own lives and how they experience their illness.

GRIEVING, HEALING AND HOPE

The language of grieving is the language of emotions. Emotions are as difficult for all of us to recognize as they are to live with. Many professionals feel uncomfortable with the emotions of their clients, but even more with how to deal with their own emotions. Medical professional education fails to teach adequate emotional vocabulary and skills in being supportively helpful in crisis situations. Good role models are not common enough in these important areas. Failure to understand leads to difficulty assisting in grieving. This, in turn, may interfere significantly with rehabilitation and healing. By *healing* we mean recovery and reintegration of the injured or ill person. The goal is to arrive at a plateau of renewed enjoyment of at least some aspects of life, to accept the unalterable limitations imposed by the disability, and to test those limits regularly.

Healing is an obviously dynamic process which involves ongoing work with new plateaus over time. Sometimes these plateaus involve lower function, sometimes higher function, depending on the illness process. Cure is not necessary for *healing* to occur. In chronic illness and in serious disabilities cure is usually not possible, even with the best medical care. True harm can be a consequence of inadequate evaluation and treatment of the emotional/psychological dimensions of illness and disability. Dr. Lown and Dr. Remen, along with many other authors, have documented many examples in their writings. Avoiding or denying suffering and related emotional responses only compound the trauma of difficult situations.

We encourage our readers to peruse at least some of the books listed as additional resources at the end of *We Cry Out*. These books, articles, and videos are presented to supplement and complement the perspective we present. They are an integral part of our book: there is much to be read which may not ordinarily be part of the resources professionals attempting to treat multiply disabled people are aware of. Some summaries and reviews we have included in our book not only illustrate our arguments, but give our readers who do not read these books the essentials of their insights.

Norman Cousins, in *Anatomy of an Illness*, writes about his unexpected recovery from a sudden devastating illness which started in 1964. It was diagnosed as ankylosing spondylitis, a rheumatologic illness in the same category as rheumatoid arthritis and lupus. He had not only painful, widespread, debilitating joint involvement, but felt very ill, severely fatigued, and generally miserable. His laboratory testing confirmed a severe inflammatory process consistent with his diagnosis. Several specialists in Rheumatology consulted by his long-time internal medicine physician told him and his physician that his prognosis was poor, and that he would progress to worse and worse debility; one specialist said that he had personally not witnessed recovery from such a severe variety of this disease. The standard anti-inflammatory, pain, and anti-anxiety medications available in 1964 were started. Norman Cousins, in consultation with his primary physician took this as a challenge rather than allowing himself to despair and panic.

After reading the medical literature and talking with physicians and researchers, and consultation with his personal physician, Norman Cousins concluded that the standard medical therapy was more likely to interfere with his body's natural ability to heal than to help him. Bothered by many of the hospital routines, he chose to leave the hospital and move to a hotel room. He talked his openminded, supportive physician into a trial of high dose intravenous vitamin C, based on some experimental uses of this vitamin. Meanwhile, he decided to mobilize all his affirmative, optimistic emotions, including hope, love, faith, laughter, and a profound will to heal and to live. His use of laughter to stimulate release of his own healing and pain managing physiologic substances has been what he is most famous for. In short, he refused to accept his grim prognosis. He profoundly believed in his body's own inherent power to heal, aided by the support of his wife and family, friends, physician, and massive doses of vitamin C, which he saw as less risky than standard medical therapy. In fact, he steadily improved and regained bodily function. He progressively felt better.

Critics said that his recovery was all due to "placebo effect". Mr. Cousins cogently argues that even if "placebo effect" had much to do with his unexpected recovery, there is nothing untoward about that. After all, this effect has been recognized as a significant aspect of healing during thousands of years of human history. He admits that good luck also helped, but is unapologetic about this as well. [22]

At the end of his book, which has the pertinent sub-title *Reflections on Healing and Regeneration*, Norman Cousins recounts a chance encounter on the streets of New York in 1974 on the tenth anniversary of his illness. He unexpectedly met one of the specialists who had told him he essentially had no chance of recovery. He describes the scenario in unforgettable terms:

> It was the sheerest of coincidences that…I should happen to meet…one of the specialists who had made the melancholy diagnosis of progressive paralysis. He was clearly surprised to see me. I held out my hand. He took it. I didn't hold back on the handshake. I had a point to make, and I thought the best way to do it was through a greeting firm enough to make an impression. I increased the pressure until he winced and asked to be released. He said he could tell by my handshake that he didn't have to ask about my present condition, but he was eager to hear what was behind the recovery.
> It all began, I said, when I decided that some experts don't know enough to make pronouncements of doom on a human being. And I said I hoped they

would be careful about what they said to others; they might be believed and that could be the beginning of the end. [23]

The power of positive or negative statements from authority figures such as physicians, certainly specialists, can cause significant benefits or harm. How an opinion of diagnosis and prognosis is expressed, with or without hope, can make a tremendous difference to a patient. It is never helpful to deny all hope; unexpected recoveries or remissions of illness, even serious illnesses, do, in fact, occasionally occur. The patient's will to heal and to live may help to provide the turning point, in conjunction with other medical therapies.

Three other books which help illustrate facets of the management of chronically ill and seriously injured people were written by Christopher Reeve and Bob Smith. In their books, the authors write about not only the facts of their experiences, but the emotional aspects of these life-altering events, and the interaction between the medical facts and their psychological and emotional responses.

In Christopher Reeve's two books, *Still Me* and *Nothing Is Impossible: Reflections on a New Life*, he wrote with emotional depth about his life with quadriplegia resulting from a fall from a horse in 1995. He emphasized the role of hope and determination in continuing rehabilitation therapy, despite the lack of scientific proof of its benefits in spinal cord injuries similar to his. His dramatic neurologic improvement starting five years after his injury was unprecedented, according to his physicians.

He was fortunate to have been a very physically fit, active, and generally optimistic person who was successful in his acting career. He had wealth, a strong loving family, and social attachments at the time of his fall, and had continued to have this support over the years since his injury. It was certainly essential that he found an encouraging, open physician, along with empathetic, competent therapists who never gave up on his potential to improve. Christopher Reeve was determined to heal as much as he possibly could. He certainly suffered, but also never abandoned his basic hope for recovery or improving his life. From his point of view, he explained the traumatic consequences of his injuries for his wife, family, and friends. If he had accepted the prognostic statements of some of his original physicians, he would not have worked as hard as he did, especially after insurance stopped paying for significant parts of his rehabilitation therapy. [24, 25]

Bob Smith's memoir, *Hamlet's Dresser*, describes the serious emotional trauma he and his family suffered following the birth of a retarded sister when he was three. His family clearly did not receive adequate sensitive medical and social support, or adequate education about the diagnosis of this beautiful disabled daughter, nor about options for her care. This child was born in the 1950's when knowledge about such matters was much less than it is now; however, insensitivity was not acceptable even in those years.

Bob Smith found salvation in the study of Shakespeare and involvement, mostly behind the scenes, in Shakespearean productions. He states unequivocally that Shakespeare literally saved his life. He never completed college, instead immersing himself in his career choice. Because of his sadness and feelings of guilt regarding his sister, he considered suicide more than once in young adulthood. From an early age, he struggled trying to cope with his mother's untreated depression, her dependence on him emotionally, as well as assisting in the physical care of his sister. He became very attached to his sister through his childhood and adolescence.

The medical advice given the family contributed to their anguish in managing their daughter's condition—specifically the strong recommendation by physicians, after an evaluation when she was a young child, that they put her in an institution and "forget about her." Her parents rejected that recommendation, but these physicians gave them no other options and no appointments for follow up. Finally, when she was in late adolescence, her aging parents felt they could no longer care for her and institutionalized her at a state facility. Bob Smith felt guilty and sad about this as well. He dealt with these feelings by not visiting her for many years. After writing this book, he was finally able to overcome his guilt and start visiting her in the institution. The most damning failure of the medical profession for this family was its failure to offer other options for caring for their daughter at home, and in not offering assistance in accessing support services to help them cope with her multiple problems. [26]

WHY HEALTH CARE IS PART OF NATIONAL SECURITY

In the United States, founded on such principles as "life, liberty, and the pursuit of happiness", a failing health care delivery and finance system threatens all three principles. These problems make this country more vulnerable to internal and external security threats. An ill population with inadequate health care is predisposed to difficulties in coping with SARS, AIDS, and tuberculosis, as well as more common health risks, not to mention a bio-terrorism catastrophe. The United States spends more as a percentage of GNP on health care than any other developed nation, according to Dr. LeBow and many other authors, yet has worse health statistics than many other developed countries. Although the U.S. has a significant advantage in availability of high technology medical procedures, many more middle-class citizens, as well as the poor, are unable to afford the care, or have to sacrifice other life priorities, even essentials, to afford it. Deferred medical care for ill people is not cost-effective, in addition to being inhumane. Heroic care late in a disease process is more expensive, often less effective in amelioration or cure of health problems, and results in more disability, and sometimes preventable death. This is tragic.

A CALL TO ACTION

Professional advice needs to be tempered by humility and humanity, by an attempt to actively listen to the ill and disabled. Dealing with the specifics of individual lives requires using the professional's own humanity to try to understand, empathize, and be flexible in attempting to provide assistance. We are calling for a more sophisticated, emotionally literate, sensitive, and humane evaluation and treatment of all chronically ill and disabled U.S. citizens—especially the multiply and severely injured and ill people whose stories are presented in *We Cry Out*. In all the books we studied, healers of all types are often seen by disabled and ill people and their families as unhelpful and sometimes harmful in their interactions with them.

Devastating crises in families require expert, respectful assistance. All of us, including family and friends, need to be enlightened about how to better understand the multiple interacting challenges in the lives of people in these difficult circumstances. It is clear to us that the U.S. health care system needs to be reorganized to provide comprehensive care to these ill and disabled people and their families. All of us who attempt to be helpful in these complex, multifaceted, interwoven individual and family crises need to be much better educated in the principles of teamwork among diverse specialties necessary for competent care.

WHAT DO THE CHRONICALLY ILL AND DISABLED KNOW THAT OTHER PEOPLE DO NOT?

All or us would agree that the entire world faces innumerable complicated and dangerous problems, only some of which are really predictable. It is also obvious that no person or group of people can claim to know any simple solutions or best approaches to ameliorate these difficulties—as none of them are truly soluble. Unknown and unexpected catastrophes are among the immutable laws of nature, allowing no effective predictability. Plans must therefore be flexible over time to take these imponderables into account.

It is therefore reasonable to consider as many perspectives as possible in approaching these predictable and unpredictable challenges. The chronically ill and disabled, as well as their families and intimate friends, see life from a very different perspective than those without such existential stresses. This difference is in the daily challenges to function that the ill and disabled face.

Insights of these kinds would be very helpful as models of flexible planning in attempting to manage world crises. Although all ill and/or disabled persons are unique in the particular constellation of difficulties they face, they nevertheless face many common obstacles in their lives requiring similar skills and attitudes to function day to day. These are precisely the skills and attitudes which governmental and non-governmental organizations need to cultivate to be more effective in meeting unpredictable recurrent world crises—the earthquakes, volcanic eruptions, severe weather-related events, illness outbreaks and epidemics, and innumerable other catastrophes. Preparing for the possible, but unpredictable, is always very difficult. Knowing how and when to react is an art as well as a science.

To help our readers to understand the type of change in vision represented by seeing the world through the lenses of the ill and disabled, we ask you now to consider the common human experiences all of us without exception face at some time in our lives: specifically, personal and family illnesses, injuries, losses, and other unexpected personal catastrophes. These events often change our attitudes from that time on, or at least for some time afterwards. The more serious the crisis the more likely it will result in life-long change in perspective. Certainly, some people choose not to learn a new perspective—instead returning to the more comfortable and familiar pre-event life view.

A second example of universal experience is to remember ourselves as children and adolescents. Most of us inevitably dramatically change our perspective by the time we are young adults, more so as we arrive at middle and old age because no life is untouched by sad and unexpected circumstances, as well as enjoyable and often unanticipated times of satisfaction and happiness. Life inevitably changes each of us over time whether we want change to occur or not.

Similar arguments could be made that taking into account the views of any minority or marginalized group of people in society is necessary to achieve realistic, reasonable approaches to world crises. These minorities also have much to teach all of us who are more privileged because they live in a truly different world—almost a parallel universe—from the dominant groups in society. They often see potential and existing problems which may not only affect them, but extend to significantly affect dominant groups as well. Women, racial and ethnic minorities, the impoverished, and children are examples of people with importantly unique world-views.

CONCLUSION

We fervently believe that not only the specific individuals and families living with disabilities and illness presented in *We Cry Out*, but society in the U.S. in general, would benefit from better care of multiply disabled people and the chronically ill. From the humanitarian viewpoint this is certainly true. It is also true from the economic point of view. We all lose from health care systems failures.

All of us benefit from attempting to grasp the multiple interacting facets of complicated problems from as many world views as possible. We anticipate that better solutions, or approaches to solutions, to individual life crises as well as world crises, would be the result of these new perspectives. All of us lose if we remain blind to new paths through the maze of our fragmented personal lives and interdependent world. We all live in the same world, whether we recognize it or not.

It seems to us that the appropriate approach involves merging the entire spectrum of human life sciences and arts, including psychological and emotional knowledge. The goal is to improve the quality of life of our clients and friends. Undoubtedly many of our friends and family members are living with chronic illnesses and disabilities, or certainly will at some time in the future, since anyone who lives long enough will eventually develop some chronic illness. With their experiences in living with difficult life problems, many would be able and willing to help others in similar circumstances.

Professionals can use all the help they can get from those affected with the illnesses and injuries inherent in life. These suffering people, their loved ones, and friends are a valuable resource because they actually live in the midst of the day-to-day, down-to-earth, aspects of life-altering experiences. Their unique knowledge is essential to better assist in the adventure of *healing* and *re-inventing* a new life, accommodating to the unalterable changes characteristic of all disabilities and chronic illnesses. Creative thinking is required. And creativity requires seeing a life problem with unique vision: the ill and disabled have this unique vision.

EPILOGUE

Susan Dahl died on February 10, 1995, just a few days after finishing her work on this book. She had been stricken in early childhood by spinal muscular atrophy, and lived most of her life in a wheelchair. She had entered the hospital a few days before her death, weak from internal bleeding. Surgeons repaired the tears in her intestinal wall, but she had developed an infection that quickly got out of control. Vital systems began to falter and shut down, and she was put on life support. The book was finally finished after 15 years of effort, and Susie was ready to leave this world. She made it clear to her doctors several times that she wanted them to give up trying and set her free. Though they had worked desperately to save her life, they finally had to agree it was hopeless. They turned off her respirator at 9 a.m. on that Friday morning, and in seconds she was gone.

Suz was 47 years old.

Her family doctor, John Campbell, told me afterwards that a normally-healthy person would have easily survived the surgery and the subsequent infection. In a sense, I believe Susie's developmental disability, thus, was what finally killed her.

But, oh, with what great dignity, good humor, kindness, and grace did she live!

This book is Susan's gift to the world. In the last few years of work on the book, I sometimes teased her (in all seriousness) that I was working slowly on the book on purpose, for I felt the book was helping keep her alive and if I worked quickly it would kill her. She always laughed when I said that, but we both knew it was the truth. As creation of the book got very near the end, I told her to begin thinking of volume two so she could live 15 more years. She didn't think that was very funny.

I sometimes feel guilty about all this, because I think she willed herself to live for this book long past the time it was good for her own well-being. I think I could have told her several months ago that the book was in good hands, that I would see it through to conclusion. She was in a great deal of pain and anxiety her last two years of life, as a result of being hit by a local handi-van as she crossed a downtown street in the crosswalk with the white "WALK" sign in her favor. She never really recovered from the accident, and the head injuries she suffered caused attacks of anxiety which made it impossible for her to work on the book more than ten minutes at a time. Tap away at the computer for ten minutes, then knit teddy-bear sweaters for the children at the rehabilitation hospital for three hours, then tap away at the computer on the book for ten minutes, then knit some more or visit with friends. An excruciatingly difficult life. She stayed alive to complete this book, at great personal cost. This book is her legacy. Her gift to others challenged by disability who inevitably will follow.

Her family asked that I as co-author be among the speakers at Susan's funeral. I wrote this letter the day before the funeral, blinded by tears, and somehow managed to read it to the hundreds of people who jammed the church to honor her:

A LETTER TO SUSIE
February 14, 1995

Dear Suz—

You are one of my very best friends on earth. I hope you know that. I tried to let you know that in the best way I could.

I'm going to miss you terribly, but since you're in my heart you'll always be around.

One thing I'll especially miss will be seeing you buzzing around town in your wheelchair or the Ford, your specially-equipped freedom-mobile. Every time I see you I have to smile to myself. There you go. Off to lunch with somebody. Off to buy a card for somebody hurting. Off to counsel someone about their love life. (This often puzzled you, because you always felt you didn't have much of a love life yourself. But, Suz, you really did, for we all loved you.)

Suz, I tried so very hard to help you finish your book up. It's a wonderful book…a wonderful book, and it will live for a long time and help a lot of people. We were only about two weeks and a downed computer from completing it and starting the process of finding a great publisher.

The Epilogue of the book is going to be about you, Suz. How you lived and how you died.

My biggest dream was to get it done, and the publisher would do a beautiful cover and your picture would be on the book with a paragraph on your accomplishments. And maybe far in the background of your photograph I'd get to stand: looking on, with a big smile.

I wanted to be able to give you that book, before you left us. I feel like I failed you. I'm terribly sorry.

I also beg forgiveness for the times your disabilities simply got the best of me. I had to hide sometimes. I just couldn't bear to listen sometimes. I felt your distress so deeply sometimes I would run away for a short while to catch my breath. I thought I was going to suffocate. I couldn't even begin to imagine how you must have felt for all these long years.

I knew you couldn't run away, but I had to. So please forgive me for that, also. I think you would agree that most of the time I did the very best I could. I'm just me, a mortal male.

By the way, you teased me about my maleness on occasion. You were good at teasing. I especially liked the card you sent me once. On the cover it said, "How come women are so damned dumb?"

I thought, "Whoa! Is that sexist, or what?"

Inside, your card answered the question why women are so damned dumb: "Because they don't have a penis to carry their brains around in."

You always had a way with words.

And you remember, Suz, how you always used to complain when people would come up to you and give you "that look." Like the little old lady in the elevator at Miller & Paine's. You rolled into the elevator, and she hobbled in after you. And as she stood next to you, uncomfortably, she patted you on the top of the head like the family dog and said, "You're such an inspiration for us all, Dear."

Now, I know you hated that. I know you didn't want to bear the burden of being an inspiration: the terrible burden of putting other people's lives in meaningful perspective at the expense of your own severe developmental disabilities.

But you did that for all of us, and you did it so well. For so long. Now you're gone and we have to bear our own burdens by ourselves.

I thank the Lord that you are finally free.

But Suz, you're still going to always be with me, doing more for me than I ever, ever did for you. You're always going to be there. Rolling down the street in your chair. Looking back a bit, beckoning to me slightly. Saying, "Come on, Old Guy. You can make it."

I love you. Good-bye.

John

ACKNOWLEDGMENTS

Countless people contribute to the creation of a book. We would like to acknowledge several who have been especially helpful:

Gladys Pilkington, Susan's friendly and faithful neighbor, who was always there in a pinch. The Child Guidance Center staff who for many years were wonderful colleagues and helped mail out questionnaires during the data-collection phase of the study. The many, many individuals who wrote personal checks to provide the modest funds to finance this effort. The people who read and edited the stories after Susan transferred them from the questionnaires to the computer: Mom, Margaret Hoffman, Barb Schliesser, Margrit Stelling, Helen Jeffery, Lenora Morrisson, Dr. George Wolcott and his great staff at Madonna, Bill Shuart, Catherine Roberts, Loek and Peter Lohnberg, Mel Luetchens, Ebb and Lucy Munden, Ginny, Nan, and Dave, Marty Tjornehoj, Mavis Johnson, Harriet Jackson, and Kevin Brown.

Dr. Lois Schwab, Susan's advisor on her Master's degree at the University of Nebraska-Lincoln in human development and family science, who encouraged Susan and generously provided insights into the research process. Drs. John Campbell, George Wolcott, and John Lonstein, who helped keep Susan alive for many, many good and fruitful years of life. The late Dr. Howard Halpern of the Child Guidance Center, who agreed to help sponsor the study along with the University of Nebraska-Lincoln, and asked the board of directors to provide modest funding. Kathleen Dubas, a Ph.D. candidate at the University of Nebraska-Lincoln, who will continue analyzing Susan's data from a statistical standpoint, finding further insights the families have provided us. The University of Nebraska-Lincoln for providing an intellectually rich and supportive environment for John to work in the past 20 years: colleagues who care about learning and about each other. Jeff and Sandi Keuss, steadfast friends/extended family over the years.

Our families: Ione Dahl, who gave Susan life and a title for this book; Ginny Flack, Nan Gellermann, and David Dahl; Nikki, Amie, Alyssa, and Erica DeFrain, and Gary Hanna; Harriet and Orville DeFrain; and Margaret Schulling. Always there when we need them, and we need them a great deal.

And, finally, the individuals and families themselves who were involved in this research and shared their wonderful stories with us.

To all, a profound and sincere thank you.

NOTES

Notes for Dr. Campbell's *Foreword* and for the final chapter of the book, *Today and Tomorrow*. Note numbers list references as they appear in the text:

[1] Sacks, Oliver. *A Leg to Stand On.* Summit Books. 1984. New York: A Touchstone Book/Simon & Schuster. 1993. Afterword. 1993.

[2] Lubkin, Irene Morof, R.N., M.S., CGNP, and Larsen, Pamela D., R.N., Ph.D., cRRN. *Chronic Illness: Impact and Interventions.* Sudbury, Mass.: Jones and Bartlett Publishers. 2002. p.3.

[3] Ibid. p. 8-10.

[4] Hymovich, Debra P., R.N., Ph.D., FAAN., and Hagopian, Gloria A., R.N., Ed.D. *Chronic Illness in Children and Adults: A Psychosocial Approach.* Philadelphia: W.B. Saunders Co. 1992. p.4.

[5] Ibid. p.6.

[6] Lown, Bernard, M.D. *The Lost Art of Healing: Practicing Compassion in Medicine.* Boston: Houghton Mifflin Company. 1996. p. xi-xii.

[7] Sacks, Oliver. *A Leg to Stand On.* (See [1] above).

[8] Sacks, Oliver. *Migraine: Revised and Expanded.* N.Y.: Vintage Books. A division of Random House, Inc. 1992. p. 229.

[9] Ibid. p. 230-231.

[10] Remen, Rachel Naomi, M.D. *My Grandfather's Blessings: Stories of Strength, Refuge, and Belonging.* N.Y.: Riverhead Books. 2000. p. 138.

[11] Ibid. p. 205.

[12] Remen, Rachel Naomi, M.D. *Kitchen Table Wisdom: Stories That Heal.* N.Y.: Riverhead Books. 1996. p. 52.

[13] Price, Reynolds. *A Whole New Life: An Illness and a Healing.* N.Y.: Athenium. 1994. p. 145.

[14] Sontag, Susan. *Illness as Metaphor*. N.Y.: Farrar, Strauss, and Giroux. 1978.

[15] Price, Reynolds. (See [13] above.)

[16] Heymann, Jody, M.D. *Equal Partners: A Physician's Call for a New Spirit of Medicine*. Boston: Little, Brown & Co. 1995.

[17] Cameron, Lindsley. *The Music of Light: The Extraordinary Story of Hikari and Kenzaburo Oe*. N.Y.: The Free Press. 1998.

[18] Newborn, Barbara. *Return to Ithaca: A Woman's Triumph Over the Disabilities of a Severe Stroke*. Rockport, Mass.: Element. 1997. P. 67.

[19] Ibid. p. 68.

[20] Sacks, Oliver. *Seeing Voices: A Journey Into the World of the Deaf*. Berkeley: University of California Press. 1989.

[21] LeBow, Bob, M.D., MPH. *Health Care Meltdown: Confronting the Myths and Fixing Our Failing System*. Boise, Idaho: JRI Press. (Self-published). 2002.

[22] Cousins, Norman. *Anatomy of an Illness as Perceived by the Patient: Reflections on Healing and Regeneration*. N.Y.: W.W. Norton & Co. Inc. 1979. N.Y.: Bantam Books. 1981.

[23] Ibid. Pp. 159-160.

[24] Reeve, Christopher. *Still Me*. N.Y.: Random House. 1998.

[25] Reeve, Christopher. *Nothing Is Impossible: Reflections on a New Life*. N.Y.: Random House. 2002.

[26] Smith, Bob. *Hamlet's Dresser: A Memoir*. N.Y.: Scribner. 2002.

REFERENCES AND RESOURCES

The references listed alphabetically below were most important in writing Dr. Campbell's Foreword to the book. A section containing additional resources follows:

Berg, Insoo Kim, and Dolan, Yvonne. *Tales of Solutions: A Collection of Hope-Inspiring Stories*. New York, N.Y.: W.W. Norton & Co. 2001.

Bridges, William, Ph.D. *Transitions: Making Sense of Life's Changes*. Reading, Mass.: Addison-Wesley. 1980.

Cameron, Lindsley. *The Music of Light: The Extraordinary Story of Hikari and Kenzaburo Oe*. New York, N.Y.: The Free Press. 1998.

Chamaz, Kathy. *Good Days, Bad Days: The Self in Chronic Illness and Time*. New Brunswick, New Jersey: Rutgers University Press. 1991.

Cousins, Norman. *Anatomy of an Illness as Perceived by the Patient: Reflections on Healing and Regeneration*. New York, N.Y.: W.W. Norton & Co. Inc.1979. N.Y.: Bantam Books. 1981.

Donohue, Paul, Ph.D., and Siegel, Mary E., Ph.D. *Sick and Tired of Feeling Sick and Tired: Living with Invisible Chronic Disease*. New York, N.Y.: W.W. Norton & Co. 1992.

Dubovsky, Steven L., M.D. *Mind-Body Deceptions: The Psychosomatics of Everyday Life*. New York, N.Y.: W.W. Norton & Co. 1997.

Falvo, Donna R., R.N., Ph.D., CRC. *Medical and Psychosocial Aspects of Chronic Illness and Disability*. Gaithersburg, Maryland: An Aspen Publication, Aspen Publishers, Inc. 1999.

Green, Stephen A., M.D. *Mind & Body: The Psychology of Physical Illness*. Washington, D.C.: American Psychiatric Press, Inc. 1985.

Heymann, Jody, M.D. *Equal Partners: A Physician's Call for a New Spirit of Medicine*. Boston, Mass.: Little, Brown & Co. 1995.

Hymovich, Debra P., R.N., Ph.D., FAAN., and Hagopian, Gloria A., R.N., Ed.D. *Chronic Illness in Children and Adults: A Psychosocial Approach*. Philadelphia, Pa.: W.B.Saunders Co. 1992.

Kleinman, Authur, M.D. *The Illness Narratives: Suffering, Healing, and the Human Condition*. New York, N.Y.: Basic Books Publishers, Inc. 1988.

LeBow, Bob, M.D., MPH. *Health Care Meltdown: Confronting the Myths and Fixing Our Failing System*. Boise, Idaho: JRI Press. (Self-published). 2002.

Lewis, Kathleen. *Celebrate Life: New Attitudes for Living with Chronic Illness*. Atlanta, Georgia: Arthritis Foundation. 1999.

Livneh, Hanoch, Ph.D., and Antonek, Richard F., Ed.D. *Psychosocial Adaptations To Chronic Illness and Disability*. Gaithersburg, Md.: Aspen Publishers, Inc. 1997.

Lown, Bernard, M.D. *The Lost Art of Healing*. Boston, Mass.: Houghton Mifflin Company. 1996.

Lubkin, Irene Morof, N.N., Ph.D., MS., CGNP., and Larsen, Pamela D., R.N., Ph.D., cRRN. *Chronic Illness: Impact and Interventions*. Sudbury, Mass.: Jones Bartlett Publishers. 2002.

Lundberg, George D., M.D. with Stacy, James. *Severed Trust: Why American Medicine Hasn't Been Fixed*. New York, N.Y.: Basic Books. 2000.

Miller, Judith Fitzgerald, R.N., Ph.D., FAAN. *Coping With Chronic Illness: Overcoming Powerlessness*. Pennsylvania, Pa.: F.A.Davis Company. 2000.

Newborn, Barbara. *Return to Ithaca: A Woman's Triumph Over the Disabilities of a Severe Stroke*. Rockport, Mass.: Element. 1997.

Pollin, Irene, MSW., with Golant, Susan K., MA. *Taking Charge: Overcoming the Challenges of Long-Term Illness*. New York, N.Y.: Times Books. Random House. 1994.

Price, Reynolds. *A Whole New Life: An Illness and a Healing*. New York, N.Y.: Athenium. 1994.

Reeve, Christopher. *Nothing Is Impossible: Reflections on a New Life*. New York, N.Y.: Random House. 2002.

Reeve, Christopher. *Still Me*. New York, N.Y.: Random House. 1998.

Remen, Rachel Naomi, M.D. *Kitchen Table Wisdom: Stories that Heal*. New York, N.Y.: Riverhead Books. 1996.

Remen, Rachel Naomi, M.D. *My Grandfather's Blessings: Stories of Strength, Refuge, and Belonging*. New York, N.Y.: Riverhead Books. 2000.

Sacks, Oliver. *A Leg to Stand On*. Summit Books. 1984. New York, N.Y.: A TouchStone Book. Simon & Schuster. 1993. Afterward. 1993.

Sacks, Oliver. *Migraine: Revised and Expanded*. New York, N.Y.: Vintage Books. A division of Random House, Inc. 1992.

Sacks, Oliver. *Seeing Voices: A Journey Into the World of the Deaf*. Berkeley, Ca.: University of California Press. 1989.

Shuman, Robert. *The Psychology of Chronic Illness: The Healing Work of Patients, Therapists, and Families*. New York, N.Y.: BasicBooks. 1996.

Smith, Bob. *Hamlet's Dresser: A Memoir*. New York, N.Y.: Scribner. 2002.

Smith, Robert C. *The Patient's Story: Integrated Patient-Doctor Interviewing*. Forward by Engel, George L., Boston, Mass.: Little, Brown, and Co. 1996.

Sontag, Susan. *Illness as Metaphor*. New York, N.Y.: Farrar, Strauss, and Giroux. 1978.

Vickers, Margaret H. *Work and Unseen Chronic Illness: Silent Voices*. New York, N.Y.: Rutledge. Taylor & Francis Group. 2001.

ADDITIONAL RESOURCES

These books, articles, and videos are a very important part of this book because they encourage the reader to explore the experience of illness and disability from many points of view. Dr. Campbell feels that many of these resources add a depth of understanding not usually found in traditional medical books and literature. For your convenience, these resources are listed in alphabetical order, and are categorized into general types of issues discussed. Some resources are listed under more than one category.

Textbooks Relating to Managing Chronic Illnesses And Disabilities for Professionals and Patients:

Donahue, Paul J., Ph.D. and Siegel, Mary E., Ph.D. *Sick and Tired of Feeling Sick and Tired: Living with Invisible Chronic Disease.* New York, N.Y.: W.W. Norton & Co. 1992, 2000.

Falvo, Donna R., R.N., Ph.D., CRC. *Medical and Psychosocial Aspects of Chronic Illness and Disability.* Gaithersburg, Md.: Aspen Publishers, Inc. 1999.

Funk, Sandra G., Ph.D., Torquist, Elizabeth M., MA, Leeman, Jennifer, D.PH., M.Div., Miles, Margaret S., Ph.D., R.N., and Harrell, Joanne S., Ph.D., R.N. *Key Aspects of Preventing and Managing Chronic Illness.* New York, N.Y.: Springer Publishing Co. 2001.

Gerteis, Margaret, Edgman-Leviton, Daley, Jennifer, and Delbanco, Thomas L., Editors. *Through the Patient's Eyes: Understanding and Promoting Patient-Centered Care.* San Francisco, Ca.: Josey-Bass Publishers. 1993.

Green, Stephen A., M.D. *Mind & Body: The Psychology of Physical Illness.* Washington, D.C.: American Psychiatric Press, Inc. 1985. (See REFERENCES section).

Hymovich and Hagopian, *Chronic Illness in Children and Adults: A Psychosocial Approach.* (See REFERENCES section for complete citation).

Kleinman. *The Illness Narratives.* (See REFERENCES section).

Livneh and Antonek. *Psychosocial Adaptations To Chronic Illness and Disability.* (See REFERENCES section).

Lubkin and Larsen. *Chronic Illness: Impact and Interventions.* (see REFERENCES section).

Shuman. *The Psychology of Chronic Illness: The Healing Work of Patients, Therapists, and Families.* (see REFERENCES section).

Vickers. *Work and Unseen Chronic Illness: Silent Voices.* (see REFERENCES section).

Mind/Body Interaction in Health, Illness and Healing:

Berg and Dolan. *Tales of Solutions: A Collection of Hope-Inspiring Stories.* (see REFERENCES section).

Bridges, William, Ph.D., *Transitions: Making Sense of Life's Changes.* Reading, Mass.: Addison-Wesley Publishing Co. 1980.

Cousins, Norman. *Anatomy of an Illness.* (see REFERENCES section).

Cousins, Norman. *Head First: The Biology of Hope and the Healing Power of the Human Spirit.* New York, N.Y.: Penguin Books. 1990.

Cousins, Norman. *The Healing Heart: Antidotes to Panic and Helplessness.* New York, N.Y.: W.W. Norton & Co. 1983.

DeBecker, Gavin. *The Gift of Fear: And Other Survival Signals that protect Us from Violence.* Boston, Mass.: Random House, Inc. 1997.

Dossey, Larry, M.D. *Reinventing Medicine: Beyond Mind-Body to a New Era of Healing.* San Francisco, Ca.: HarperCollins Publishers. 1999.

Dubovsky. *Mind-Body Deceptions: The Psychosomatics of Everyday Life.* (see REFERENCES section).

Eisenberg, David, M.D. with Lee, Thomas. *Encounters with Qi: Exploring Chinese Medicine.* New York, N.Y.: W.W. Norton & Co. 1985.

Green. *Mind & Body: The Psychology of Physical Illness.* (see REFERENCES section).

Gutkind, Lee, editor. *Healing: 20 Prominent Authors Write about Inspirational Moments of Achieving Health and Gaining Insight.* New York, N.Y.: Penguin/Putnam, Inc. 2001.

Janiger, Oscar, M.D. and Goldberg, Philip. *A Different Kind of Healing: Doctors Speak Candidly about their Successes with Alternative Medicine.* New York, N.Y.: G.P. Putnam's Sons. 1993.

Kübler-Ross, Elizabeth, M.D. *The Wheel of Life: A Memoir of Living and Dying.* New York, N.Y.: Scribner. 1997.

Lappe, Marc, Ph.D. *The Tao of Immunology: A Revolutionary New Understanding of Our Body's Defenses.* New York, N.Y.: Plenum Trade. 1997.

Mehl-Madrona, Lewis, M.D. *Coyote Medicine.* New York, N.Y.: Scribner. 1997.

Milburn, Michael P., Ph.D. *The Future of Healing: Exploring the Parallels of Eastern and Western Medicine.* Freedom, California: The Crossing Press. 2001.

Moyers, Bill. *Healing and The Mind:* 5 videos—Vol. 1: *Mystery of Chi;* Vol. 2: *The Mind-Body Connection;* Vol. 3: *Healing From Within;* Vol. 4: *The Art of Healing;* Vol.5: *Wounded Healers.* David Grubin Productions, Inc. and Public Affairs Television Inc. 1993.

Moyers, Bill. *On Our Own Terms: Moyers on Dying.* Program one: *Living with Dying;* Program two: *A Different Kind of Care;* Program three: *A Death of One's Own;* Program four: *A Time to Change.* 4 videos. Films For the Humanities and Sciences. 2000.

Northrup, Christine, M.D. *Women's Bodies, Women's Wisdom: Creating Physical and Emotional Health and Healing.* New York, N.Y.: Bantam Books. 1998.

Perrone, Bobette, Stockel, H. Henrietta, and Krueger, Victoria. *Medicine Women, Curanderos, and Women Doctors.* Norman, Oklahoma: University of Oklahoma Press. 1989.

Siegel, Bernie S., M.D. *Peace, Love, and Healing: Bodymind Communication and the Path to Self-Healing: An Exploration.* New York, N.Y.: Harper & Row. 1989.

Sternberg, Esther M. and Gold, Phillip W. *The Mind-Body Interaction in Disease.* From *The Hidden Mind:* Special Edition *Scientific American*, Vol. 12, No. 1, June 2002. P.82.

The Ailing U.S. Health Care System, and the Art and the Science of the Practice of Medicine:

Alvord, Lori Arviso, M.D. and Van Pelt, Elizabeth Cohen. *The Scalpel and the Silver Bear: The First Navajo Woman Surgeon Combines Western and Traditional Healing.* New York, N.Y.: Bantam Books. 1999.

Cassell, Eric J., M.D. *Doctoring: The Nature of Primary Care Medicine.* New York, N.Y.: Oxford University Press. A Copublication with the Milbank Memorial Fund. 1997.

Funk, Sandra G., Ph.D., Torquist, Elizabeth M., MA., Leeman, Jennifer, Dr.PH., M.Div., Miles, Margaret S., Ph.D., R.N., and Harrell, Joanne S., Ph.D., R.N. *Key Aspects of Preventing and Managing Chronic Illness.* New York, N.Y.: Springer Publishing Co. 2001.

Groopman, Jerome, M.D. *Second Opinions.* New York, N.Y.: Viking. 2000.

Halpern, Jodi, M.D., Ph.D. *From Detached Concern to Empathy: Humanizing Medical Practice.* New York, N.Y.: Oxford University Press. 2001.

Heymann, Jody, M.D. *Equal Partners: A Physician's Call for a New Spirit of Medicine.* (see REFERENCES section).

Hunter, Kathryn Montgomery. *Doctor's Stories: The Narrative Structure of Medical Knowledge.* Princeton, NJ: Princeton University Press. 1991.

Kaufman, Sharon R. *The Healer's Tale: Transforming Medicine and Culture.* Madison, Wisconsin: The University of Wisconsin Press. 1993.

LeBow, Bob, M.D., MPH. *Health Care Meltdown: Confronting the Myths and Fixing Our Failing System.* (see REFERENCES section).

Lown, Bernard, M.D. *The Lost Art of Healing.* (see REFERENCES section).

Lundberg, George D., M.D. with Stacy, James. *Severed Trust: Why American Medicine Hasn't Been Fixed.* (see REFERENCES section).

Nuland, Sherwin B., M.D. *The Mysteries Within: A Surgeon Reflects on Medical Myths.* New York, N.Y.: Simon & Schuster. 2000.

Platt, Frederic W., M.D. *Conversation Failure: Case Studies in Doctor-Patient Communication*. Tacoma, WA.: Life Sciences Press. 1992.

Smith, Robert C., M.D. *The Patient's Story: Integrated Patient-Doctor Interviewing*. Forward by Engel, George L., M.D. Boston, Mass.: Little, Brown & Co. 1996.

Staton, Jana, Shuy, Roger and Byock, Ira. *A Few Months to Live: Different Paths to Life's End*. Washington D.C.: Georgetown University Press. 2001.

About Surviving the Experience of Chronic Illness, Disabilities, and Other Life Traumas and Disasters—Grieving and Healing:

Bolen, Jean Shinoda, M.D. *Close to the Bone: Life-Threatening Illness and the Search for Meaning*. New York, N.Y.: Scribner. 1996.

Breslin, Rosemary. *Not Exactly What I Had in Mind: An Incurable Love Story*. New York, N.Y.: Villard Books/Random House. 1997.

Cameron, Lindsley. *The Music of Light: The Extraordinary Story of Hikari and Kenzaburo Oe*. (see REFERENCES section).

Carter, Betsy. *Nothing to Fall Back On: The Life and Times of a Perpetual Optimist*. New York, N.Y.: Hyperion. 2002.

Cassell, Eric J. *The Nature of Suffering and the Goals of Medicine*. New York, N.Y.: Oxford University Press. 1991.

Charmaz, Kathy. *Good Days, Bad Days: The Self in Chronic illness and Time*. New Brunswick, NJ.: Rutgers University Press. 1991.

Cousins, Norman. *Anatomy of an Illness*. (see previous citations).

Cousins, Norman. *Head First*. (see previous citations).

Cousins, Norman. *The Healing Heart*. (see previous citations).

DeBecker, Gavin. *The Gift of Fear*. (see previous citation).

Deits, Bob. *Life After Loss: A Personal Guide Dealing With Death, Divorce, Job Change, and Relocation*. Tucson, Arizona: Fisher Books. 1988.

Donahue and Siegel. *Sick and Tired of Feeling Sick and Tired.* (see previous citation).

Duff, Kat. *The Alchemy of Illness.* New York, N.Y.: Bell Tower. 1993.

Fox, Michael J. *Lucky Man: A Memoir.* New York, N.Y.: Hyperion. 2002.

Frank, Anne. *The Diary of a Young Girl: The Definitive Edition.* Edited by Otto Frank and Miriam Pressler. Translated by Susan Massotty. New York, N.Y.: Bantam/Random House. 1997.

Frank, Arthur. *At the Will of the Body: Reflections on Illness.* Boston, Mass.: Houghton Mifflin Co. 1991.

Frank, Arthur. *The Wounded Storyteller: Body, Illness, and Ethics.* Chicago, Ill.: The University of Chicago Press. 1995.

Frankl, Viktor E. *Man's Search for Meaning: An Introduction to Logotherapy.* Boston, Mass.: Beacon Press. 1992.

Griffin, Susan. *What Her Body Thought: A Journey Into the Shadows.* San Francisco, Ca: Harper. 1999.

Jamison, Kay Redfield. *An Unquiet Mind: A Memoir of Moods and Madness.* New York, N.Y.: Vintage Books/Random House. 1995.

Jennings, Kate. *Moral Hazard: A Novel.* New York, N.Y.: Fourth Estate/HarperCollins. 2002.

Kaufman, Miriam, M.D. *Easy for You to Say: Q & A's for Teens Living with Chronic Illness or Disability.* Toronto, Canada: Key Porter Books. 1995.

Kerrey, Bob. *When I Was a Young Man: A Memoir.* New York, N.Y.: A James H. Silberman Book/Harcourt, Inc. 2002.

Kleinman, Arthur, M.D. *The Illness Narratives.* (see previous citation REFERENCES).

Kubler-Ross. *The Wheel of Life.* (see previous citation).

Lerner, Max. *Wrestling With the Angel: A Memoir of My Triumph Over Illness.* New York, N.Y.: W.W. Norton & Co. 1990.

Lewis, C.S. *A Grief Observed.* Forward 1994. San Francisco, Ca.: Harper. 1961.

Lewis, Kathleen. *Celebrate Life: New Attitudes for Living with Chronic Illness.* Atlanta, Georgia.: Arthritis Foundation. 1999.

MacPherson, Myra. *She Came to Live Out Loud: An Inspiring Family Journey Through Illness, Loss, and Grief.* New York, N.Y.: A Lisa Drew Book/Scribner. 1999.

Miller, Judith Fitzgerald, R.N., Ph.D., FAAN. *Coping With Chronic Illness: Overcoming Powerlessness.* Philadelphia, Pa.: F.A. Davis Co. 2000.

Mardell, Harvey, M.D. and Spiro, Howard, M.D., editors. *When Doctors Get Sick.* New York, N.Y.: Plenum Medical Book. 1987.

Mullan, Fitzhugh, M.D. *Vital Signs: A Young Doctor's Struggle with Cancer.* New York, N.Y.: Farrar, Straus, Giroux. 1982.

Neumayr, Anton. *Music & Medicine: Haydn, Mozart, Beethoven, Schubert.* Translated by Clarke, Bruce Cooper. Bloomington, Ill.: Medi-Ed Press. 1994.

Newborn. *Return to Ithaca.* (see REFERENCES section).

Pensack, Robert, M.D. and Williams, Dwight. *Raising Lazarus: A Memoir.* New York, N.Y.: G.P. Putnam's Sons. 1994.

Pollin, Irene, MSW., and Golant, Susan K., MA. *Taking Charge: Overcoming the Challenges of Long-Term Illness.* New York, N.Y.: Times Books/Random House. 1994.

Price, Reynolds. *A Whole New Life.* (see REFERENCES section).

Reeve, Christopher. *Nothing is Impossible.* (see REFERENCES section).

Reeve, Christopher. *Still Me.* (see REFERENCES section).

Register, Cheri. *Living With Chronic Illness: Days of Patience and Passion.* New York, N.Y.: The Free Press/MacMillan, Inc. 1987.

Remen. *Kitchen Table Wisdom.* (see REFERENCES section).

Remen. *My Grandfather's Blessings.* (see REFERENCES section).

Rosenbaum, Edward, M.D. *A Taste of My Own Medicine: When the Doctor is the Patient.* New York, N.Y.: Random House. 1988.

Sacks, Oliver. *A Leg To Stand On.* (see REFERENCES section).

Sacks, Oliver. *An Anthropologist On Mars: Seven Paradoxical Tales.* New York, N.Y.: Vintage/Random House, Inc. 1995.

Sacks, Oliver. *Awakenings.* New York, N.Y.: Harper/Perrennial. 1990.

Sacks, Oliver. *Migraine.* (see REFERENCES section).

Sacks, Oliver. *The Island of the Colorblind; and Cycad Island.* New York, N.Y.: Vintage Books/RandomHouse. 1997.

Sacks, Oliver. *The Man Who Mistook His Wife for a Hat and Other Clinical Tales.* New York, N.Y.: Simon & Schuster. 1998.

Sacks, Oliver. *Seeing Voices: A Journey Into the World of the Deaf.* Berkeley, Ca.: University of California Press. 1989.

Sacks, Oliver. *Uncle Tungsten: Memories of a Chemical Boyhood.* New York, N.Y.: Alfred A Knopf. 2001. Thorndike Press. 2002.

Schmookler, Andrew Bard. *Living Posthumously: Confronting the Loss of Vital Powers.* New York, N.Y.: Henry Holt & Co. 1997.

Shuman. *The Psychology of Chronic Illness.* (see REFERENCES section).

Smith. *Hamlet's Dresser.* (see REFERENCES section).

Sontag. *Illness as Metaphor.* (see REFERENCES section).

Sparks, Nicholas. *The Notebook.* New York, N.Y.: Warner Books. 1996.

Sparks, Nicholas. *Message in a Bottle.* New York, N.Y.: Warner Books. 1998.

Staton, Shuy, and Byrock. *A Few Months to Live.* (see previous reference in RESOURCES section).

Terkel, Studs. *Will the Circle Be Unbroken?: Reflections on Death, Rebirth, and Hunger for a Faith.* New York, N.Y.: The New Press. 2001.

West, Paul. *A Stroke of Genius: Illness and Self-Discovery*. New York, N.Y.: Viking/Penguin. 1995.

Zazove, Philip, M.D. *When the Phone Rings, My Bed Shakes: Memoirs of a Deaf Doctor*. Washington, D.C.: Gallaudet University Press. 1993.

978-0-595-38733-5
0-595-38733-0

www.ingramcontent.com/pod-product-compliance
Lightning Source LLC
Chambersburg PA
CBHW030256290526
45785CB00001B/104